GARDEN CRAFT
IN EUROPE

André le Nostre, Che.r de L'Ordre S.t Michel Con.er du Roy
Controlleur general Ancien des Bastimens de sa Majesté
Jardins, Arts & Manufactures de France.

GARDEN CRAFT IN EUROPE

BY

H. INIGO TRIGGS

Author of
"Formal Gardens in England & Scotland."
"The Art of Garden Design in Italy."
etc.

CLASSIC EDITIONS

This edition digitally re-mastered and
published by JM Classic Editions © 2008
Original text © H Inigo Triggs 1913

ISBN 978-1-906600-05-1

All rights reserved. No part of this book subject
to copyright may be reproduced in any form or
by any means without prior permission in writing
from the publisher.

PREFACE

THE love of gardens is an old characteristic of our race. "The Englishman has ever felt the lure of green things growing," wrote the author of *Piers Plowman* more than six centuries ago, and though fashions have come and gone in gardens as in everything else, this interest, far from having died out, is nowadays stronger than ever.

Since Mr. J. D. Sedding wrote his poetic essay on Garden Craft, and for the first time treated the subject from the standpoint of the best architectural taste, there has been an extraordinary revival in garden craft (or as the French express it, *jardinage*, that is, the art of designing gardens as distinct from horticulture) and the old nineteenth century naturalistic ideas of garden design are fast losing their hold upon the public.

When my work on *Formal Gardens in England and Scotland* appeared ten years ago, it met with so gratifying a reception that I felt induced to extend my studies to the Continent, and especially to Italy. Many opportunities of travel in France, Germany, Holland and Spain have since enabled me to collect the material for the present work. In all these countries examples of old garden craft are but rarely to be met with, and considering the changes wrought by succeeding fashions, this is hardly to be wondered at. Few people realize how fragmentary are the remains that exist, and it is difficult to grasp the original lay-out and the various changes that have taken place on a visit even to such gardens as Versailles and Fontainebleau. I have preferred, therefore, to take my illustrations as far as possible from contemporary engravings, in the collection of which I have been assisted by the Librarians of the *Bibliothèque Nationale*, Paris, by M. de Nolhac, the curator of Versailles, by Mr. Leonard Springer, of Haarlem, and by my publisher, who has in his possession numerous rare books on the subject. To all of these

PREFACE

my thanks are due. Particulars of my indebtedness to those who have supplied material for illustration will be found in the Note of Acknowledgment.

The first history of Garden Craft was written in 1770 when Hirschfeld published his *Théorie de l'Art des Jardins*; this was followed in 1824 by an interesting series of historical references in Loudon's *Encyclopedia*. An instructive little work by George Riat, entitled *L'Art des Jardins*, was published in Paris a few years ago. With these few exceptions I know of no work tracing the historical development of garden craft in Europe. Mr. Forbes Sieveking's work, *The Praise of Gardens*, contains a valuable and interesting collection of citations on gardens, from authors of all ages, and in glancing through this fascinating collection it is curious to note how very modern some of the old writers seem to be. They did not distinguish the subject as that of "Formal" gardens, because in the view of most garden lovers, at any rate until the middle of the eighteenth century, all gardens were necessarily formal and regarded as essentially artificial productions and not merely a strip of nature, captured and railed off.

Miss Amherst's *History of Gardening in England*, issued in 1896, and Mr. Blomfield's small book on *The Formal Garden in England*, 1892, together with my own folio work upon the English and Scotch gardens, have made it unnecessary to deal with English gardens as fully as I otherwise should.

This short account of the development of garden-craft in Europe does not profess to be exhaustive. The field is a wide one, and in order to have achieved such a purpose it would have been necessary to have extended the size of the work to at least several volumes. I have not given more than a passing glance at the gardens of Norway, Sweden and Russia; the development of garden design in these countries occurred in the decadent period of the eighteenth century and such gardens as were carried out were usually poor imitations of the school of Le Nôtre or of the all-pervading English landscape style. The Bibliography at the end of the volume will assist those who desire to make a special study of any branch of the subject.

H. INIGO TRIGGS.

LITTLE BOARHUNT
  LIPHOOK,
    February, 1913.

NOTE OF ACKNOWLEDGMENT

I HAVE to thank Messrs. Longmans for permission to include some subjects from my work on *The Art of Garden Design in Italy*, published by them, and Mrs. Aubrey le Blond has been good enough to place at my disposal the negatives which are reproduced on the plates facing pages 34, 46, and 50. My publisher has permitted the reproduction of several subjects from works published by him. Mr. Martinus Nijhoff, of The Hague, has kindly supplied from *Oud-Nederlandsche Tuinkunst* the illustrations of the subjects from the Grimani Breviary, included among Mediæval Gardens, as well as several subjects in the chapters on Dutch and German Gardens. An acknowledgment is due to the authorities of the British Museum, the Victoria and Albert Museum, the Bodleian Library, and the *Bibliothèque Nationale* (*Cabinet des Estampes*) for engravings and drawings photographed from their collections. Mr. B. Zweers, of Haarlem, has furnished the negatives for the subjects reproduced on pages 169, 191, and 196. I have to acknowledge Mr. A. E. Walsham in connection with the illustrations on pages 122, 145, and the plates facing pages 88, 130, 134, and 150, and Mr. H. N. King, of Hammersmith, has allowed me to reproduce several of his photographs of English work, which will be found on pages 208 (lower subject), 214, and 231, and on the plates facing pages 226 and 306. Mr. Charles Latham photographed the subjects illustrated on page 221 and on the plates facing pages 203 and 205. To Mr. Thomas Lewis is due the photographs reproduced on page 208 (upper subject) and on the plate facing page 228.

CONTENTS

CHAP.		PAGE
	PREFACE	v
I	ANCIENT GARDENS IN EUROPE	1
II	THE GARDENS OF THE MIDDLE AGES	13
III	THE ITALIAN GARDEN	28
IV	FRENCH GARDENS OF THE SIXTEENTH AND EARLY SEVENTEENTH CENTURIES	65
V	LE NÔTRE AND VERSAILLES	86
VI	FRENCH GARDENS OF THE LATER SEVENTEENTH AND EIGHTEENTH CENTURIES	121
VII	GARDEN DESIGN IN THE NETHERLANDS	159
VIII	ENGLISH GARDENS OF THE SIXTEENTH, SEVENTEENTH AND EIGHTEENTH CENTURIES	203
IX	GERMAN AND AUSTRIAN GARDENS	232
X	GARDEN DESIGN IN SPAIN	264
XI	THE ENGLISH LANDSCAPE SCHOOL AND ITS INFLUENCE ON THE CONTINENT	288
	BIBLIOGRAPHY OF SELECTED WORKS ON EUROPEAN GARDEN DESIGN	312
	INDEX TO TEXT AND ILLUSTRATIONS	322

CHAPTER I

ANCIENT GARDENS IN EUROPE

THE art of garden design, like all the decorative arts, extended with civilization from East to West. The Greeks drew their earliest inspirations from Egypt, Persia, and Assyria, and in their turn passed on the tradition to the Romans. Upon the banks of the Nile horticulture flourished from the tenth to the third century B.C., and there is no lack of evidence to show that garden design was practised as an art from the very earliest ages and flourished especially during the fourth, twelfth and eighteenth dynasties.

Under the rule of the Ptolemies and in the early years of Roman domination, Egypt was one of the most fertile regions of the world, and in the Augustan Age the public and private gardens of Alexandria are said to have covered more than a quarter of the city area. From the many graphic records that have been brought to light in modern times, it is not a difficult matter to obtain a very accurate idea of the plan of these ancient Egyptian gardens. In order to facilitate irrigation they were usually laid out, either upon the banks of the Nile or upon canals fed by it, and took the form of a rectangular area, surrounded by an embattled wall or palisade, the entrance being by means of high gates or *pylons*, whose lintels and jambs were decorated with hieroglyphic inscriptions. The walks were shaded by palms or by tunnels of trained plants, similar to the pleached alley that was so prevalent a feature of the seventeenth century gardens; small canals traversed the gardens and fed the numerous tanks, whilst here and there gaily painted pavilions and bowers, lightly constructed of trellis, were reflected in the tranquil pools, glistening with the lotus and tenanted by a large variety of fish, ducks, cranes and other aquatic birds.[1]

---

[1] See Charles Joret, *Les Plantes dans l'antiquité et au moyen âge.* Paris, 1897.

From the flat nature of their situation the gardens of ancient Egypt must always have lacked variety; this element, however, was not wanting in the gardens of ancient Greece, where the physical character of the country gave far greater scope for artistic display. To a nation like the Greeks, so eager to take advantage of every device for embellishing their surroundings, the cultivation of beautiful gardens became a prime necessity in setting off their architecture. They always preserved a studied symmetry in laying out their gardens, which were planned to meet the principal requirements of shade, coolness, fragrance and repose. The idea of imitating nature does not seem to have been seriously entertained, and though Homer, in describing the Garden of Calypso, speaks of the capricious winding of silver streams and generally indicates an informal or natural garden, the description refers more to one of those sacred and mysterious retreats, everywhere to be found, dedicated to the gods of the waters and of the woods, or else to some local divinity. The deities favourable to gardening were, above all, Aphrodite, venerated at Athens, where her statue was set up in a grove of oleanders, and Dionysus, to whom Xenophon dedicated a temple near Olympia. Secondary to these were the Graces or Charites.

In Athens, amongst other famous public gardens, was one known as the Lyceum. This was also the resort of a great school of philosophy and was famous for the plantations laid out by the orator, Lycurgus. Theophrastus and Demetrius built a museum in its groves, and here it was that Aristotle used to walk with his disciples. The most ancient allusion to a Greek garden is in Homer's account of the palace of Alcinous, where the Gods were pleased to dwell and upon which Ulysses had gazed with admiration. The description, which appears to have been written from nature, is worth transcribing here.

"And without the courtyard hard by the door is a great garden, of four plough gates, and a hedge runs round on either side. And there grow tall trees blossoming, pear-trees and pomegranates, and apple-trees with bright fruit, and sweet figs, and olives in their bloom. The fruit of these trees never perisheth, neither faileth winter nor summer, enduring through all the year. Evermore the West Wind blowing brings some fruits to birth and ripens others. Pear upon pear waxes old, and apple on apple, yea and cluster ripens upon cluster of the grape, and fig upon fig. There too hath he a fruitful vineyard planted, whereof the one part is being dried by the heat, a sunny plot on level ground, while other grapes men are gathering, and yet others they are treading in the wine-press. In the foremost row are unripe grapes that cast the blossom, and others there be that are growing black to vintaging. There too, skirting the furthest line, are all manner of garden beds, planted trimly, that are perpetually fresh, and therein are two fountains of water, whereof one scatters his streams all about the garden, and the other runs over against it beneath the threshold of the courtyard, and issues by the lofty house, and thence did the townsfolk draw water. These were the splendid gifts of the gods in the palace of Alcinous." [1]

About the sixth century B.C. the effect of foreign influence began to make itself felt, and travellers returned with glowing accounts of the " Paradeisoi " of the Persian kings and of the wonders of Babylon and Egypt. On account of the smallness of the Greek cities and their democratic rule it was vain to attempt any approach to Eastern magnificence ; but although unable to compete in extent or display, the Greek gardens by the beauty of their statuary and architecture equalled, if they did not surpass, their larger prototypes. The principal apartments of a Greek dwelling were planned upon the opposite side to the entrance, and the garden was usually enclosed by the rear wings of the house. At the further end would probably be a high bank of earth planted with sweet-smelling shrubs, roses, myrtles and agnus-castus, in order that the scent might be freely wafted across the garden area. Upon one side was often a cool shady wood, thickly planted like the Italian *bosco*. The art of forcing and retarding flowers was considerably practised by the Greeks, who thus ensured a continuous supply throughout the year. Democritus speaks of the lentisk and of freshly cut branches of the vine being used to form soft springy couches upon which to enjoy the midday rest. Flowers were cultivated upon an elaborate scale, each variety being as a rule in separate beds. In the collection of writings known as the " Geoponica " there are frequent allusions to the varieties of plants and also to the general planning of Greek gardens. Myrtles, violets, roses, lilies, hyacinths and iris were largely grown. The narcissus was used for crowning the statues of goddesses ; actors and dancers often wore crowns of flowers, and at every feast it was the custom for guests to adorn themselves with chaplets and garlands. The temples and altars

[1] *Odyssey*, VII, Translation of S. H. Butcher and A. Lang.

were also hung with flowers. Pindar bestowed upon the City of Pallas the poetic appellation of " the brilliant city of violet wreaths."

There is no doubt that Roman garden craft was largely borrowed from the Greeks; the same strictly formal type appears to have everywhere prevailed, and the technical terms in use are frequently of Greek origin. The Roman gardens of the Republican period were comparatively simple and largely used for the growth of fruit and vegetables, but amenity and formality were the groundwork of the design, and even the stern Cato demanded that gardens, especially if in or near the city, " should be planted with all kinds of ornamental trees, bulbs from Megara, myrtle on palisades, both white and black, the Delphic and Cyprian laurel. . . . A city garden, especially of one who has no other, ought to be planted and ornamented with all possible care." Of the earliest Roman gardens very little can be gathered from ancient authors. One of the first mentioned in history is that of Tarquinius Superbus, 534 B.C. It adjoined the royal palace and abounded in flowers, chiefly lilies, roses and poppies.

Four hundred years later we have records of the gardens of Lucullus, which were laid out at a time when the great General, fresh from his victories over Mithridates and Tigranes, deserted by his men and superseded by Pompey, retired to his sumptuous houses and carried out the immense garden works described by Plutarch. Lucullus may be said to have been the real creator of the princely garden and set an example which was quickly followed by other Roman nobles. His gardens were conceived upon a most lavish scale at Cape Misenum near Baiae, and in their magnificence rivalled the splendid pleasure gardens of the East. He expended vast sums of money in cutting through hills and rocks, and finding insufficient scope for his labours upon land, must needs throw out advanced works into the sea.

Cicero, both by his writings and his example, introduced a greater moderation of taste. In his villa at Tusculum he had covered alleys and terraces, and in imitation of the philosophic gardens of ancient Greece he called one the Academy and another the Lyceum. Neither Virgil nor Horace have left us descriptions of the gardens of their time, and although we have frequent allusions to sylvan beauties and to flowers, these authors give us no information as to the artistic disposition of gardens. But, among Roman writers of the classical period, we have three, Varro, Columella and Pliny, who have all left valuable accounts of the gardens of their day. Varro's well known work[1] mostly deals with agriculture, but in the third book he describes his villa at Casinum which, amongst other features, contained an aviary of rare birds, arranged within a portico over which a hempen net was spread. Pliny's descriptions of his two villas are so well known that it is unnecessary to do more than refer to them here. He owned several villas and loved to spend his leisure in seclusion where, as he says, " there is no need to put on your toga, no one wants you in the neighbourhood, everything is calm and quiet, and this in itself adds to the healthfulness and cheerfulness of the place, no less than the brightness of the

THE LAURENTINE VILLA OF PLINY THE YOUNGER, FROM A RESTORATION BY HAUDEBOURT.

sky and the clearness of the atmosphere."[2] The two principal villas described were known as the Laurentine and the Tuscan. The former (illus., pp. 5 and 6), was situated some fifteen miles to the south-west of Rome upon the sea coast, and the description shows the care with which the position was chosen to embrace the splendid view commanded by the *cœnatio* or dining-room. An enclosed portico, with a range of windows overlooking the sea on one side and the garden on the other, was arranged so ingeniously that in windy or bad weather either side could be thrown open and acted as a protection to the *xystos* or flower garden " fragrant with sweet scented violets."

[1] See *De Re Rustica*, § VIII.
[2] A good translation with restored plans is given in R. Castell's *Villas of the Ancients*, 1728.

The Tuscan country seat, described in his letter to Apollinaris, was his favourite villa, and whereas the Laurentine house was used in the modern sense of a villa in the suburbs, this was intended more as a summer resort and was situated about a hundred and fifty miles from Rome.

Pliny's writings afford us the finest descriptions extant of Roman villas, and it is remarkable how similar in many points these villas must have been to those of the Italian Renaissance. Some learned restora-

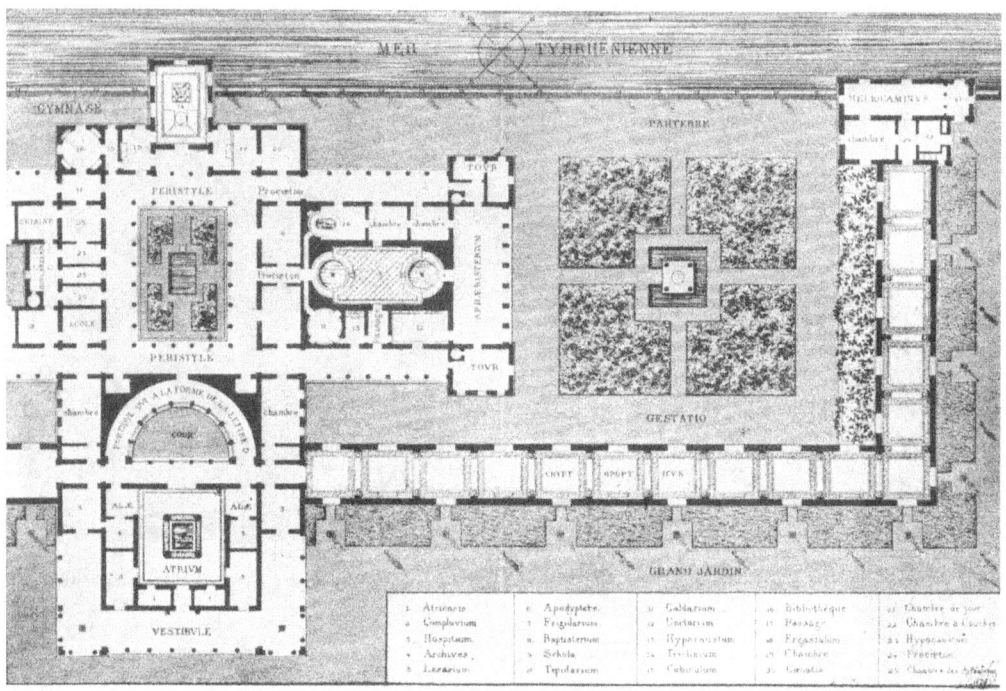

PLAN OF PLINY'S LAURENTINE VILLA, AS RESTORED BY HAUDEBOURT.

tions on paper have been made by servants. Scamozzi, Félibien, Castell, Marquez, Haudebourt and Bouchet have all endeavoured to reconstruct their glories. The restoration made by Haudebourt in 1852 is in many respects the best, and is conceived in a very architectural spirit, both in reference to its building and in the rectangular nature of its lines.

This type of villa was known as the *Villa Urbana,* and the neighbourhood of Rome abounded in examples, each one differing in plan from

Pliny's descriptions only as the exigencies of the situation demanded. Their sites were invariably well chosen, especially with regard to the season of the year during which they were to be occupied. A hillside has always been the most attractive situation to the Italians for their villas, and apart from its healthiness, it affords great opportunities for garden display in the construction of terrace walks and in the arrangement and distribution of water. On the other hand, a level site affords greater opportunities for extensive display. The *villa rustica* was a smaller type of country house, more of the nature of a pleasure farm.

The whole of the Campagna round Rome was studded with such villas, arranged in zones or districts according to their size. The Roman love of the country during autumn still survives in the annual *villeggiatura*, which is so essential a feature in the life of a modern Italian.

In the neighbourhood of Rome the favourite situations for country villas were upon the slopes of the Sabine and Alban mountains, at Tibur (the modern Tivoli), Laurentium, Sublaqueum (Subiaco), where Nero had a large villa, Antium, upon the sea coast, Centumcellæ (Civita Vecchia) and Præneste. The last named was a very famous summer resort under the Emperors on account of its bracing climate, and together with Tibur and Baiae is much extolled by Horace. Pliny describes the roses of Præneste as being the finest in Italy, and they were grown in enormous quantities for the Roman market. Another favourite district for villas was along the shore of the Bay of Naples, especially Baiae, where Nero, Pompey and Cæsar all had sumptuous villas. Here all restraint was thrown off and life entirely given up to pleasure and luxury.

The larger country villas and their farms often covered an area of several hundred acres. The house itself being taken as the key to the situation, the courts round it were arranged to conform to its architecture. The various courts and *loggie* merged into the *atrium*, which was usually enclosed by a colonnade adorned with statuary. The principal parts of the garden plan were separated from each other by thick hedges or shady pergolas. The most important feature was the hippodrome, a place devoted to running and equestrian exercise, divided longitudinally by hedges of box ornamented with topiary work. The Hippodrome survived even to the days of the Renaissance, and an excellent example may still be seen in the gardens of the Villa Borghese at Rome. Next in importance was the *xystos* or flower garden, consisting of a parterre composed of beds and paths. The Romans in borrowing the word from the Greeks had altered its meaning; with the Greeks it meant a covered gallery, and Vitruvius expressly notes the difference. Sometimes the bed was raised above the level of the path, in which case it was called a *pulvinus* or *torus*. If the bed was not raised it was often outlined with box or rosemary. A *rosarium* or rose garden and a labyrinth were planned adjoining the *xystos*, and the fruit and vegetable garden, with trees arranged quincuncially,[1] frequently formed part of the garden scheme. A finely organized system of aqueducts brought water from the hills to supply the summer fountains and pools.

The staff required to keep in order such a villa garden was very large. First came the *topiarii*, chief of all the slaves whose primary duty was to exercise their art in the clipping and pruning of trees into all kinds of fantastic shapes. In addition to these were the *viridarii*, whose work lay probably more within doors; the *aquarii*, who had charge of the fountains and waterworks; the *vinitori*, presiding over the vineyards; and the *olitori*, who looked after the olive yards.

The most characteristic ornament of the classic garden was its topiary work (*opus topiarum*), and the plants chosen for this work were those that preserved their foliage in winter, as the box and cypress. They assumed a variety of shapes; cut into quite low hedges, they traced the letters forming the name of the artist or proprietor, an idea we may still see in the gardens of the Vatican; or, when required to accentuate certain points of the *xystos*, they were cut into pyramids, cones, and other geometrical forms, figures of men and animals were often employed, and in some cases a hunt or an entire fleet was represented in topiary.

All the larger Roman villas had a number of garden buildings collected within the enclosure of the park and garden, and Hadrian's Villa at Tivoli is an astonishing example of their extent and variety; besides several theatres were the Hippodrome, the Academy, Baths, a building known as the *Canōpus* containing a number of Egyptian statues, some of which are now in the Vatican, the so-called Elysium, the *Prytaneum*, the *Nymphæum* and *Palæstra*. The most luxurious and expensive materials, such as marble, porphyry and precious woods, were used in the construction of the *triclinia* and

[1] Quincunx is the name given to a mode of planting in rows so that in a plot of ground thus planted the trees appear in rows in four directions.

garden pavilions, which were by no means the ephemeral constructions of the Egyptians and Greeks. The finest sculpture was employed in the statues of philosophers, athletes, gods and goddesses, satyrs, muses, centaurs and animals, and in the decoration of vases. In fact, much of the best ancient sculpture adorned these sumptuous gardens of the age when Imperial Rome was in her glory.

Conservatories and hot-houses for the protection of the more tender plants are mentioned as early as the first century, though we do not know the technical name by which they were designated. Some of the references in ancient authors may refer to mere frames, but others are more explicit and indicate that substantial buildings were erected to shelter plants in winter; otherwise some of the more tender plants imported from the East could hardly have acclimatized themselves. As the taste for exotic plants came more into vogue the necessity arose for more elaborate buildings. They were enclosed with *specularia* or windows of talc and heated by means of flues. In the Villa of Maecenas at Rome, a building was excavated in 1874 which is supposed to have been such a conservatory; it had masonry tiers for displaying the plants and was heated. Martial once sarcastically wrote that " he wished he were his friend's apple tree, rather than his guest, for it was protected from the cold by glass or talc, whilst his bedroom had none."

HOUSE OF SALLUST, POMPEII.

The principal features of the villas which have been described were to be found upon a grander scale in all the great imperial palaces; the most stupendous of these being Hadrian's villa, the ruins of which still exist. It was begun about twelve years before Hadrian gave up the administration of public affairs, and occupied an area of about 160 acres. The gardens were mostly confined to courtyards and terraces commanding glorious views over

HOUSE OF SALLUST, POMPEII.

the beautiful vale of Tempe, within sight of Rome, yet away from its noise. It was customary in the larger villas to erect models in miniature of celebrated monuments, triumphal arches, etc. After having frequented the streets of Rome during the winter the fashionable world liked to find reproductions of its monuments in their gardens during the summer. The idea was revived during the Renaissance, and in the garden at the Villa d'Este at Tivoli there still exists a model of part of ancient Rome with temples, Forum and triumphal arches.

In Rome itself there were a considerable number of beautiful gardens surrounding the town houses, which were mostly used during the winter months or during the Roman season until, as Pliny says, "the appearance of spring was a signal for the aristocracy to disperse to their country seats." The Pincian hill was occupied by the magnificent gardens of Acilius Glabrio. Upon the Janiculum stood the gardens of Julius Caesar, and on the Tiber's banks were those of Augustus, Pompey, Nero and Caligula. Domitian laid out his gardens upon the Palatine Hill in imitation of the gardens of Adonis, and their plan has been discovered, incised on marble slabs. Upon the site of the Vatican were the *Horti Agrippinae*.

In the restricted areas of the less pretentious town gardens, every square yard of available space was turned

HOUSE OF MARCUS LUCRETIUS, POMPEII.

to good account. Terraces, balconies and roof-gardens (*solaria*) helped to satisfy the desire for fresh air, and where space permitted were laid out with beds of flowers or even fruit trees. In almost all town houses the living apartments were arranged round one or more open courtyards; the smaller of these was the *atrium* and the larger, which only existed in more important houses, was known as the *peristyle*. Many examples may be seen at Pompeii where even the smallest *atrium* was laid out in some fashion as a garden. In the centre was an *impluvium* or shallow pool, which received the water of the roof, and was enclosed by a low coping hollowed out to contain lilies and aquatic plants, or bordered with fresh green moss, its rippling fountain merrily spurting in the sunlight. Sometimes the larger court or *peristyle* was laid out with beds of flowers and shrubs and ornamented with statuettes, fountains, and mosaic or shellwork grottos, and tables or basins of marble were scattered about. Many examples of such decorative features are

MOSAIC NYMPHAEUM AT POMPEII.

to be seen in the museum at Naples, and others still remain in their original position at Pompeii, where the authorities have very wisely reconstructed several of the ancient gardens, as may be seen in the illustrations, showing how delightful an effect may be produced within the smallest compass.

In many of the wall paintings, both at Herculaneum and Pompeii, various ephemeral structures are depicted, summer-houses (illus., p. 12), *nymphaea*, shrines, temples and aviaries, generally of wood, and enclosures of trellis, with angle posts carved and decorated. Such structures were painted in the gayest colours, an example which might with advantage be followed to-day. The pergola has always been a great feature in Italian garden design and, by the use of marble columns with carved and painted beams, was capable of great elaboration.

TRELLIS ARBOUR FROM A FRESCO AT POMPEII

With the fall of Rome and the incursions of barbaric tribes the sumptuous villas did not long survive destruction, often being converted into fortified abodes where there was little opportunity for gardening. The best traditions, however, passed on to the Eastern Empire, and under the influence of Byzantine taste, were never entirely lost. In Italy and the West of Europe generally, the art of horticulture was only kept from entire degeneration by the monks in the comparative peace afforded by convent walls, and by their untiring labours whole districts in Italy, France and Spain were fertilized after having been abandoned in consequence of the ravages of Goths and Saracens. Nevertheless, the influence of Pliny and other writers on agriculture was felt through all these centuries. The Herbal of Apuleius, founded on Pliny's works, was compiled in the fourth century and later translated into Anglo-Saxon.

CHAPTER II

THE GARDENS OF THE MIDDLE AGES

URING the dark ages that followed the downfall of the Roman Empire, all taste for country life was soon extinguished. War once more became the ruling passion, and in Italy agriculture fell upon bad times. In the South of France the Gallo-Roman establishments did not disappear so completely. Sidonius Apollinaris, the Bishop of Clermont, mentions several beautiful gardens of this epoch, and takes pleasure in describing the delights to be found in them. The wise policy of the early Church in respecting pagan customs by turning them to the profit of the Christian religion was instrumental in the development of horticulture and incidentally created a demand for the cultivation of flowers for use at festivals. Thus the garlands which young girls used to weave for the pagan festivals of the *Ambarvalia,* under the new *régime* were used to adorn Rogation processions.

The growth of monastic life also helped the progress of gardening. To the monks, entirely shut off from the world, the most human and universal taste for gardening served well as an outlet for the expression of their love of beauty, and filled a void in their lives, so debarred from all participation in earthly pleasures.

The gardens of the royal villas belonging to the Merovingian dynasty were not of any great importance, being little better than clearings on the outskirts of forests, and the cultivation of palatial gardens does not appear to have made very great progress until the ninth century, when Charlemagne, having warred successfully against Saracens, Lombards and Saxons, built his sumptuous palaces at Aix la Chapelle and at Ingelheim on the Rhine. Besides these he had vast estates throughout the whole extent of his empire, from which he drew a large proportion of his revenue. He interested himself very much in agriculture and horticulture, and in 812 issued his famous capitulary, *De villis et curtis*, in which particular directions are given concerning the maintenance of orchards and gardens, together with a list of trees and plants that should be cultivated. This is one of the most valuable and explicit documents relating to the art of gardening in these early centuries that has been preserved. We find enumerated all the plants which the Emperor had grown himself, and the culture of which he recommended to his subjects; they were principally fruit trees and medicinal herbs, but a certain number of ornamental plants are also described.[1] An important feature in these gardens of Charlemagne was the great menagerie; wild animals were much prized as royal gifts, and we read that the King of Persia presented Charlemagne with an elephant which was brought to the menagerie at Aix-la-Chapelle. How such a bulky present journeyed across Europe it would be interesting to know.

MONKS' GARDEN AT THE CERTOSA, PAVIA.

The plans of the Abbey of St. Gall, situated near the lake of Constance, give very exact information as to early monastic gardens in general; here the *hortus* is indicated as a regular enclosure, with a central path leading from the gardener's house, and nine long and narrow beds of equal size upon each side; the *herbularis*, or physic garden, is smaller with a border of plants round the wall, and four beds on both sides of a central wall, the plants contained in each of these beds are carefully noted. At the monastery

---

[1] This capitulary is dealt with at length in the *Magasin encyclopédique*, by MM. Sereau et Harman, An VIII, tomes III et IV.

THE GARDENS OF THE MIDDLE AGES

of Monte Cassino the Benedictines created the earliest school of medicine, the forerunner of the great botanic gardens of the sixteenth century.

The tenth century was an age of great depression over the larger part of Europe, and horticulture passed through a period of decline, from which it did not emerge until the beginning of the next century when, owing to the great religious revival and the stimulating effects of the crusades, gardening, in common with all the arts, made considerable progress.[1] It was much to the advantage of Western Europe that at this crisis it should have become acquainted with the marvels of the East, of Egypt, and the North of Africa. Many hitherto unknown plants and fruits were brought back by the Crusaders and acclimatized in Europe, adding a new impetus to gardening, such as it had not experienced for centuries.

Some of the architectural features, such as the bathing-pools (illus., p. 16) that are so frequently met with in mediaeval drawings, can be directly traced to oriental influence; they were

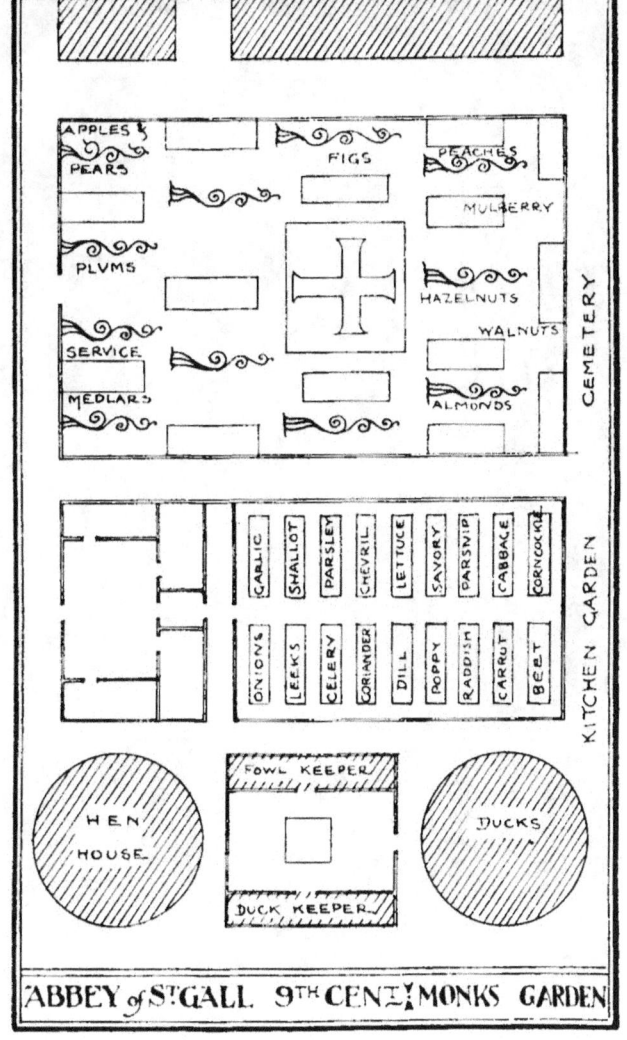

ABBEY of St GALL. 9TH CENT. MONKS GARDEN

[1] See Léopold Delisle, *Etude agricole en Normandie au moyen âge.* Evreux, 1851.

usually quite shallow pools approached by several steps. Another garden accessory that owes its origin to the East is the tent, pictures of which may often be found in miniature paintings.

The flower garden now had a definite place allotted to it, and the space which had hitherto been devoted to the orchard became more curtailed. Many new varieties of flowers were introduced. The yellow Persian rose is said to date its introduction into Europe from this period, and the damask rose, or rose of Damascus, also betokens its Eastern origin. The jessamine was brought from Arabia by way of Spain, and very soon the tulip, fritillary, ranunculus, balsam, hyacinth, lilac and mimosa were imported from Turkey and Asia Minor, whilst many other exotics, now almost considered indigenous to Europe, were introduced by the Crusaders.

A BATHING-POOL, FROM AN ILLUMINATED MS. IN THE BRITISH MUSEUM.

THE GARDENS OF THE MIDDLE AGES

About 1270 Jacob van Maerlant, a Flemish poet, wrote *De Naturen Bloeme,* a treatise in verse on plants, beasts and minerals; it is illustrated by coloured drawings and claims to be based on the work of Albrecht van Keulen; it was written in thirteen books, of which three deal respectively with trees, medicinal plants and herbs.

Life in a feudal castle had much monotony, and it may easily be imagined what diversion the small *verger*, or private garden gave to the *châtelaine* and her ladies, who no doubt often found their greatest pleasure in carefully tending some little plot of ground hidden away in the recesses of the castle.

Our knowledge of mediaeval gardens can only be acquired from casual references in old chronicles or from stray pictures to be found in breviaries, missals, and Books of the Hours. Though considerable allowance must be made for the fluent fancy of the artists, these little sketches assist us in reconstructing the quaint pleasaunce of the middle ages

A MEDIAEVAL GARDEN SCENE.

with its babbling, sparkling fountain, its curious seats and arbours, its low wattled hedges and quaint topiary works. In the beautiful fifteenth-century manuscript of the "Romance of the Rose" preserved in the British Museum we find a considerable number of garden sketches. In one of these (illus., p. 19) the pleasaunce is laid out with grass plots divided by a fence. Here we see a variety of fruit trees and a fountain throwing up jets of water which fall into a basin, while the *châtelaine* sits with her music, singing to the accompaniment of a troubadour. In another picture, illustrated above, a gay company of knights and ladies is seen in an orchard surrounded by a high embattled wall, walking in procession to the accompaniment of minstrels.

Although the use of statuary was so general in Roman gardens, it does not seem to have been known at all, as a form of garden ornamentation, during the middle ages. Wherever statues appear, they belong either to the house itself or to some purely architectural feature, such as a fountain, a wall, or a bridge.

Plants in pots are often seen in representations of mediaeval gardens, and, as rare foreign plants were one of the earliest luxuries of garden lovers, the use of ornamental pots was frequently resorted to and these were themselves made objects of beauty. A French illumination in the *Bibliothèque de l'Arsenal*, entitled *The instruction of a young prince*, shows a round vase containing a curiously cut shrub. Other mediaeval drawings show gardens embellished with flowering plants in low pots either of metal or earthenware and painted blue and white. The Grimani breviary illustrates several pots of this character.

Water in a variety of forms was introduced into the garden as often as possible. The fountain was the central and most ornamental feature; it was generally gilt and decorated in brilliant colours, and its design gave scope for many different forms of architectural treatment. From the fountain little channelled ways branched off in several directions, leading the water to pools scattered about the garden.

The fish ponds and pools were planned away from the castle and were often very extensive; they were generally encircled by a wall or by a continuous arbour extending round the four sides. In the manuscript *Les très riches Heures du Duc de Berry* preserved in the Museum at Chantilly such a delightful little water garden is represented, encircled by an arbour and having a parterre divided off by low wattled screens.

Little or no garden furniture is to be found in representations of mediaeval gardens; people sat on the lawns or upon the resting-places round the boundary walls. These consisted either of brick seats cushioned with turf, or earth banked up round a tree and kept in position by wattled reeds; such seats were about two feet wide and eighteen inches above the ground, and sometimes, instead of the grass seat there were beds of roses, camomile, and other plants. A Dutch painting of the fourteenth century in the Rijks Museum at Amsterdam shows a large U-shaped seat, with grass upon brick-

GARDEN FROM THE BRITISH MUSEUM MS. OF "THE ROMAUNT OF THE ROSE,"
SHOWING TREILLAGE SCREEN AND FOUNTAIN.

work, placed away from the walls in the middle of a cloister garden. In another example, shown in a woodcut of 1487, the child Jesus is seated upon a turfed seat with attendant figures on the grass at His feet. Two illustrations from *Der Meister des Liebesgartens* show a table set out for a feast and a canopied throne for the lady personifying Love. The mediaeval custom of raising the flower bed well above the ground was a very pleasing one and worthy of imitation nowadays.

The parterre was subdivided into compartments of trellis work, square or diamond-shaped (illus., p. 27), or else of rough lattice, the angle posts often gaily decorated in colour, while the main paths and alleys were either of grass or loosely covered with sand. Wooden galleries, their structure concealed by flowering shrubs or vines, often encircled the garden.

Sauval, the historian of Paris, tells us that the town gardens of Paris in the fifteenth century were surrounded by hedges, kept within bounds by crossed stakes or else by tunnels of verdure framed in a similar way. Guillebert de Metz, in his description of Paris in 1422, relates that on the fortifications of the Petit Châtelet the Parisians cultivated curious hanging gardens in this way. In the *Ménager de Paris*,[1] composed about 1393, we find an account of the plants, flowers and vegetables usually cultivated in town gardens.

A TRELLIS ARBOUR FROM "THE ROMAUNT OF THE ROSE."

From very early times labyrinths were laid out in gardens. At first merely winding paths cut in the ground, they later on developed into walks entirely enclosed by hedges. Charles V laid out a famous labyrinth known as the *Maison de Dédale* in the gardens of the Hôtel Saint Paul, at Paris, where amongst other curiosities was a collection of bay-trees which at

[1] Published by the *Société des bibliophiles français*.

this time were considered quite a novelty. The garden was reconstructed in 1431 by the English Regent, Bedford, who, we are told, introduced holly trees and planted many hundred elms. Charles V appears to have been a great patron of gardeners, and a rare volume dedicated to him, entitled *Des prauffits Champestres et Ruraulx*, by one Pierre de Croistens, was recently sold from the library of the Earl of Cork and Orrery. It deals at length with

RAISED SEAT SURROUNDING AN ENCLOSURE FROM "THE ROMAUNT OF THE ROSE."

A GARDEN POOL AND CHANNEL FROM "THE ROMAUNT OF THE ROSE."

flower gardens, with the planting and pruning of trees, ploughing, and threshing corn.

During the reigns of Charles VIII and Louis XII great changes took place in garden design in France. As property became more secure, life became more sedentary. Considerable progress was made in the cultivation of plants, and above all the increased use of artillery necessitated great alterations in the planning of castles. They were made much more habitable and a less severe aspect was given to them, but still a large space was invariably left free immediately round the castle to prevent sudden attack and in order that a look-out might be kept in all directions. It was not until the seventeenth century was well advanced that the moat could be dispensed with in safety. Old plans of the castles of Commines and Viniers show the gardens beyond the outermost fortifications, connected with the ramparts by a bridge, and laid out in geometrical patterns. Frequently these outside gardens were left quite undefended or at most protected by a slight wall or palisade.

The development of gardening in Italy during the middle ages generally followed the lead of France. The incessant wars, resulting in the mingling of so many different nations on Italian soil, ravaged the length and breadth of the country and hardly permitted the same development of horticulture that we see in the more northern parts of Europe. It is not until the latter half of the thirteenth century, when Pietro Crescenzi compiled his great work, *Opus Ruralium Commodorum*, that we have any very definite account of garden design.

The work of Crescenzi was by far the most important treatise upon agriculture produced during the middle ages, and stands quite alone in the literature of gardening; it was founded upon the works of the ancient agrimonists, Cato, Varro and Columella and on the author's own personal observation. It remained in manuscript for more than a century and a half and was first printed in 1471 in Latin, but was afterwards translated into Italian, French and German. The eighth chapter treats of the laying out of gardens, which the author divides into three classes. Firstly, he deals with small herb gardens, under which term he includes small orchards, and gardens of fruit trees and herbs pleasing to the sight. After giving minute directions as to the preparation of the soil, he recommends that the garden be square. In its bor-

FIFTEENTH-CENTURY GARDEN FROM THE GRIMANI BREVIARY.

GARDEN CRAFT IN EUROPE

ders should be planted every species of odoriferous herb, such as goats-rue, sage, basil, marjoram, mint and the like. The paths were to be of grass, and against the wall a high bank of earth arranged as a seat, blossoming and beautiful, whilst pergolas of vines gave to the charming spot a cool and delightful shade. " As in trees of this kind the shade is sought rather than the fruit, they must not be dry or manured because it would hurt the neighbouring herbs and flowers, ... and care must be taken that the trees neither be too many nor grow too thickly, because the shutting off of air corrupts the health of the place, also because the garden requires a free current of air."

He recommends the use of sweet-scented and shady trees, and advises that " in the middle of the lawn there should be no trees, but the fresh level of the grass left alone in a pure and glad air, and if possible a clear fountain, to add pleasure and gaiety by its beauty."

Crescenzi then proceeds to deal with gardens for ordinary persons from two to four acres in extent ; these, he suggests, should be surrounded by trenches of prickly shrubs and white briars, with a hedge beyond of pomegranates in hot countries, and of hazel nuts or quinces in cold. He also suggests an arbour or trellis bower made in the fittest and most convenient plan, " like unto a pavilion." Thirdly, the treatise deals with the gardens of kings and other rich persons for, " whereas such persons having great riches and power can in these worldly things entirely satisfy their wills, most times only lack the industry and the science of ordering them. ... On the northern side let there be planted a forest of different trees where the wild animals let loose in the garden can run and hide. On the southern side let there be built a beautiful palace where the king or queen will dwell when bent on escaping serious thoughts and renew their soul with comfort and mirth. ... Also

A FLOWER GARDEN, FIFTEENTH CENTURY, GRIMANI BREVIARY.

in some part of this garden can the orchards be planted. And let a fishpond be made in which many generations of fish shall be fed, and also let there be hares, stags, roebucks, rabbits and such animals as are not rapacious. And at the top of some small trees near the palace let there be built a kind of house having a roof and walls of copper wire finely netted, where shall be put pheasants, partridges, nightingales, blackbirds, goldfinches, linnets, and all kinds of singing birds. And let the rows of the trees in the garden of the palace be far from the forest, in order that from the palace it may be seen what the animals in the garden are doing. There also ought to be made in this garden a dwelling-place, with walks and bowers of trees only, in which the king or the queen may sojourn with their barons in dry weather."

The early Britons owed to the Romans all the knowledge they possessed of horticultural science. Strabo, writing in the fourth century, says "The people of Britain are entirely ignorant of the art of cultivating gardens as well as of the other parts of agriculture." With the fall of the Roman Empire a death-blow was struck to horticulture, and gardening as an art of design entirely disappeared during the stormy centuries that succeeded. Shelter and defence are implied by the etymology of our words "yard" and "garden," and such were the leading characteristics of the little enclosed spaces devoted by our Saxon ancestors to such plant culture as then obtained.

In the latter half of the eleventh century the advent of the Normans added considerably to the general comforts of living, but again during the troublous period following the Conquest the quiet pleasures of a garden could hardly be enjoyed.

The earliest writers on horticulture in England were monks, and the most valuable authority upon

A CASTLE COURTYARD, FIFTEENTH CENTURY, GRIMANI BREVIARY.

the subject of early English gardens is Alexander Neckham, Abbot of Cirencester. He was born at St. Albans in 1157 and died in 1217, and in early life was a professor at the University of Paris. His account consists of a series of notes entitled *De Naturis Rerum* (a kind of contemporary encyclopædia). His description of the herbs, fruits and flowers to be found in a garden of his day is interesting, and gives a good idea of what was considered necessary for the support of a monastic establishment of the time. Neckham was a compiler rather than an observer or a thinker, and his knowledge of gardens was drawn more from writers of another age and climate than from practical experience in his own country. Classic authors, such as Pliny, were studied for directions as to culture rather than for information on laying out, and so Neckham is silent on the subject of garden design.

Other writers of this period were Bishop Grosseteste of Lincoln and John de Garlande, an Englishman who resided in Paris during the first half of the thirteenth century and who has left a description of his garden there. From this and other accounts it is evident that both in matters of taste and in horticulture France had advanced further than England in garden craft. The two countries were so intimately connected at this period that the accounts already given of French gardens would equally apply to English, at any rate as far as the more important gardens were concerned.

One of the most important of the gardens surrounding the royal palaces was that of Woodstock, where Henry III carried out many improvements. He commanded the Bailiff of Woodstock " to make round about the garden of our Queen, two walls good and high so that no one may be able to enter, with a becoming and honourable herbary near our fish-pond in which the same Queen may be able to amuse herself."

There were also royal gardens at Windsor, Westminster, Whitehall and the Tower. The old maps of London show what a number of magnificent gardens there were belonging to the palaces that bordered the Strand and extended in terraces to the River Thames.

Considerable advances in horticultural science were made in the reign of Edward I, when the mediaeval prosperity of the English may be said to have culminated. The King and all the nobility devoted much attention to the cultivation of their demesnes, and, at the same time, a class of smaller landowners was growing up who, gradually throwing off allegiance to their feudal lords, built for themselves small farms and manor-houses which they surrounded with orchards and gardens, so that, by the end of the fourteenth century, almost every small manor and farm had its pleasaunce. During the Wars of the Roses much that civilization had gained in horticulture was lost, and progress was not continued until the restoration of peace under the Tudors.

HORTUS CONCLUSUS, GRIMANI BREVIARY.

CHAPTER III

THE ITALIAN GARDEN

HE account of Pietro Crescenzi, quoted in the last chapter, enables us to form some idea of the state of garden design in Italy during the latter half of the thirteenth century. Throughout the whole of the fourteenth and fifteenth centuries the work of Crescenzi stands alone in the history of gardening. As the Renaissance in architecture proceeded, villas sprang into being upon all sides, the result of a period of peace and comparative security, and during the fourteenth century the craze for gardening grew apace, and had become quite a passion when Boccaccio sketched from life the delightful picture of the garden of his time in the introduction to the third day of the *Decameron*. He describes a garden breathing the spirit of the Ancients, one which might have been laid out quite as well in the days of Pliny as in the middle of the fourteenth century. The garden of the fairy palace to which Pampinea conducts her gay company has been identified as that of the Villa Palmiera, some few miles outside Florence. The spot was well known to Boccaccio, and from his habit of taking many of his sketches direct from life it may readily be assumed that he faithfully portrays the Italian garden of his time.

Such gardens as Boccaccio has described are frequently found in paintings of the period. The well-known " Massacre of the Innocents " in the Academy at Florence shows a courtyard enclosure, upon the walls of which is a pergola with low round bowls alternating between the columns. In Lorenzo Lotto's picture of " Christ's farewell to the Virgin " is a garden with pleached alleys leading to a circular arbour (see annexed figure), and in Pinturicchio's picture of " Susanna and the Elders " the garden is shown, surrounded by a low red wall and a hedge of roses trained upon a lattice of gilded reeds. Long before the Renaissance had fully matured the classic passion for beautiful gardens reasserted itself with renewed vigour as a growing sense of safety and an influx of wealth permitted the pleasures of country life to become more and more appreciated by the noble families of the day, and so great an impetus was given to the movement that the whole countryside round Florence and other great cities soon became studded with villas and pleasure grounds.

A GARDEN FROM LORENZO LOTTO'S PICTURE OF "CHRIST'S FAREWELL TO THE VIRGIN."

Chief amongst the makers of princely gardens were the Medici at Florence, and Cosimo de Medici was one of the first great princes to turn his serious attention to garden design. In 1417 he purchased a country seat at Careggio, which he entirely rebuilt and laid out from the designs of Michelozzo Michelozzi; the villa still exists, though little of Cosimo's work remains. Here he spent the last years of an arduous life, seldom moving abroad, and here he died in 1464. According to Vasari, Michelozzi also laid out the fortress villa at Cafaggiuolo, but no vestige of these gardens now exists. The example of Cosimo de Medici was soon followed by other members of his family, each vying with the other in efforts to create more grandiose schemes, so that in addition to the great palace in Florence they had no less than

A COVERED FOUNTAIN.   TOPIARY DESIGNS.

A TREILLAGE SCREEN.

GARDEN DETAILS FROM "POLIPHILI HYPNEROTOMACHIA."

eleven magnificent villas in the immediate vicinity. The Boboli garden, laid out upon the hillside behind the Pitti Palace, was begun in 1549 by Eleonora de Medici, who commissioned Buontalenti and Il Tribolo to design the gardens extending to the south and west of the palace. The character of these has been but little altered, and nowhere are we better

ITALIAN FOUNTAIN : SIXTEENTH CENTURY

able to study an Italian garden of the sixteenth century. The palace is situated at the foot of a steep hillside which has been considerably excavated. Instead of a parterre the principal apartments overlook an immense amphitheatre with six tiers of stone benches, set off by a background of laurel hedge behind which rise the ilex-clad slopes of the upper garden.

This amphitheatre was designed to show off the superb spectacles given from time to time by the Medici, and is a feature rarely to be seen in Italian gardens. The engravings of Della Bella illustrate the great fêtes that took place here, when all Florence flocked to see the entertainments.

Another beautiful feature of the Boboli garden is the *Isolotto*, an oval-shaped island at the foot of the long cypress alley dividing the garden. It is laid out as a lemon garden, connected by two bridges, and is surrounded by a balustrade in which orange trees in large red pots alternate with short lengths of balustrading. In the middle is John of Bologna's gigantic fountain surmounted by a figure of Oceanus.

THE AMPHITHEATRE OF THE BOBOLI GARDEN ON THE OCCASION OF A GRAND FÊTE, FROM AN ENGRAVING BY DELLA BELLA.

A delightful picture of a city garden in Florence during the halcyon days of the sixteenth century is given by Bocchi, an author who, writing about the middle of the century, thus describes the garden of one of the Acciaiuoli palaces: "There is a garden on strong arches about fifteen cubits high, in a street close to the Arno and looking due south, where the air is soft and pleasant. There in pots and on espaliers are such delightful greenery and fruits, such as lemons and pomegranates, that although the space is not really large, yet the delight it gives is so great that it appears so. Above this and behind, rising yet higher, is another terrace filled with similar trees; it is marvellous to see the quantity of fruit produced and what good condition it is in. Above, and still further back, is yet another terrace, more than thirty cubits from the ground, and the view thence is so beautiful that the soul is rejoiced; wherever a man turns he enjoys the sweet air, full of the perfume of fruit and of flowers which are ever abundant according to their season. Water is lifted by ingenious devices from below up to the garden on the third terrace so that when dried up by the heat the moisture may be quickly restored."

THE ISOLOTTO, BOBOLI GARDEN, FLORENCE.

The most important Medicean villas remaining outside Florence are those of Castello and Petraja, now the property of the Royal Family; they lie side by side, resting against the hillside amid beautiful surrounding woods of ilex. The great parterre at Castello lies behind the low façade of the Casino that Buontalenti built for Pier Francesco de Medici, and is backed by a noble terrace, its brilliant whiteness admirably contrasting with the rich tones of the dark ilex woods behind. In the centre of the parterre is the fountain of Hercules, a work of consummate art and one of the finest fountains in Italy. It is generally supposed to have been executed by John of Bologna. Beyond lies the orange garden, enclosed on three sides by the terrace. One of the grottos, that devised by Il Tribolo, still remains in working order; it is probably the finest of its kind in Italy and is decorated with arabesques of different coloured shells and pebble-work with life-sized animals. The garden was everywhere adorned with exquisite bronzes

THE MODERN WATER PARTERRE AT VILLA GAMBERAIA, NEAR FLORENCE.

of animals and birds; several of them have been removed and are now among the treasures of the Bargello museum; upon the topmost terrace is a colossal recumbent figure representing the Apennines shrinking beneath the shower of water thrown by a jet high into the air.

The villa of Petraja has suffered more from the ravages of time than Castello. It was a favourite resort of Cosimo I, and here he spent his honeymoon with Camilla Martelli. Il Tribolo's fountain, brought from

VILLA CASTELLO, near FLORENCE.

THE WATER GARDEN, VILLA MARLIA.

FOUNTAIN BY IL TRIBOLO AT VILLA PETRAJA, FLORENCE.

Castello, still adorns the parterre, but the whole garden has been allowed to run riot.

Both Castello and Petraja were planned upon what the Italians considered the ideal garden site, as described by Ferrari in his *De Florum Cultura*: "First let the man whose nature exults in the culture of flowers, choose for his flower garden a plot exposed to a healthy climate, and remote from marshes, lest the gardener himself, among the gaily coloured flowers, should by breathing pestilential air be overcome by the pale hue of death; not facing a river lest he should breathe cold and damp, and therefore unhealthy air; and if possible close to his house so that he may have a golden age of eternal spring at home, and may see a paradise of flowers laid out below his windows; as large as possible, lest the various and manifold nation of flowers should be too closely crowded; sheltered from the north, whose deadly cold might be breathed by the tender plants in winter; turning towards the south, whose warm, humid, gentle-blowing breath is the life

ENTRANCE TO THE VILLA PIA, VATICAN.

of the flowers. So let not the little garden be inferior in the amenity of its site to Italy herself, which, sheltered from the cold of the sterile north wind by her Alpine walls, seemed to Varro to be one orchard spread out towards the fertile warmth of the southern sky."

Poggio a Cajano, some ten miles beyond Florence, was laid out about

A COURT IN THE GARDENS OF THE VATICAN.

1485 from the designs of Giulio di San Gallo, and was famous for its plantation of mulberry trees and for its wonderful parks, where Lorenzo de Medici formed a collection of all kinds of rare birds and animals. He was also keenly interested in the study of plants, and owing to his efforts Italy may claim to be the creator of botanical gardens. The grounds of his villa at Careggio might almost be called a botanical garden, as they contained countless specimens of trees and shrubs. The collection of rare animals soon became a princely occupation, and by the end of the fifteenth century menageries (*serragli*) were reckoned part of the suitable appointments of every court. "It belongs to the position of the great," says Matarazzo, "to keep horses, dogs, mules, falcons and other birds, court jesters, singers, and foreign animals."

THE PARTERRE AT THE VATICAN.

Towards the end of the fifteenth century the famous Orti Orcellari, at Florence, were laid out by Bernardo Rucellai, the kinsman of Lorenzo il Magnifico. Here it was that the celebrated Platonic Academy held its meetings and Niccoló Machiavelli read his discourses.

At the same time that these villas were being laid out in the neighbourhood of Florence, many of the best artists of the day were engaged upon the princely villas in and about Rome. Raphael, San Gallo, Bramante, Peruzzi, all giants in art, who knew how to combine the attainments of painter, architect and engineer, did not consider it beneath them to be also the designers of gardens. Amongst the most beautiful villas were those of Cardinal d'Este at Monte Cavallo, the Villa of Pope Julius, the Farnese gardens, and those of Cardinal Riario at Trastevere and of Cesio outside the Porta del Popolo. Bramante was engaged in laying out the gardens of the Vatican; and Raphael, with San Gallo, was creating the Villa Madama

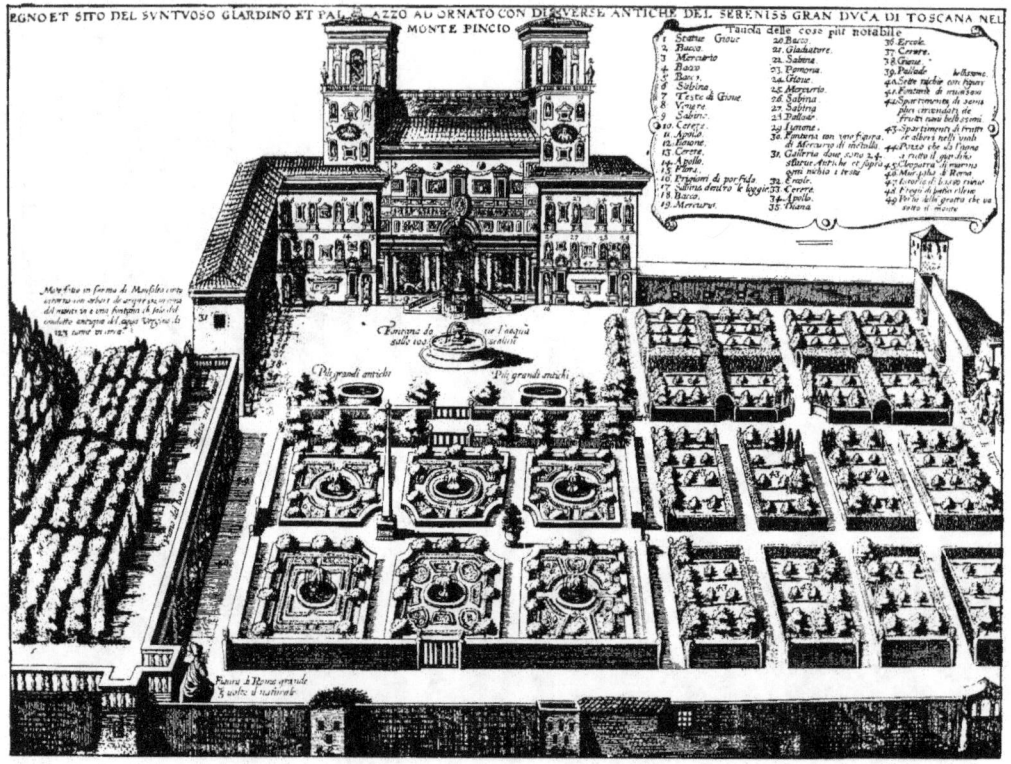

THE VILLA MEDICI IN THE SEVENTEENTH CENTURY. FROM AN ENGRAVING BY FALDA, 1670.

for Margaret, Duchess of Parma, upon the slopes of Monte Mario just outside Rome. In spite of the alterations that have taken place from time to time the Vatican gardens retain many traces of the works carried out at this period. Quite their most interesting feature is the delightful little garden pavilion known as the Villa Pia (of which the entrance is illus., p. 37). There are few more charming examples of garden architecture than this exquisite little work which Pirro Ligorio designed for Pope Julius IV in 1560.

It lies in a hollow against a rising background of ilex woods, and is said to have been built in imitation of the old Roman villa architecture; in fact, it embodies exactly the descriptions of Pliny.

The Villa Medici (illus. opposite), now the home of the French Academy in Rome, has preserved its characteristics untouched for many years. It was begun about 1540 from the designs of Annibale Lippi, and the gardens were laid out at the same time. They are approached from the piazza in front of the Casino by a shady drive ascending to the parterre, which is thus arranged upon the same level as the *piano nobile* of the house. The parterre is divided into sixteen plots, shaded by ilex trees and stone-pines, and traversed by hedged alleys. Falda's drawing of the garden in 1670 shows that it remains to-day in very much its original condition. There is a mount surrounded by an ilex *boschetto*, and

THE VILLA MEDICI, ROME

from its summit a grand view of Rome may be obtained. The mount is a feature rarely to be met with in Italian gardens, though we occasionally find it in the North of Italy at a later date. There are few gardens in Italy that can be compared with the Villa Medici, or which exhibit to a greater extent the good taste and simplicity characteristic of the best period of Italian garden-craft. Everywhere one feels a sense of quiet repose, due principally to the fact that no effort has been made to produce the violent contrasts in tree planting that so often quite destroy the charm of modern gardens. Stone-pine and ilex give a pleasing setting to the cool greys and green tones of the Casino at all seasons of the year.

THE AVIARY   VILLA BORGHESE, ROME

In the early years of the seventeenth century Scipione Borghese, the nephew of Pope Paul V, began to lay out the Villa Borghese. The Casino was designed about 1618 by Giovanni Vansanzio, a Flemish architect, and the grounds were originally laid out by Rainaldi and afterwards extended and remodelled. The gardens were famous in the seventeenth century for their wonderful fountains and grottos, and for a collection of " simples,"

TERRACE OF THE VILLA PAMPHILI DORIA, ROME, FROM AN ENGRAVING BY FALDA.

THE LOGGIA AT VILLA ALBANI, ROME.

cultivated in the enclosures upon either side of the Casino. The parterre still remains surrounded by gigantic caryatid figures, but most of the other features have been scattered.

The Villa Pamphili (illus. opposite), is just outside the city walls on the Janiculum hill. The casino was built about 1650 by Olimpia Pamphili for her son Camillo, and as Goncourt says " has the appearance of one of Benvenuto Cellini's chests in burnished silver, with little white statues standing out against the deep blue sky, as sentinels from Olympus, set in the midst of dark indigo trees, and surrounded by grass plots, white in springtime with daisies, and terraces with huge vases of bluish aloes or great camellia bushes."

There is no lack of documentary evidence to show the princely magnificence of these pleasure houses in and about Rome. Besides the many descriptions given by travellers they have been the subject of numerous engravings. Falda's work *I Giardini di Roma* is of considerable interest, in spite of the somewhat coarse character of the engraved plans and bird's-eye views, as it shows records of gardens which have now been entirely swept away or altered beyond recognition.

FOUNTAIN IN THE COURTYARD OF THE PALAZZO BORGHESE, ROME.

AN ITALIAN SEVENTEENTH CENTURY VASE FROM AN OLD MODEL.

In the beginning of the nineteenth century Percier and Fontaine published the plans of many of the most famous Roman gardens as they existed before the craze for natural gardening had wrought such havoc.

In addition to their villas in Rome many of the great cardinals had sumptuous establishments in the country. In the little mountain village of Caprarola, Cardinal Alessandro Farnese built his fortress palace upon an eminence looking out over the broad Campagna. The garden stretches behind up to a single crowning architectural conception, a quadrangle of gigantic figures standing out against the skyline. The palace and garden were designed by Giacomo Vignola, and nowhere is his genius seen to better advantage. Fortunately it has been handed down to our time in a state that presents a vivid picture of the magnificent splendour of the Princes of the Church in the glorious *cinquecento*. The palace is approached by a magnificent stairway and surrounded by a moat, walls of massive masonry three miles in circuit effectually shutting it out from all intrusion. The plan is arranged in the form of a pentagon enclosing a circular court. Round four sides of the palace stretches a broad terrace, and from two of the sides, stairways lead to square parterre gardens joined by a central loggia and fountain. Huge barocco statues, bearing baskets of fruit (illus., p. 49), and elaborately wrought balustrades complete the design. Upon one side is an immense grotto, worked in stucco and pebbles, its walls sustained by six gigantic sylvan figures. The ground rises gently behind these parterres,

ANOTHER FORM OF VASE.

THE PARTERRE, VILLA CAPRAROLA.

VILLA CAPRAROLA, NEAR VITERBO.

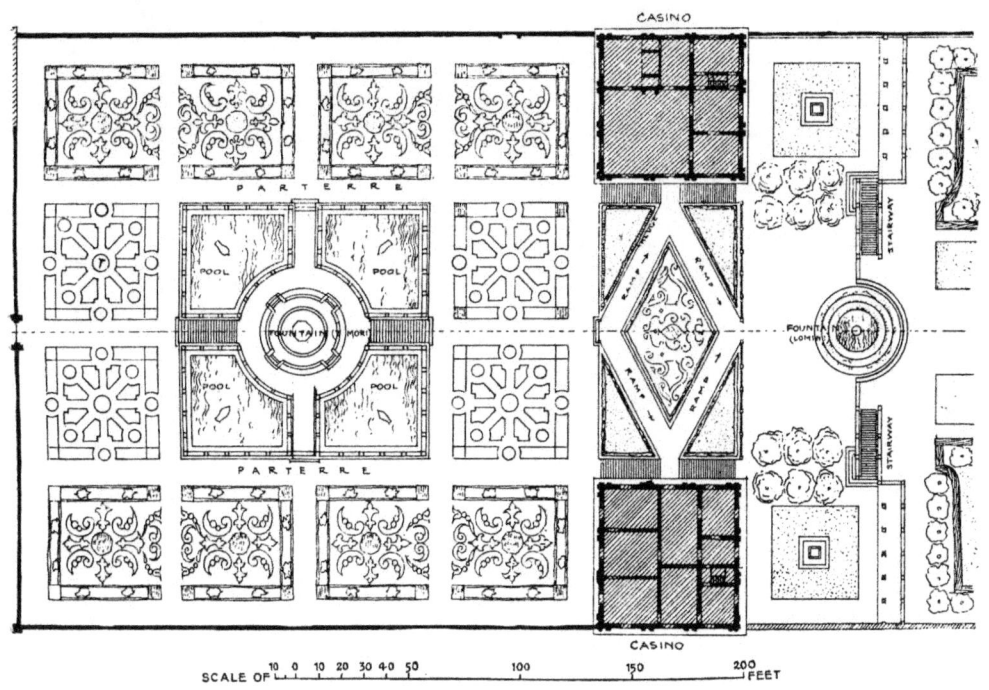

PLAN OF GARDEN AT VILLA LANTE.

and an avenue of cypresses leads to a graceful little casino known as the Villa Farnese, laid out some seventy years later than the palace by Cardinal Odoardo Farnese. At the extremity of the cypress avenue is a square courtyard with a circular pool, and on both sides are grottos, between which a broad ascent leads to a series of parterres cut out of the hillside.

The Palace of Caprarola set a fashion in villa building that was quickly followed by Cardinal Ippolito d'Este at Tivoli, and by Cardinal di Gambara in the Villa Lante near Viterbo. At the Villa Lante (illus., p. 47), almost within sight of Caprarola, Cardinal Gambara devised the interesting garden scheme that still remains in almost the same condition as when first constructed. It is reputed to have been designed by Vignola, and is one of the most pleasing gardens in Italy. The lower parterre is arranged as a water garden with beautifully proportioned balustrades leading up to the central fountain of bronze figures supporting the *stemma* of the family. The square twin villas stand out on both sides of a series of stairways and waterworks, ascending the hillside. Caprarola is a complete epitome of an Italian nobleman's country-house—

ON THE TERRACE OF VILLA CAPRAROLA, VITERBO.

a place of retirement when the summer heat, unbearable in cities, begets a craving for shade amid the sound and sight of water, which everywhere occupies a foremost place in the garden scheme.

It was in 1549 that Ippolito d'Este, Cardinal of Ferrara, having been appointed governor of Tivoli by Pope Paul III, decided to take up his residence there; he called to his aid Pirro Ligorio, the architect of the pictur-

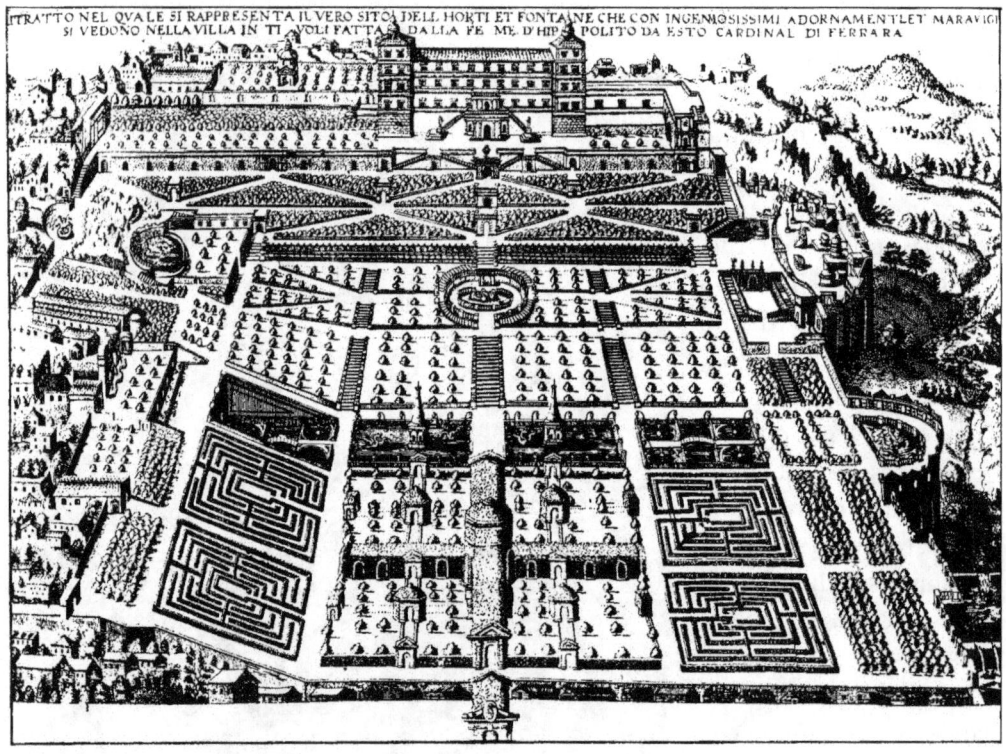

VILLA D'ESTE, TIVOLI, IN 1573.

esque little Villa Pia in the Vatican garden. The Villa is most beautifully situated with an extensive view over towering cypress spires and silvery waves of olive woods and ilexes to the vast stretches of the Campagna, and the Sabine mountains faint on the distant horizon. Much of the land had to be acquired from the municipality to lay out the garden, and according to Uberto Faglietta, writing in 1629, a considerable part of the village had to be demolished. The Villa was intended only as a summer residence, and

THE WATER PARTERRE, VILLA LANTE.

VILLA LANCELLOTTI, FRASCATI.

BOX PARTERRE AT VILLA LANCELLOTTI.

we see it to-day in an incomplete state, void of all architectural embellishment—a barrack-like structure planned to house a cardinal and his suite, numbering, it is said, as many as two hundred and fifty persons. Though the Casino was never entirely completed, no effort was spared in laying out the gardens, which were the joint design of Pirro Ligorio, Giacomo della Porta, and the famous hydraulic engineer, Orazio Olivieri. The River Anio flowed into Tivoli from the mountain heights, and a part of its waters was diverted to supply the enormous amount required for the multitude of fountains, cascades and hydraulic surprises that excited so much wonder and admiration when in the heyday of their glory, and as they appeared when Evelyn saw them: " We went to the Palace of Este. In the garden are sixteen vast conchas of marble, jetting out water, before the ascent of the Palace is the famous fountain of Leda and not far from that four sweet and delicious gardens. Descending thence are two pyramids of water and in a grove of trees near it the fountains of Tethys, Esculapius, etc. The cupids pouring out water are most rare and the grots are richly paved with 'pietra-commessa' shells, coral, etc. A long fountain walk led to a curious model of ancient Rome with temples and streets all in miniature, and in another part was the great water organ, which, as Montaigne complained, always played the same tune. This was effected by means of water, which, falling in a large body, and with a sudden descent into a round arched cave, strikes upon the air in it, and compels it to make its exit through the pipes of the organ which are thus supplied with wind. Another fall of water turns a broad wheel furnished with teeth so fixed in it as to strike in due order the keys of the organ and thus produce the tune to which the wheel is set."

The Casino stands upon a wide terrace some four hundred and fifty yards long, high above the garden; in the centre opposite the Casino, one descends to the next terrace below and by means of ramps and stairways to the level of the great fountain terrace, or gallery of a hundred fountains. The balustrades to the stairways are ingeniously formed of a series of basins and jets of water, leaping from step to step.

At one end of the great fountain terrace is a large *théâtre d'eau*, known as the fountain of Arethusa, and an adjoining grotto, with bathing rooms; at the other end is a miniature representation of an ancient city, supposed to represent old Rome with its little streets, temples and theatres.

Frascati has long been famous for its villas and pleasure grounds, and since ancient days the undulating country at the foot of the Alban Mountains has been the favourite resort of the citizens of Rome wishing to escape from the heat and bustle of the great city.

The Villa Aldobrandini stands grandly upon a succession of broad terraces with three main avenues of approach. It was built in 1598 for the nephew of Pope Clement VIII, Cardinal Pietro Aldobrandini, from the designs of

ARCHITECTURAL TERMINATION TO THE CASCADE, VILLA ALDOBRANDINI, FRASCATI.

Giacoma della Porta, famous as the architect who completed the dome of St. Peters. For the best contemporary account of the villa we must again turn to the description of John Evelyn, who saw it soon after completion. He gives a picturesque description of the water theatre that Giovanni Fontana and Orazio Olivieri designed behind the palace. " From the summit of the hill, falls a cascade precipitating into a large theatre of water (illus. p. 55). Under this is an artificial grotto, wherein are curious rocks, hydraulic organs,

CASCADE AT THE VILLA ALDOBRANDINI.

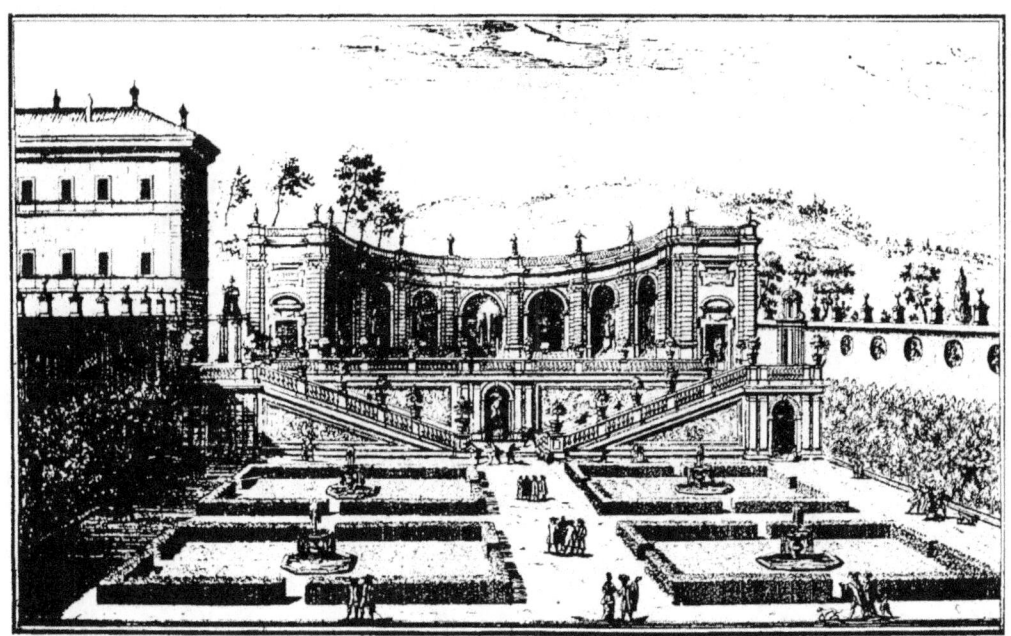

GIOVANNI FONTANA'S GARDEN THEATRE AT VILLA MONDRAGONE, FRASCATI.

and all kinds of singing birds, moving and chirping by force of the water, with several other pageants and surprising inventions. In one of the theatres of water is an Atlas spouting and in another a monster makes a terrible roaring with a horn. The steep hillside upon which the villa stands was

GARDEN THEATRE AT THE VILLA GORI, SIENA.

formed into a long platform some 300 yards long and 40 wide, and upon the edge of this space the casino was built with bosquets upon either side." During the last century the garden has fallen upon evil days, like most of the Frascati villas, but we can still trace enough of its former glories to form a good idea of its appearance in the seventeenth century.

The Villa Torlonia belonged originally to the Conti and later passed by marriage into the Torlonia family. The garden consists entirely of ilex *boschi* laid out upon the hillside in rectangular forms divided by mossy alleys. Here and there, at the intersections of the walks, are fountains sending up high jets of water, and these, seen at the termination of long vistas, give a very pleasing effect. The two principal features are a fine terrace extending the entire width of the gardens and the great cascade (illus. opposite). Another famous Frascati garden is that of the Villa Mondragone (illus., p. 55) built in 1567 for Cardinal Marco d'Attempo. The garden is now much neglected, but the fine *théâtre d'eau* terminating the parterre still remains. Other villas at Frascati which have now all practically disappeared were the Villa Falconiere built for Cardinal Ruffini, the Villa Pallavicini and the Villa Muti.

A WELL-HEAD AT VICOBELLO, SIENA.

Around Siena are several most interesting old Tuscan villas. The Villa Gori still has its long dense ilex tunnels radiating from the Casino across the farmlands; one leads to a circular decoy arranged upon a small hill covered with thickets, and another tunnel conducts to the Garden theatre (illus., p. 57), a charming feature often found in Italian gardens. The stage was a grass platform, rows of clipped cypresses forming the wings, and framing the whole. A rather larger example of a garden theatre is just outside Siena at the Villa Sergardi, and in this case it is so arranged that the audience need not trouble themselves to leave the house, as the stage is placed in full view of the first floor windows.

In the South of Italy and in Sicily old formal gardens are not so often to be met with. There are a few in the neighbourhood of Naples, but these date chiefly from the eighteenth century and cannot be compared with the

FONTANA SVPERIORE IN CIMA LA SCALA E CASCATA DI SOPRA AL TEATRO NEL BOSCO DEL GIARDINO LVDOVISI A FRASCATI.

FOUNTAIN AT VILLA TORLONIA, FRASCATI.

VEDVTA IN PROFILO ET PER FIANCO DELL ANTECEDENTE TEATRO DELLE FONTANE NEL GIARDINO LVDOVISI A FRASCATI

TERMINATION TO THE CASCADE, VILLA TORLONIA.

Roman gardens. The most famous is at the Palace of Caserta between Naples and Rome; this is one of the largest palaces in Europe and recalls the Escurial in its vastness and desolation.

The finest gardens in the North of Italy are to be found round the Lakes of Garda, Maggiore and Como, and principally date from the late seventeenth and eighteenth centuries. Isola Bella upon Lake Maggiore (illus., p. 63) is perhaps the most famous. Romantically situated upon one of the Borromean Islands, it is a most fascinating study in garden planning. The garden was begun in 1632 by Count Carlo Borromeo under the direction of Carlo Fontana, but the whole work was not completed until 1671. Although the conception of Isola Bella is undoubtedly good there is a great falling off in the architectural detail, which is often coarse and lacks the refinement of the Roman and Florentine villas.

The whole district round Milan, especially the neighbourhood of Varese,

FOUNTAIN AT VILLA CARLOTTA, CADENABBIA.

abounded in large country villas, built in the seventeenth century. The flatness of the ground, which nowadays consists mostly of marshland, was ill-suited to the making of gardens, but nevertheless in the rare volumes of Alberto dal Ré, *Ville di Delizia di Milano*, we find an interesting series of villas, all more or less laid out in the style of Le Nôtre. Most of these have since been abandoned for more beautiful situations on the Italian lakes. A few, however, still remain, and of these the Villa of Castellazzo is a well preserved specimen. Upon Lake Como the well-known Villa Carlotta still attracts many sightseers. It is a characteristic example of the way in which the Italian villa has been so often spoiled, and we would fain see the beautiful terraces and pavilions that Dal Ré engraves instead of the present meaningless plan. The water approach alone remains of all the former beauties of this garden.

All along the Italian Riviera were beautiful villas; their situations, with the mountain scenery behind and the blue Mediterranean in front, could hardly fail to inspire a garden designer. In the environs of Genoa, and especially at the fashionable suburb of Sampierdarena, were many fine villas with stately gardens, pleasure houses of the merchant princes of Genoa, who in the sixteenth century commissioned such artists as Galeazzo Alessi, Giacoma della Porta, Pirro Ligorio, and Annibale Lippi to build their sumptuous palaces. With very few exceptions these have long since disappeared, but fortunately an excellent series of records of the finest villas was made in 1832 by M. Gauthier.[1] The situations were in some respects unsuited to gardens, the soil being barren and rocky, and the designers resorted more especially to architecture in order to obtain their effects, and instead of *boschi* which are so general in Italy, we find an extensive use of pergolas, in order that all parts of the garden might be reached in shade.

[1] See *Les plus beaux Edifices de la Ville de Gênes et de ses Environs*, par M. P. Gauthier. Paris. 1832.

SEVENTEENTH-CENTURY
TERRA-COTTA VASE AND STAND.

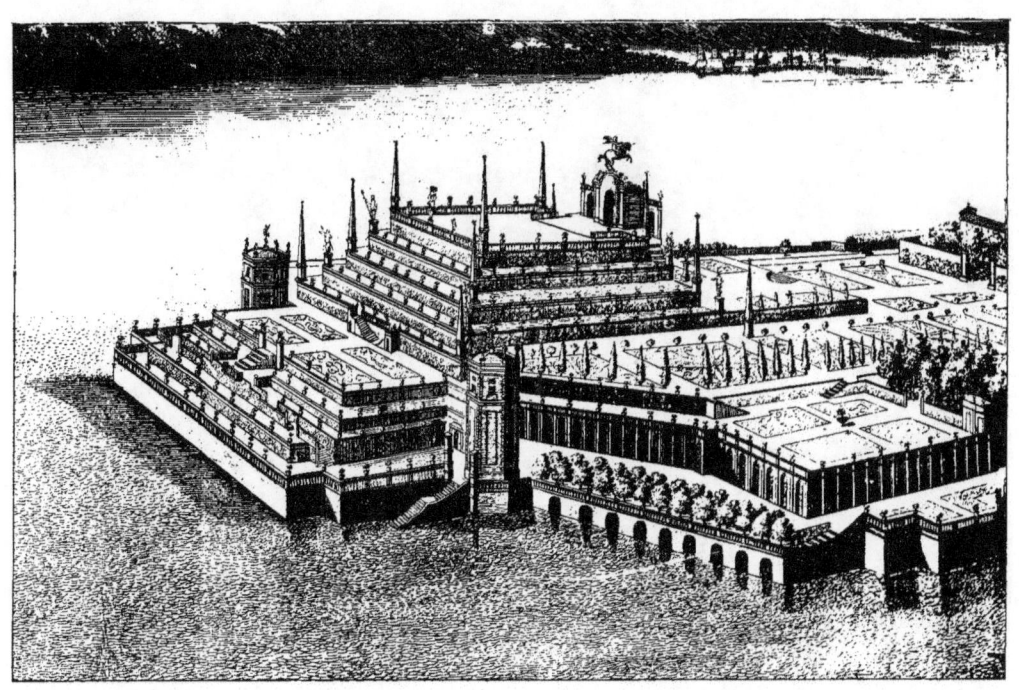
ISOLA BELLA IN THE EIGHTEENTH CENTURY FROM AN ENGRAVING BY DAL RÉ.

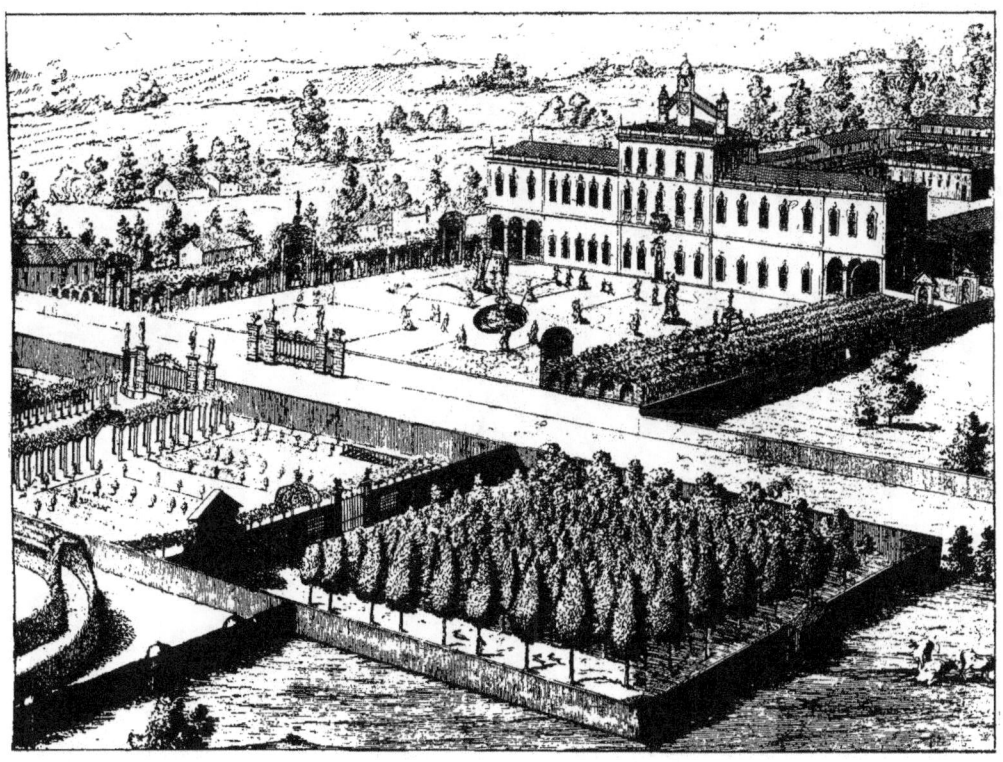
A VILLA NEAR MILAN IN THE EIGHTEENTH CENTURY FROM AN ENGRAVING BY DAL RÉ.

CHAPTER IV

FRENCH GARDENS OF THE SIXTEENTH AND EARLY SEVENTEENTH CENTURIES

IN France the art of garden design had a very definite beginning with the reign of François I, and its development continued without interruption during the next two centuries until the culminating point was reached under Le Nôtre and his school. Chambord, Fontainebleau, and Saint Germain were the principal creations of François I, who, like his great successor Louis XIV, appears to have been always fortunate in attracting the best artists of the day to his court. Few kings have shown an equal amount of discrimination and taste, or exercised a more powerful influence on the art of their country. From Italy he drew the greatest talent of the day, and employed such artists as Il Rosso, Primaticcio, Serlio and Vignola, who handed on the finest traditions of the Italian Renaissance to a most brilliant school of Frenchmen, a school numbering in its ranks Pierre Lescot, Jean Goujon and Philibert de l'Orme.

In laying out the gardens of Fontainebleau (illus., p. 67), François I introduced many Italian features, and although at the present time hardly anything remains of the gardens as they existed at this period, Du Cerceau's plan of about 1570 enables us to form a very accurate idea of them. The great parterre must have been a most delightful garden, an admirable complement to the irregular outline of the quaint collection of turrets and pavilions that constituted the palace. The gardens were not long allowed to remain as François left them. Henri IV considerably extended the boundaries and employed Francini, an Italian designer, to rearrange the great parterre or King's Garden, which was now known as *le jardin du Tibre*, from a colossal allegorical statue placed in the centre. Henri IV also added the canals and planted avenues upon both sides.

The splendid Château de Chenonceaux was another of the palaces of François I. It passed into his hands in 1524, but he did not reside here very much, and Henri II presented it to Diane de Poitiers, who, in 1556, employed Philibert de l'Orme to remodel the building and lay out the gardens. In later years Bernard Palissy, whose work we shall consider presently, created a garden, the description of which reads like a fable. He completely abandoned himself to his exuberant fancy for rockeries, basins, and grotesque ornaments.

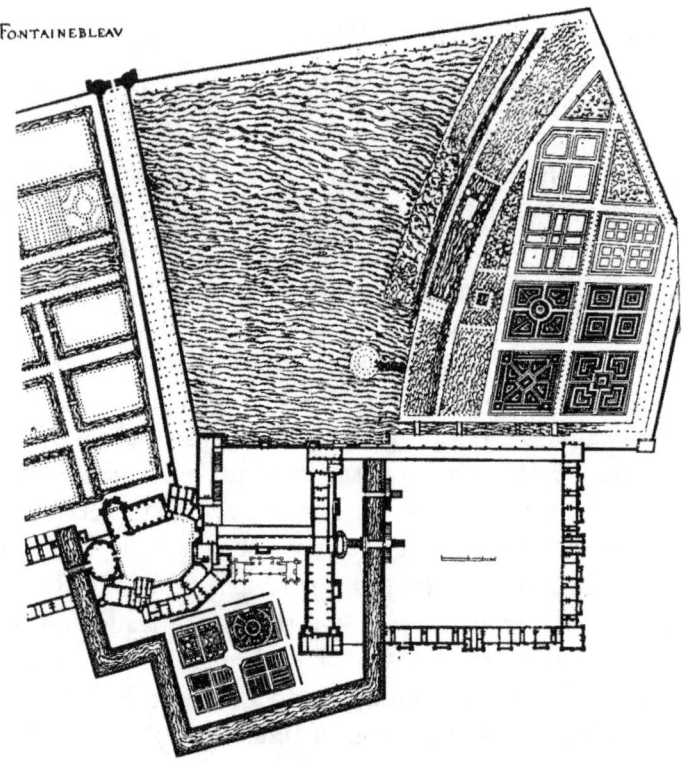

FONTAINEBLEAU IN THE SIXTEENTH CENTURY FROM THE PLAN BY DU CERCEAU.

About the year 1538 the Constable Anne de Montmorency began the improvement and rebuilding of the Château de Chantilly, near Paris. The property had passed into his hands in 1522 and soon after this date, at a period when he was estranged from the Court, he conceived the idea of converting the castle into a rich and agreeable dwelling, surrounded with gardens and parterres, and enlarging and planting the park.

A most important addition to gardening literature appeared in 1545, when Charles Estienne (1504–1564), a physician of Paris and member of a

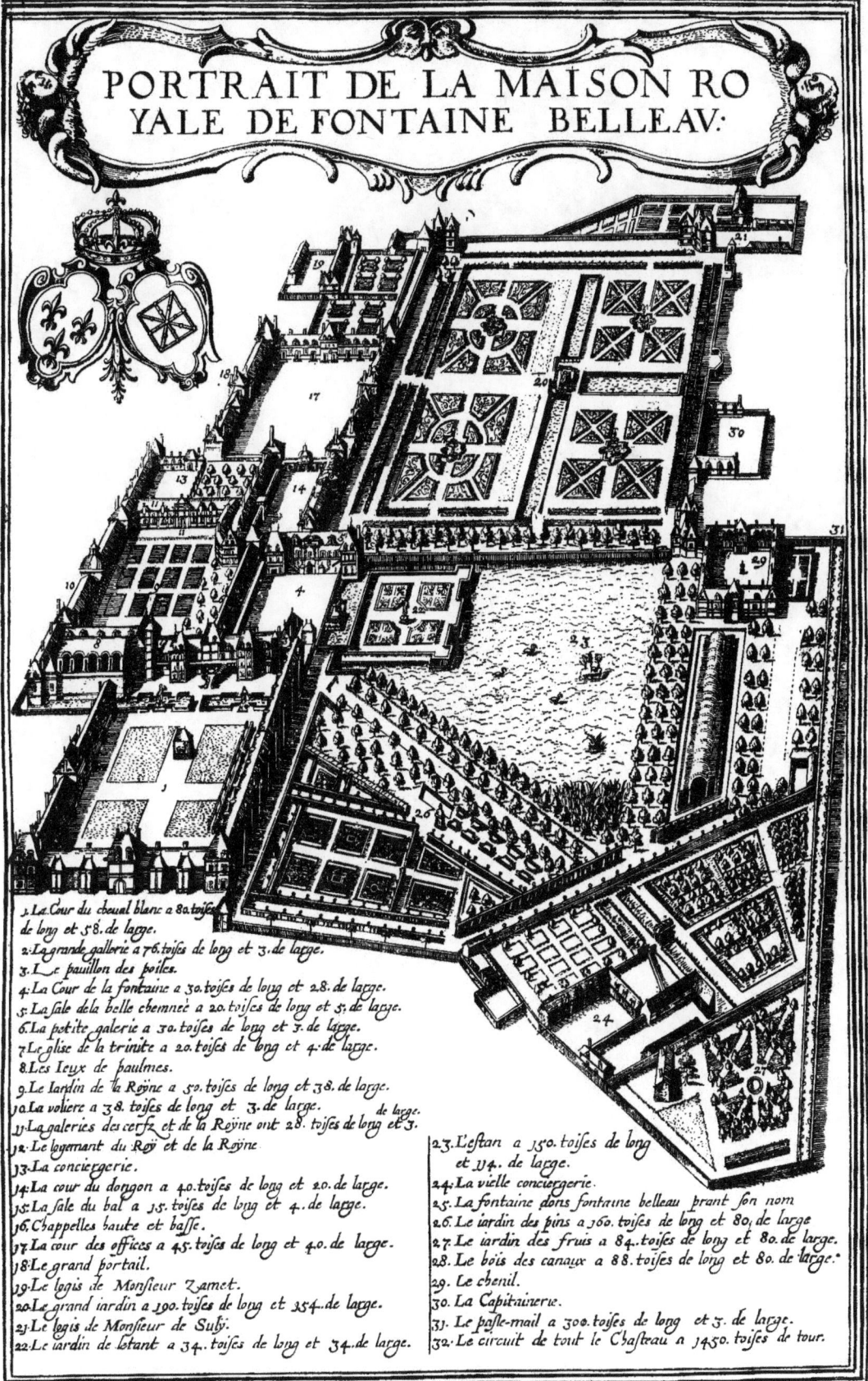

FONTAINEBLEAU IN THE SEVENTEENTH CENTURY.

FRENCH GARDENS: 16TH AND EARLY 17TH CENTURIES

family of famous printers, published his treatise on agriculture. In 1570 he published in conjunction with his father-in-law, Jean Liebault, a work entitled *La Maison Rustique*. This book went through upwards of thirty editions, and was translated into English in 1600 by Richard Surflet, and was reprinted in 1616 by Gervase Markham. " It is a commendable and seemely thing," says the author, " to behold out of a window manie acres of ground well tilled and husbanded, whether it be a Medow, a Plot for planting of

A FOUNTAIN AT THE CHATEAU DE VERNEUIL, FROM DU CERCEAU.

Willowes, or arable ground: but yet it is much more to behold faire and comely Proportions, handsome and pleasant Arbors, and, as it were, Closets, delightfull borders of Lavender, Rosemarie, Boxe, and other such like."

In the middle of the sixteenth century, Androuet du Cerceau began the wonderful series of surveys for his great work *Les plus excellents Bastiments de France*, many of the original drawings for which are now preserved in the British Museum.

The work of Du Cerceau gives an excellent *résumé* of French architecture under the last of the Valois, and shows the extraordinary activity in château building that characterized a period of between fifty and sixty years of comparative peace. From these designs we realize the undoubted influence of the Italian taste, but not even Italy can show us so marvellous a series of buildings produced within so short a space of time.

Of this wonderful series the châteaux of Madrid, Creil, Montargis and Verneuil no longer exist. The Louvre, Vincennes, Coussy, Gaillon, Blois, Amboise, Fontainebleau, Villers-Cotterets, the Tuileries, Chantilly, Anet, are all more or less mutilated by alterations and restorations. Chambord, Ecouen, Saint Germain, Ancy-le-Franc, Chenonceaux, Dampierre have still much of their original appearance left.

A FOUNTAIN AT THE CHATEAU DE GAILLON.

The irregular shapes of the castle buildings rendered it almost impossible for the French garden designers to imitate the Italians in laying out their gardens upon a main axial line with the house, and the gardens illustrated by Du Cerceau are in most cases designed quite irrespective of the château, as is the case at Blois and Gaillon. On the other hand, at Ancy-le-Franc and Verneuil both château and garden are designed as a whole.

The parterres are almost invariably square, and the designs for the flower borders of simple geometric form. They are often surrounded by a low balustrade with posts supporting heraldic beasts, gilt or picked out in gay colours. This craving for colour, which was so characteristic a feature of the mediaeval garden, disappeared in the seventeenth century, since when garden woodwork has lost considerable charm by its lack of colour. A central feature, such as a fountain or sundial, often gains much when richly coloured or gilt.

The Château of Gaillon (v. illus. opposite), on a hill overlooking the wind-

FRENCH GARDENS: 16TH AND EARLY 17TH CENTURIES

THE GREAT PARTERRE AT THE CHATEAU DE GAILLON, FROM DU CERCEAU.

ings of the Seine about thirty miles south-east of Rouen, was erected between 1497 and 1510 and was the most sumptuous private residence in France. "In the eighteenth century people said of a fine country seat 'C'est un petit Versailles'; in the sixteenth the saying was:—'C'est un petit Gaillon.' Its creator was George of Amboise, Cardinal Archbishop of Rouen and Prime Minister to Louis XII, the chief of a group of enlightened prelates who did much to spread Renaissance culture in France."

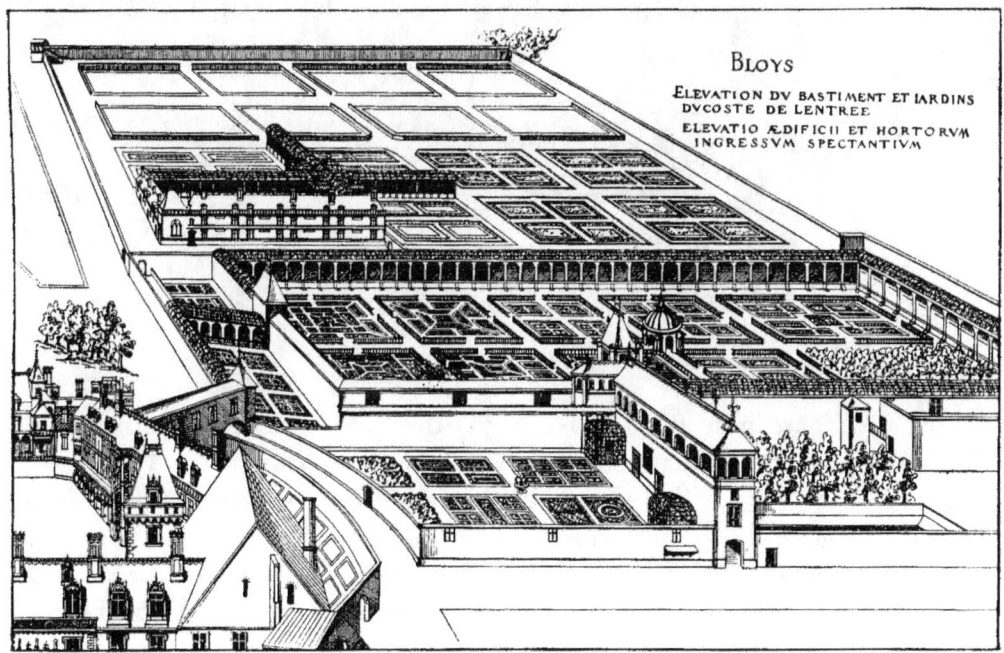

THE CHATEAU DE BLOIS.

Amongst other curiosities of the Château de Gaillon were the Hermitage and an island retreat known as *La Maison blanche,* a shining white garden pavilion that glistened in the sun, surrounded by fairylike parterres. The magnificent octagonal marble fountain reproduced on page 70 from Du Cerceau's drawing had three large basins, the water spouting from one to the other through satyr masks; the lower panels were richly sculptured with armorial bearings.

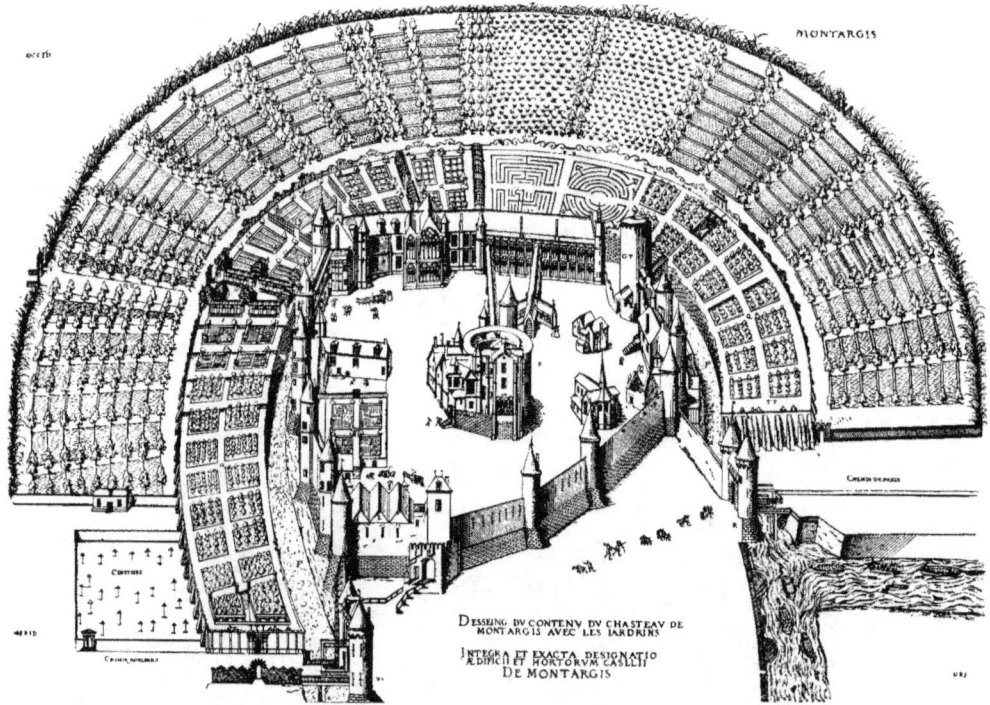

THE CHATEAU DE MONTARGIS.

At the Château de Blois (illus., p. 71) the garden scheme consisted of three principal large gardens with several smaller ones attached. The largest of all had a central pavilion similar to that at Gaillon and was divided into a series of square flower parterres, each enclosed within a low railing. It was entirely surrounded by a wooden gallery for the training of plants, and similar galleries leading from one garden to the other made it possible to reach almost any part under cover, protected from rain or sun. These also appear in the garden at the Château de Beauregard, illustrated from Du Cerceau's drawing.

FRENCH GARDENS: 16TH AND EARLY 17TH CENTURIES

The Château de Creil, which was commenced by Charles V and destroyed by the Prince de Condé before the Revolution, was planned on a little island in the river Oise in Picardy. The garden shown in Du Cerceau's plan is not extensive and consists of four enclosures divided into simple knots, each garden surrounded by a high wall and one containing a pavilion overlooking the river.

Montargis (illus., pp. 72 and 74) was, in the words of Du Cerceau, "un demesne vrayment Royale." Situated upon the junction of the Loing and

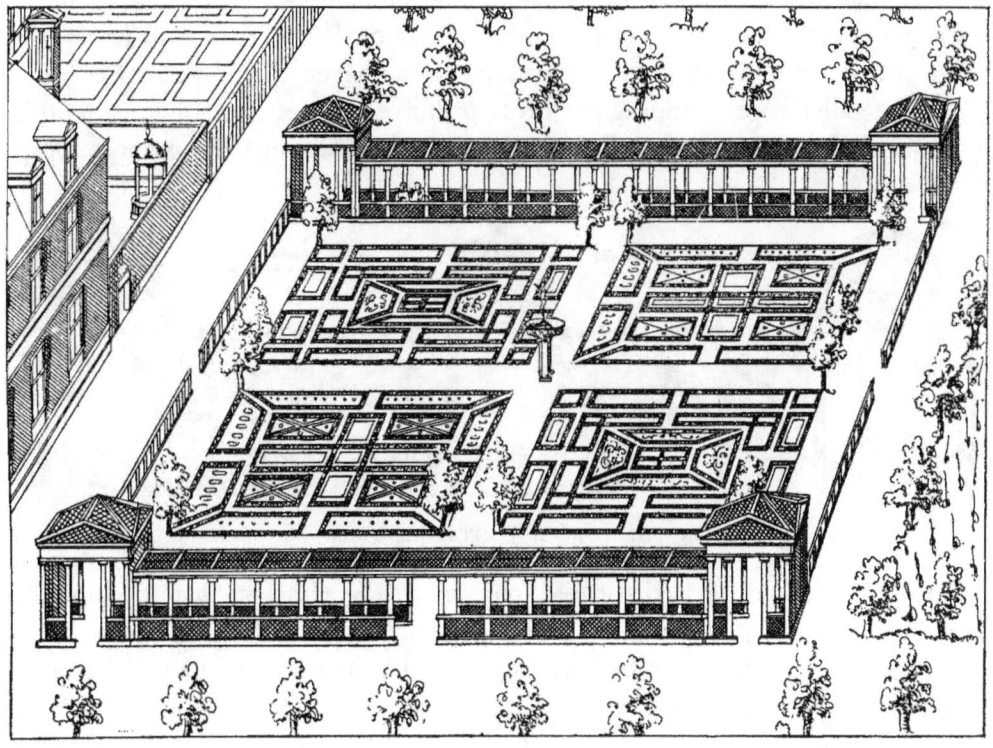

THE CHATEAU DE BEAUREGARD.

Vernisson, it had one of the most beautiful sites in France. Its group of buildings of different periods, clustered round a central keep, were sheltered from the east by great forests. During the Revolution the greater part of the château was destroyed, and nothing now remains save the fine buttressed terrace. Upon the original plan is a note that the small garden within the castle was known as the *Jardin d'Orléans*; it was probably used as a herb or medicinal garden. Du Cerceau's view shows how the *Grant jardin*, or pleasure garden, was divided from the château by a ditch and again from the orchards and more utilitarian gardens by a high buttressed wall. The pleasure garden was divided by great *galeries de charpenterie*, elaborate and massive architectural constructions, which were probably intended to be covered with plants.

As yet flowers were seldom grown in gardens for decorative purposes, and it will be found that their cultivation for these purposes, without regard to their medicinal uses, was very much neglected. The famous gardens of Vauquelin des Yveteaux in the neighbourhood of Paris are said to have contained more melons than tulips and more cabbages than hyacinths.

The galleries surrounding the great parterre at Anet were of considerable architectural pretensions; they were vaulted, and lighted by large open

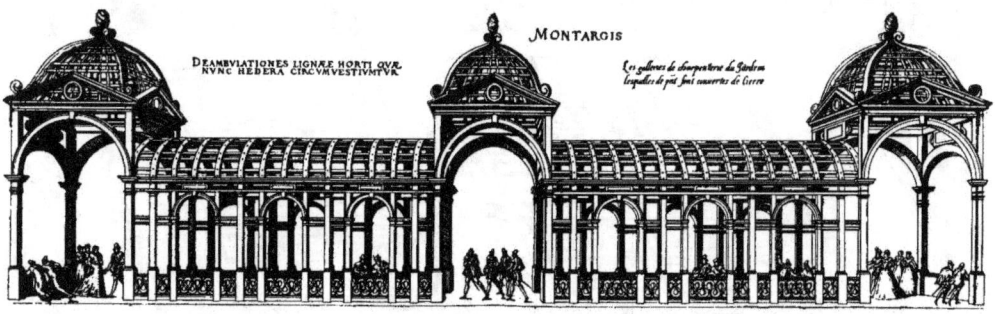

A WOODEN GALLERY AT MONTARGIS, FROM DU CERCEAU.

windows decorated with rusticated pilasters; the windows had pediments, and the floor was paved with a pattern of cut stone and brick. The great parterre in the middle was divided into twenty-four large unequal squares, some laid out in regular geometric patterns, others of grass, box and aromatic plants. Two square pavilions occupied the angles of the gallery and overlooked the deer park; they were designed by Philibert de l'Orme. "I have had made," says De l'Orme, "in the Château d'Anet for Madame la Duchesse de Valentinois two little pavilions overlooking the park where may be put the players of cornets and trumpets and other instruments to give pleasure to the King and to the Princes." The gardens were celebrated for their wonderful collection of plants formed under the supervision of the famous gardener Mollet—the first of the great family of French gardeners—who by purchase and exchange brought together an immense variety of the rarest plants of his day. In 1685 the park and gardens were almost entirely destroyed by Le Nôtre, and the beautiful decorations of the sixteenth century nearly all annihilated.

Besides Du Cerceau the principal professional garden designers of the sixteenth and early seventeenth centuries were Bernard Palissy, Olivier de Serres and the three Mollets.

Bernard Palissy has been described as a man "obscurely great amongst the prominently little." In 1563 appeared his most important work, the *Recepte véritable*.[1] We find him also employed as a garden designer at Ecouen, Chaulnes, and Nesle in Picardy, Reux in Normandy, Madrid in the environs of Paris, and the Château de Chenonceaux.

BERNARD PALISSY.

The *Recepte véritable* is essentially original and full of charm; it gives very important information of the garden design of this period and is written, as he says in the preface, "that the simple may be instructed by the wise, in order that we may none of us

[1] *Recepte véritable par laquelle tous les hommes de la France pourrent apprendre à augmenter leurs Trésors avec le Dessin d'un jardin délectable et Utile.* Rochelle, 4to., 1563.

be rebuked at the last day for having hidden talents in the earth." It takes the form of a dialogue in which he represents the speakers as Theory and Practice. The first part of the book deals entirely with agriculture, and in the second part Palissy lays down his plan for a delectable garden which is in reality a description of the garden he laid out at Chaulnes in Normandy. First of all he recommends that a hilly site be chosen that water may be easily brought down from the high ground; he then proceeds to give minute details of the eight *cabinets*, or garden houses that were to mark the angles,

A SURPRISE FOUNTAIN.

and the termination of the four cross walks of the great parterre. He proposes to form the rock upon the mountain sides to the north and west of the garden into a series of chambers, with aspects exposed to the sun in order to protect tender plants during the winter months. He directs that the terrace is to be bordered by a balustrade on which are to be damask roses, violets, and the most fragrant flowers, in enamelled pots.

Although Palissy, like Bacon, professes to dislike the hydraulic surprises so dear to the fashionable world of his day, he nevertheless suggests that place should be found in his garden for a statue holding a vase of water in one hand

and an inscription in the other, so placed that when any one steps forward to examine the inscription he may have the vase of water emptied on his head. The surprise fountain illustrated on p. 76 consisted of a revolving dragon, emitting a jet of water that could be made to play in any direction by a concealed operator. In describing the arrangement of the trees to form the *cabinets de verdure* or natural summer houses, he says that young elms should be planted at even distances, trained upward, and lopped until their trunks are grown to a sufficient height to form the columns of a little temple; they are then to receive, above and below, circular wounds which will cause a deposit of fresh wood, and natural protuberances corresponding to the bases and capitals of ordinary columns. The branches which shoot from the capitals of these living pillars are to be trained in the first instance, and elaborately worked into the pattern of an architectural frieze. Evidently fearing the ridicule with which these ideas might be met, Palissy goes on to say that whereas in these days men admired gardens abounding in dragons, cocks, and other absurdities, even soldiers on horseback, cut out of rosemary and other plants, how much more should they admire his living house, which when established would not need attention more than about twice a year.

Olivier de Serres (1539-1619) was another great gardener of the period, though he is famous more as a practical horticulturist than as a designer. He published in 1599 his *Treatise on the Silkworm* and in 1600 the *Théâtre d'Agriculture*.

The Mollets may be said to have formed a dynasty in their art. The first was the chief gardener at the Château d'Anet, where he laid out the famous gardens that we have already described and formed a collection of rare flowers and herbs for the Duc d'Aumale. His son, Claude Mollet, was born in 1563 and succeeded his father as the designer of the Royal gardens of Henri IV and Louis XIII. He is said to have been the first in France to create the *parterres à compartiments de broderie* (v. p. 125). In 1595 we find him employed at Saint Germain-en-Laye and a few years later at Monceaux, Fontainebleau and also at the Tuileries. He left two sons, Claude and André, both of whom were famous gardeners, the latter being appointed head gardener to James I. In 1651 André Mollet published his great work, *Le Jardin de Plaisir*. He was the first author to recommend the extensive planting of avenues, a fashion destined to effect great changes in the garden craft of both France and England. He insists that

Parterres des costes de la fontaine du Mercure a St Germain a laye.

the first adornment of a Royal palace should be a grand double avenue or triple row of elms or limes, "which ought to be laid out at right angles with the front of the house; at the beginning of the avenue there should be a large semicircle or square, so that the general design can be better observed. Then at the back of the house there should be constructed *parterres en broderie* near it so that they can be easily enjoyed from the windows without any obstacles of trees, palisades or any other high objects that might impede the eye from seeing their full extent."

PARTERRES AT ST. GERMAIN-EN-LAYE, DESIGNED BY CLAUDE MOLLET.

Another garden author of the sixteenth century was André Mizauld, who published many works, chiefly in Latin. The first one which relates to gardening appeared in 1564; it was followed by other pamphlets and the whole was collected by Caille, a physician, and published in 1578 in French.[1] The work was translated into German and printed at Basle in 1675. Mizauld was known in his day as the *Esculape de France*, and his writings were held in great repute, but the descriptions relating to the design of gardens cannot compare in charm with those of Bernard Palissy.

In examining the maps of Paris at this period it is astonishing to find the large number of beautiful gardens that existed in the sixteenth and seventeenth centuries, of which hardly any trace now remains. Their sites, that might have been used to so great advantage for the creation of public squares, have in many cases been built over, and in this respect Paris has suffered much more than London. The plan of Gomboust, 1642, shows the botanic garden of Nicholas Houel, famed for its pavilions and fountains;

---

[1] *Le jardinage de Mizauld contenant la manière d'embellir les jardins et comment il faut enter es arbres et les rendre médicinaux.* Paris, 1578. André de la Caille. Another edition published in 1607 is entitled *La Maison Champestre*, by E. Vinet et A. Mizauld.

the parterres of Nicholas d'Yveteaux and of Conrart, described in the Clélie of Mlle. de Scudéry, where the founders of the Académie Française first met together. Many of the great abbeys of the seventeenth century had parterres that rivalled the large palaces in their magnificence. The royal abbey of St. Denis had in additon to a most elaborate *parterre de broderie*

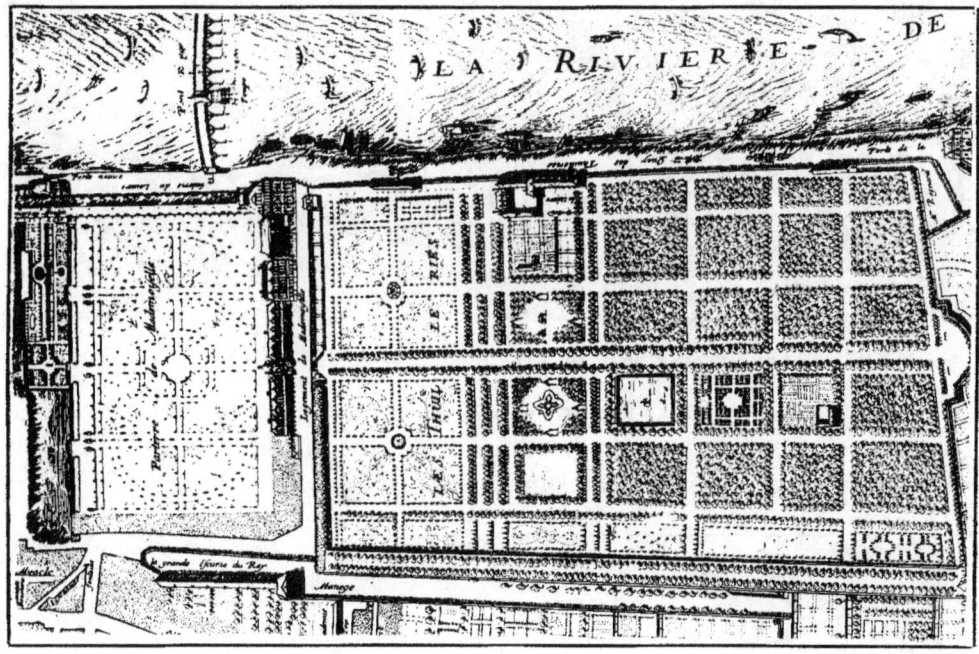

THE TUILERIES GARDEN FROM GOMBOUST'S PLAN, 1642.

within the cloisters, another splendid parterre garden with long avenues stretched out in the form of a gigantic cross.

The two most important Parisian gardens were those of the Tuileries and the Luxembourg; the first was laid out by Catherine de Medici, in the latter part of the sixteenth century, and the second by Marie de Medici some years later. Both princesses delighted in their gardens, and in their childhood's days had revelled in the charming country villas of their family at Pratolino and Castello in the neighbourhood of Florence, and also in the magnificent Boboli garden adjoining the Pitti Palace. It was therefore only natural that in later life they should have shown so great a taste for horticulture.

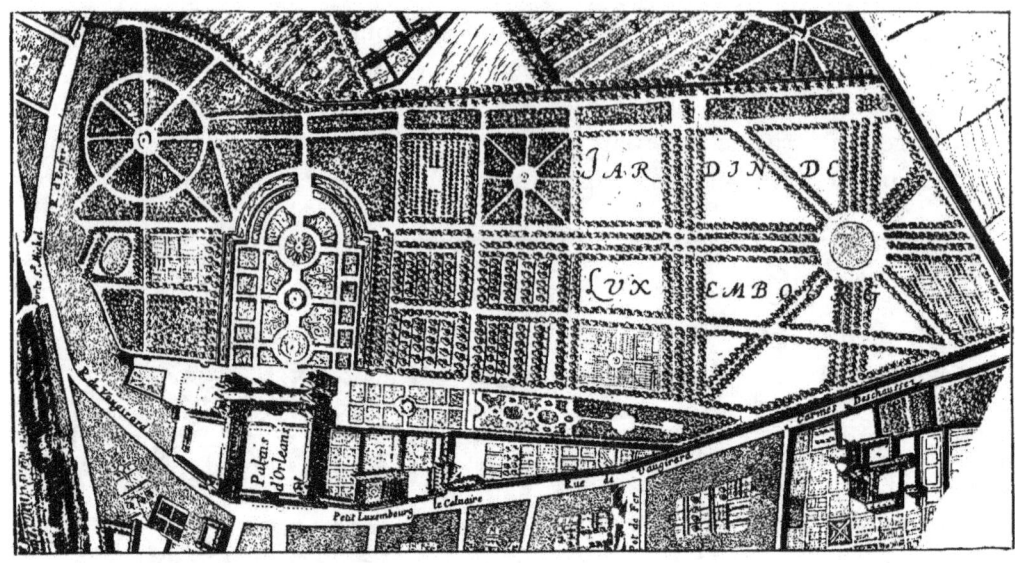

THE LUXEMBOURG GARDEN IN 1642 FROM GOMBOUST'S PLAN OF PARIS.

The Palace of the Tuileries (illus., p. 79) was created by Catherine de Medici as a retreat from the bustle and business of the Louvre. Here life might be enjoyed at greater ease, untrammelled by the etiquette of the Court.

THE LUXEMBOURG GARDEN IN THE SEVENTEENTH CENTURY, FROM I. SILVESTRE.

FRENCH GARDENS: 16TH AND EARLY 17TH CENTURIES 81

From the plan of the gardens of this period by Du Cerceau we see that they were laid out upon a piece of meadow-land alongside the Seine, known as the Tuileries on account of the tile-yards long established upon the spot. They had elaborate *compartiments de broderie*, designed by Claude Mollet near the palace, and there was a small *bosquet* and a rectangular basin beyond. A plan by Mérian shows the gardens as they existed in 1615, with a series of quaint *treillage* pavilions. The *volière* or aviary, consisting of several buildings, was planned in the middle of the Quai des Tuileries. The most famous feature of the garden was the "echo," a kind of grotto with numerous hydraulic surprises, the work of Palissy. Here it was that the gallants of the day betook themselves to serenade their mistresses. Some little distance from the "echo" was the *ménagerie*, containing a collection of wild animals. A contemporary account of a visit of the Swiss Ambassadors to the garden

"LA FONTAINE DE MEDICIS," LUXEMBOURG GARDEN.

relates that: "In the morning the Ambassadors set out for the garden of the Queen called the Tuillerie. The garden is very large and very pleasant. A broad path divides it into two parts, planted on each side with tall trees, elms and sycamores, which afford shade to the walkers. There is a labyrinth designed with such art that, once inside, exit is difficult. There are tables made of branches and leaves, beds, etc. The astonishing thing is that this labyrinth is almost entirely formed of bent cherry trees. There are several fountains with nymphs and fauns, holding urns from which the water flows. One is especially remarkable. It is a rock over which run various reptiles, serpents, snails, tortoises, lizards, frogs, etc.

They also poured water—one would have said the rock itself exuded water."

In building the Palace of the Luxembourg (illus., pp. 80, 82), Marie de Medici was particularly desirous that it should resemble the architecture of the Pitti Palace which belonged to her family. It was one of the earliest instances in France of a palace and garden being considered as one whole design. There was a magnificent scheme of fountains, and the water supply was brought from Arcueil in a monumental aqueduct. The " Fontaine de Médicis " (p. 81), said to have been designed by Rubens, may still be admired to the east of the palace. It represents Polyphemus surprising Acis and Galatea. The parterre at the Luxembourg, as shown in the engravings of Israel Silvestre, must have been a marvellous creation. John Evelyn says that—" it is so rarely designed and accurately kept cut, that the embroidery makes a wonderful effect to the lodgings which front it."

"AUTUMN," IN THE LUXEMBOURG GARDEN.

The most famous garden in the neighbourhood of Paris before the creation of Versailles, was that of Saint Germain-en-Laye, which was justly considered one of the marvels of the age. The old fortress of St. Germain was rebuilt in 1367 by Charles V, and again in 1540 by

FRENCH GARDENS: 16TH AND EARLY 17TH CENTURIES 83

François I. The engraving shows the garden as it appeared in 1654, laid out for Henri IV. The gardens were designed by Dupérac and laid out by Claude Mollet.

A splendid series of terraces, arcades and stairways led down to the river Seine, two hundred feet below. The grottos under the terraces were decorated with shellwork, painting and statuary, and contained many curious

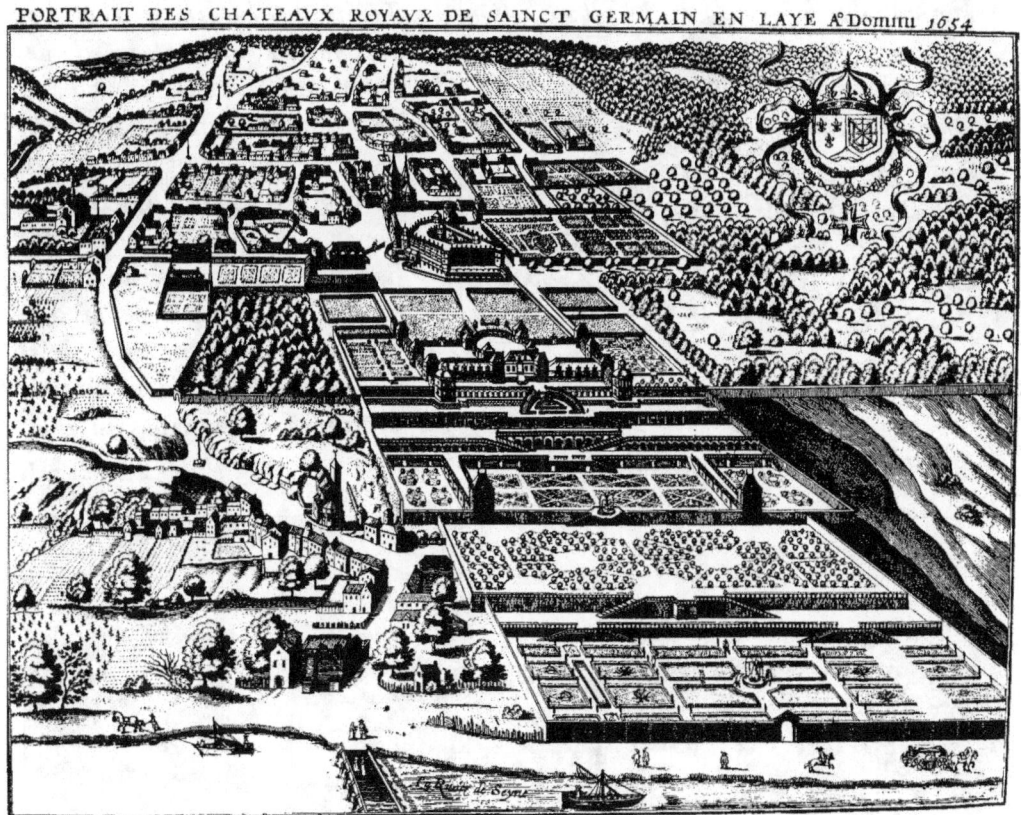

SAINT GERMAIN-EN-LAYE IN 1654.

mechanical contrivances and fanciful waterworks invented by the great Florentine *fontainier*, Thomas Francini, who was brought from Italy by Henri IV. A description of them was published by André Duchesne in 1610, and they have also been engraved by Abraham Bosse.

Before considering the work of Le Nôtre and his school there is one garden designer to whom attention must be drawn. Jacques Boyceau,

A PARTERRE BY JACQUES BOYCEAU.

Sieur de la Baradière, was one of the gardeners of Louis XIII and also of Louis XIV during his minority. He is chiefly celebrated as the author of a rare volume, *Traité du Jardinage selon les Raisons de la Nature et de l'Art*, 1688. In the first part he deals with the elements in general, and with the qualities that go to make a good gardener, who, he says, should have had training in the art of design, or failing this, the design of a garden should be left in the hands of the architect. Writing on the shapes suitable to gardens, he disapproves the continual use of straight lines and square par-

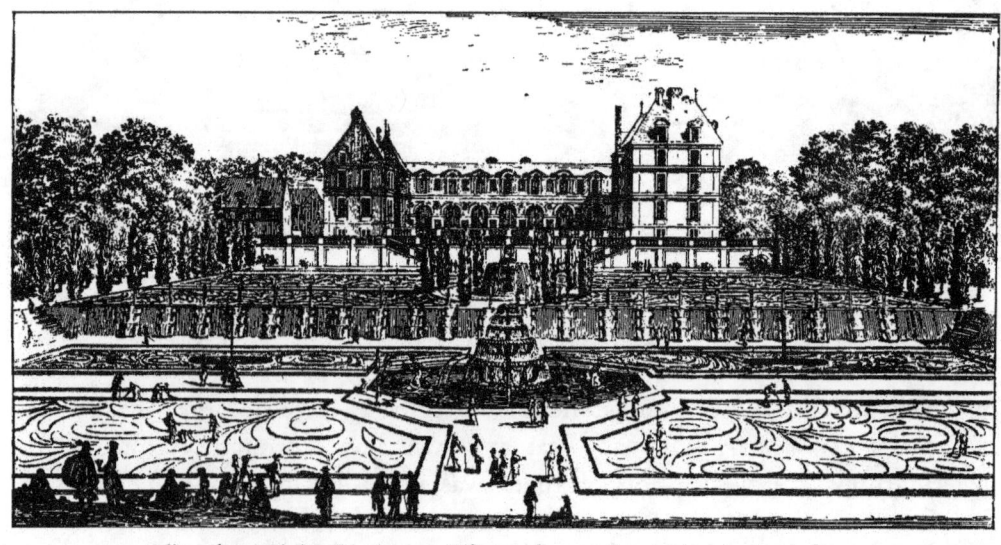

Face du costé des Cascades   Ædium prospectus versus præcipites aquarum lapsus

THE CHATEAU DE REUX, FROM I. SILVESTRE.

FRENCH GARDENS: 16TH AND EARLY 17TH CENTURIES

terres and recommends a greater use of circles and curves to give variety to the plan; he further recommends the designer to take care that all the walks communicate with one another so that it is unnecessary to return by the same route by which one came. He says that alleys are necessary to gardens, as much to serve for promenades as for the growth of those plants that are usually cultivated in them. The width of avenues should be proportionate to their length; if they exceed a length of three or four hundred *toises* they should be from 7 to 8 *toises* in width.[1] In preference, oaks, elms and limes were to be used, planted in two or more rows; if walnuts or chestnuts, one row would suffice. As the alleys approach to the centre of the garden they should diminish in width. Parterres, he says, give grace to a garden, especially when placed that they may be seen from an elevation; they should be composed of various coloured shrubs and low growing plants fashioned into all manner of compartments, the variations of their designs being produced by flowers, grass and coloured sands. He gives a very large number of designs for parterres, including those he laid out at the Louvre, the Tuileries, St. Germain-en-Laye and Versailles.

[1] The *toise* may be reckoned as 6·395 feet.

CHAPTER V

LE NOTRE AND VERSAILLES

WE now reach a period when for more than a century the art of garden design was entirely dominated by one strong individuality, whose influence extended over the whole of Europe; André le Nôtre, "the gardener of kings and king of gardeners," under whom the art of formal or architectural gardening attained its highest point.

Le Nôtre was born in Paris in 1613; his father, Jean le Nôtre, was one of the gardeners employed at the Palace of the Tuileries under Marie de Medicis. The father was anxious that his son should become a painter, and André was apprenticed early in life to Simon Vouët, the King's painter. The training he received in Vouët's atelier stood him in good stead in after life, and besides the companionship of his fellow students, Le Sueur, Mignard and Le Brun, a powerful influence over his artistic development was exercised by his constant inter-

VAUX-LE-VICOMTE.

course with the great artists of the day who often visited the master's studio. These influences, taken in conjunction with a practical knowledge of gardening, inherited from his father, enabled him to start on his career singularly well equipped for the great task that lay before him.

After leaving Vouët he worked quietly with his father in the royal gardens for many years, always studying horticulture and the practical

THE PARTERRE, VAUX-LE-VICOMTE.

science of gardening, and drawing a small salary as an under gardener, his work being confined to the care of an *espalier* of Spanish jessamine and white mulberries.

Le Nôtre is said to have made some designs for Richelieu's château of Rueil and for Gaillon, but the first work which brought him into prominence was the garden at Vaux-le-Vicomte, between Paris and Fontainebleau, where Fouquet raised his superb château upon a scale of magnificence that ultimately caused his downfall. He is said to have spent eighteen million francs at Vaux, an enormous sum even for the present day, proving, as a contemporary writer said, that the Chancellor served himself with no more economy than he served his King. Fouquet had the good fortune to be the patron of Charles Le Brun, who introduced his fellow student Le Nôtre, and the two artists worked amicably together, both being artists great enough to inspire one another. The work was begun in 1656 and was sufficiently advanced by 1661 for the famous fête which was given to Louis XIV on August 17 of that year. This was the most brilliant event of a period of brilliant festivities, when the *fête champêtre* reached the zenith of magnificence. The lavish entertainment of his King caused the ruin of the great financier, who was arrested three weeks afterwards; but for Le Nôtre it meant the rise to fame, for the renown of these gardens, together with those of Chantilly, brought him into such prominence that he was soon afterwards invited to assist in the laying out of the new Versailles.

THE THEATRE D'EAU, VAUX-LE-VICOMTE.

The Château at Vaux was planned upon a scale that had never before been attempted in France. It is approached through a vast courtyard with extensive dependencies planned on either side; the enormous parterre (illus., p. 86) stretches to the south and is terminated by a broad sheet of water and *théâtre d'eau*. Perhaps the most interesting feature of the plan is the very able way in which Le Nôtre dealt with the variations in level of the parterre, which besides sloping to the south had a considerable fall from west to east; this has been cleverly concealed by a *bosquet* on one side and a balancing terrace upon the opposite side. In the centre of the parterre is

THE PARTERRE. VAUX-LE-VICOMTE.

a magnificent *pièce d'eau*, to the right was a maze, and to the left a splendid cascade. The entrance front of the *cour d'entrée* is closed by a wrought-iron grille with a series of stone terms modelled by Poussin. Le Nôtre had for chief *fontainier* one Claude Roubillard and for gardener Antoine Trumel. The gardens still retain many of their *berceaux* and *palisades* just as Le Nôtre left them, and have been less changed than any of his other great schemes; the parterres have been altered, but the terraces, the fountains, and charming perspectives are perhaps more beautiful than in Fouquet's day, having an added beauty in their setting of large trees.

Before considering the work of Le Nôtre at Versailles it is important to follow him at Chantilly, where he carried out very extensive designs for the great Condé. It is also important to note that the works at Chantilly are of earlier date than Versailles, and great as may be the difference in size of the two it is nevertheless certain that it was after his famous visit to Condé at Chantilly that Louis XIV determined to entrust the whole of the works at Versailles to Le Nôtre.

VAUX-LE-VICOMTE.

We have already seen how a century earlier the Constable Anne de Montmorency remodelled the gardens. They remained in this form until the great Condé took up his residence, and like his ancestors employed his leisure in completely transforming and beautifying the château. Natural conditions of the soil gave Le Nôtre greater opportunities than he had had at Vaux. He transformed a rapid stream, "La Nonette" into a broad canal and *pièce d'eau* known as "La Manche," which advanced towards the château and divided the two great parterres. An aqueduct supplied the fountains and the moat, and an elaborate system of machinery was devised for pumping the water. The canal was nearly as large as the one at Versailles and the great cascades were considered amongst the most wonderful of their day. At the same time the great esplanade was constructed, long avenues were cut through the park with *pattes d'oie*, or goose feet,[1] very characteristic of the formal gardens of the day.

The plans of the whole scheme are preserved in the *Bibliothèque Nationale*, and a comparison of these with those made by Du Cerceau in the previous century gives an idea of the gigantic work. Le Nôtre began

THE PARTERRE AT CHANTILLY.

operations in 1663, assisted by his nephew Desgots,[2] Daniel Gitard the architect, La Quintanie the gardener and the water engineer Le Manse.

The *Maison de Sylvie* (illus., p. 93) was constructed in 1670. It was so named after the Duchesse de Montmorency and still exists, a delightful cool retreat, amidst secluded woods. Condé spent much of his time at Chantilly, especially at those periods when he was forced to hold himself aloof from public affairs. Here he died in 1686, after having transformed a fortified castle

[1] The "goose foot" consisted of three or more avenues radiating from a small semicircle.
[2] Desgots afterwards worked for Charles II and also designed the gardens of the Palais Royal, and the parks of Bagnolet and St. Maur.

Veüe et perspective de la Grande Cascade de Chantilly

THE GRAND CASCADE, CHANTILLY

LE CANAL DE CHANTILLY est aussi remarquable par son etendue considerable et par l'abondance de ses eaux que par les belles allées d'arbres de haute futaye dont il est environné. On voit ici la partie circulaire du canal en forme de demi lune qui fait face au parterre d'eaux avec le bras du canal qui s'avance dans le milieu de ce mesme parterre. Dans le lointain on apperçoit le bassin de la gerbe au pied du grand escalier et la statue du Connestable de Montmorency qui est en face de l'entrée du grand Château.

THE CANAL AT CHANTILLY.

into a palace, the splendours of which can only be gathered from the engravings of Perelle. The château is now a Museum, the gigantic *parterre d'eau*, although shorn of its surrounding flower beds and therefore not so beautiful as formerly, being still impressive by its size. Would it were possible to restore in some measure the beautiful designs of Le Nôtre for the gardens!

Le Nôtre was fortunate in his patron, and Louis XIV, although he constantly interfered with the works of other artists whom he employed, was sufficiently astute to realize the talent of Le Nôtre. He afforded him the noblest opportunities, and heaped benefits and honours upon him. He

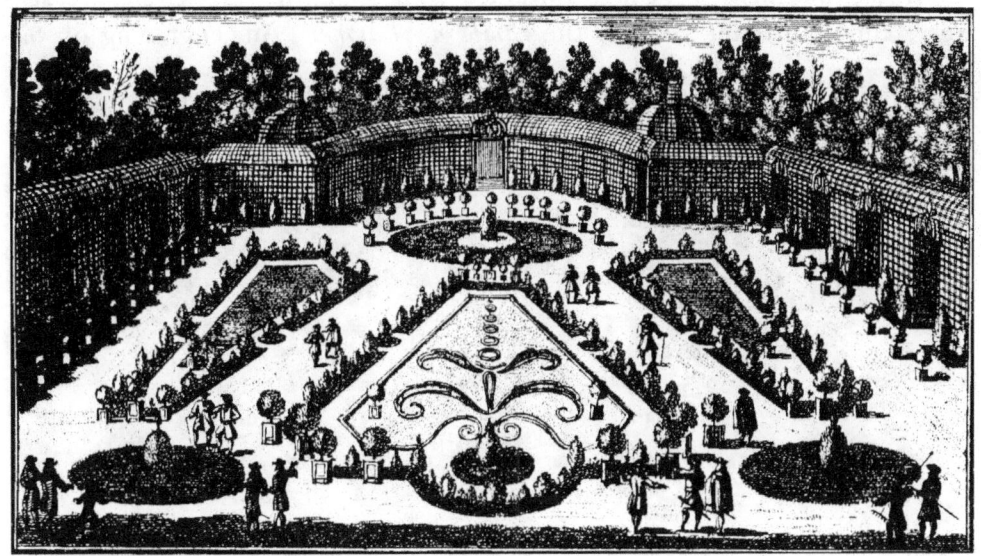

Les Berceaux du jardin de Silvie

TREILLAGE BERCEAUX AT CHANTILLY.

employed him for a period of forty years, and when at the age of eighty-six Le Nôtre was obliged to resign, he was frequently visited by the King. In addition to the fine portrait of him at Versailles, there is a bust by Coysevox and statues at the Louvre and at Chantilly. When Le Nôtre was sixty-two, Louis XIV insisted on making him a chevalier of the Order of St. Michael, and suggested that he should adopt a coat-of-arms, which suggestion he laughingly declined, saying that he had one ready made—three snails surrounding a spade and surmounted by a cabbage leaf. Le Nôtre died in 1700 and was buried in the church of St. Roch.

It is difficult to fix the exact date when Le Nôtre was first employed at Versailles, but it is probable that he submitted his preliminary sketches to the King soon after 1662. About this time the spoliation of Fouquet's garden was proceeding apace; during the previous winter no less than 1,200 trees were transplanted from Vaux and the greater part of the statuary there was removed, and became the nucleus of the superb collection of sculpture for which the gardens soon became famous.

Between 1662 and 1663 a commencement was made, by altering Boyceau's *parterre de broderie*, and preparing the huge artificial plateau which is now known as the *parterre d'eau* maintained by a gigantic semi-circular earthwork, known in later years as the *rampe de Latone*. An engraving of Sil-

VIEW FROM THE TERRACE AT VERSAILLES.

vestre (p. 95) shows the ramp with the fountain of Latona, and the palace in its second stage before the long wings had been added on both sides. In the same year the central walk, or *Allée Royale*, was laid out, but it was afterwards widened and extended and named the *Tapis vert*, terminating in a small pond that later became the *Bassin d'Apollon* (illus., p. 100). By 1665 the principal lines of the garden had been established, and up to this date the enormous sum of 1,500,000 livres had been spent upon the works. The brothers Francini were busily employed in constructing their first hydraulic effort, " The Grotto of Tethys " dedicated to the " Glory of the Sun," a most beautiful construction carried out in perfect taste *en rocaille*. The grotto existed only for a few years and was destroyed in 1686.

Veüe du Chasteau de Versailles du costé du Jardin.

Versaliarum Palatii a parte horti Prospectus.

VERSAILLES IN 1674, BEFORE THE ADDITION OF THE WINGS, FROM AN ENGRAVING BY SILVESTRE.

THE FOUNTAIN OF LATONA IN 1678.

A great many changes took place in the planning of the great parterre in front of the Palace. Boyceau's original design consisted of a *parterre de broderie* with ten *plates bandes* in arabesque arranged round a circular basin. In 1664 Perelle's engraving shows a parterre of four squares flanked right and left by clumps of trees, and a plan made by La Pointe in the same year shows two *plates bandes* of grass bordered with box; the next change took place about 1674, when the grass *plates bandes* gave way to fountains and the name was changed to the *parterre d'eau*. The plan reproduced above is preserved at Versailles, and shows an alternative scheme of Le Nôtre for this parterre. The idea appears to have been to create a water parterre, the design of which was traced by multi-coloured currents.

LE NÔTRE'S DESIGN FOR THE PARTERRE D'EAU, FROM HIS ORIGINAL DRAWING.

"THE RHONE," BY TUBY. ONE OF THE EIGHT FIGURES SURROUNDING THE PARTERRE D'EAU, VERSAILLES.

The idea was never carried out, and in its stead Louis XIV formed the two large pools enclosed within marble kerbs that mirror on their surface the long lines of the white palace. Around this kerb are placed a series of bronzes without equal in Europe,— each one a masterpiece of grace and dignity. The angles of each basin are marked by four recumbent figures representing the rivers of France by Tuby, le Hongre, Regnaudin, and Coysevox, and between are graceful figures of recumbent nymphs alternating with playful groups of

THE FOUNTAIN OF APOLLO.

children. In this immense garden, to quote the words of Louis XIV, there is "childhood everywhere." The whole of the wonderful series of bronzes was cast by the Brothers Keller of Zürich. "They will do honour to the France of the last two centuries as long as an artist lives to visit them, and as long as thoughtful minds take pleasure in the places where the figures of history can be made to live and move."

In a part of the garden known as the *Salle du Conseil* was the piece of

GROUPS OF CHILDREN ROUND THE PARTERRE D'EAU, BY LESPIGNOLA.

THE "THEATRE D'EAU," VERSAILLES, FROM AN ENGRAVING BY RIGAUD.

water called the *Obélisque*. Here water pipes were arranged to make an effect of a regular obelisk three yards in diameter at its base, and twenty-seven yards high; owing to the careful adjustment of the pipes the colour of the water as it fell was as white as snow. Among the green walks diverging from the *Bassin de Neptune* Le Nôtre planned the bosquet of the *Théâtre d'Eau* (illus., p. 102). It took its name from the three cascades that met in a

L'OBELISQUE D'EAU, FROM RIGAUD.

central oval space; the effects of the hundreds of water jets in the cool greenery of the bosquet were unequalled, but nothing now remains of this marvellous work, except engravings and paintings. The *Théâtre d'Eau* disappeared in the middle of the eighteenth century, and in its place is a large cup-shaped hollow covered with turf.

In addition to the *Théâtre d'Eau* there was another theatre known as

Les trois fontaines (illus. opposite), so called from three basins arranged on different levels; the lowest was octagonal with sixteen jets of water, some forming huge arches, others rising as single jets.

The next work to be undertaken was the cutting of the grand canal, which was devised in order to enlarge the view, and at the same time to drain the marshy area of the low-lying ground. When seen from the upper terrace it is difficult to realize that this canal is more than a mile long, and one can only grasp its extent from seeing a plan of the grounds. It is probable that Le Nôtre felt this himself, for he afterwards broke up its straight length by cutting two arms which branch off about the middle as transepts, one leading to the Trianon and the other to the Ménagerie.

There is an authentic list of no less than ninety-five sculptors, including all the famous men of the day, who were employed to carry out the decorative works in the gardens of Versailles. This band of artists was presided over by the genius of Le Brun, who bestowed the greatest pains upon every detail, and "little by little, grove by grove, fountain by fountain, the magic of this most beautiful spot in the world was born." Models were first made in plaster, then put into position, coloured to represent bronze or marble and left for the decision of the King as to the nature of the final material. Among the earliest works of sculpture are the two charming groups of children riding on sphinxes which now overlook the *parterre des fleurs*. They were modelled in 1660 by Jacques Sarrazin, the earliest sculptor employed at Versailles. When first set up they were gilt, but this was afterwards removed in order to make them more in harmony with the bronzes that surround the two large ponds.

About 1669 that part of the gardens which descends to the *bassin du Dragon* was rearranged, and this important work involved a whole series of magnificent fountains, the pyramid by Girardon and the charming series of fourteen fountains known as the *Allée d'eau*. The *Allée d'eau* was quite a new form of water decoration devised by Claude Perrault, and as first designed consisted of fourteen small fountains (illus., p. 109) ranged upon both sides of the grass *allée*; each fountain was of gilt metal and consisted of beautifully modelled groups of children supporting a dish of fruit and flowers. The famous fountain of the Pyramid adorns the entrance to the *Allée d'eau* from the Parterre du Nord; it is one of the most original and beautiful fountains in the gardens, and was carried out by François Girardon. M.

THE BOSQUET DES TROIS FONTAINES, FROM AN ENGRAVING BY RIGAUD.

A NYMPH, BY LE HONGRE, PARTERRE D'EAU.

BASSIN DE LA GERBE.

Pierre de Nolhac says that " the general idea was devised by Le Brun, who gave the most minute attention to the work. . . . It is composed of the flora and fauna of the ocean, amongst which sirens and tritons are disporting themselves. Upon the lead, which was originally gilt, as much workmanship has been employed as though it were a specimen of the goldsmith's art. Under the quivering foam the sea-gods seem to be alive as they laughingly chase each other in the running water."

AMORINI IN THE ALLEE D'EAU.

Another famous work of Girardon was the Bath of the Nymphs of Diana, a composition of eleven graceful nymphs disporting themselves on the borders of a river.

The fountains of Ceres and Flora by Tuby were set up in 1672–75, the

"SUMMER," LEADEN FOUNTAIN GROUP.

Mirror pond in 1672, the fountain of Bacchus from 1673–1677, the Royal Island 1674–1683, the fountain of Enceladus, 1675–76. The figure of the giant is by Marsy; from its mouth issues a jet of water seventy-eight feet high. The *Bosquet de l'arc de triomphe* and also the *Bosquet des trois fontaines* were constructed between 1679 and 1683. The new orangery (illus., p. 112) was begun in 1670 and finished in 1687. Louis XIV had a passion for orange trees, and as the old building was unable to house the enormous collection that had been got together by Le Nôtre, plans were prepared by Mansart for the new orangery while Le Nôtre made the designs for the parterre. Le Nôtre brought 3,000 young trees from Italy and rare varieties were also sent from San Domingo and from Flanders, and in the summer of

FOUNTAIN GROUP OF AMORINI.

L'ORANGERIE DE VERSAILLES. TITRE DU LIVRE DE LOIRE PAR CARTOUCHE

PLAN OF THE ORANGERY.

1687 the collection from Fontainebleau was added to the newly finished building. The Orangery comprises a central gallery and two side galleries, the former being 506 feet long by 40 feet wide. The building was frequently used for entertainments, and at the present day is sometimes employed for the same purpose.

The parterre in front of the Orangery (illus. opposite) had many fine pieces of sculpture in marble and bronze, and some beautiful examples of leaden vases still adorn the surrounding terraces. Lespignola modelled a series of fourteen baskets of fruit and flowers, and to Le Gros and Le Comte were entrusted the colossal stone groups that rest on the pillars of the double entrance to the gardens. Inside the parterre were numerous decorative sculptures in marble and bronze,

FOUNTAIN IN THE ALLEE D'EAU, 1688, BY MAZELINE.
For contemporary engraving v. p. 109. The basin has been replaced.

but of these only four are left. Not far from the Orangery was the Labyrinth, which has now disappeared. It was famous for its series of thirty-nine leaden figures representing scenes from the Fables of Aesop, and

THE BASSIN DES SIRENES, PARTERRE DU NORD.

was composed of a complicated network of alleys cutting one another at right angles or forming curves of the most puzzling character.

THE COLONNADE, DESIGNED BY MANSART IN 1688.

A LEADEN VASE.

A BRONZE VASE BY BALLIN.

LEADEN VASES, BASSIN DE NEPTUNE.

LA SALLE DU BAL, FROM JEAN RIGAUDS' ENGRAVING.

The *Salle du Bal* (illus. opposite) placed in a bosquet near by, was one of the most charming features of the garden; it was elliptical in shape, and had a cascade of rockwork at one end from which fell silvery sheets of water, producing a scintillating effect when brilliantly lit up on the occasion of a ball. The orchestra were seated above, and the spectators ranged themselves opposite upon tiers rising from the arena where the dancing took place.

The great sheet of water known as the *Pièce des Suisses* was completed in 1683. It serves most effectively to continue the perspective beyond the Orangery parterre and reflects upon its surface the hills of Satory beyond. It was made by Le Nôtre out of a swamp which the engineers had tried in vain to drain. In 1688, with the completion of the *Salle du Bal* and the Colonnade, the colossal work of laying out the gardens appears to have been achieved, and although changes continually took place afterwards, these did not materially destroy the general lines of the design.

GROUP OF CHILDREN, BY LE GROS.

Of all the groves, with their delicate *cabinets de treillage* and frail *rocaille* fountains, the *Salle du Bal* and the *Colonnade* alone remain in anything like their old completeness and elegance.

The Gardens of Versailles remained much as Le Nôtre had left them for the next half century, though under the Regency the palace was deserted and they were not kept up. An interesting picture, painted in

THE CONDITION OF VERSAILLES IN 1775, FROM A PAINTING BY HUBERT ROBERT.

1775 by Hubert Robert, shows in a most realistic way the havoc that had been wrought by this period several years before the Revolution added the finishing touch to their ruin. Although to-day the garden is not kept up as it should be, it is fortunate that it escaped the doom threatened during the *Directoire*. A plan that was made during the Revolution for the partition of the garden actually exists in the Bibliothèque Nationale.

A GARDEN SCENE AFTER LE BARBIER.

CHAPTER VI

FRENCH GARDENS OF THE LATER SEVENTEENTH & EIGHTEENTH CENTURIES

ESIDES the immense garden schemes at Vaux, Chantilly and Versailles, Le Nôtre in the course of his long and busy life laid out gardens over the whole of France, and established a standard and tradition of garden design in the "grand manner" which were accepted as a matter of course throughout Europe. Plans sufficient to fill several volumes exist of the work he carried out, and either he or his pupils were at some time or other engaged upon nearly all the most important estates in France. His invention seems inexhaustible, and his gardens display an astonishing variety, for to each one he was able to give a different charm, as he always carefully studied the site and adapted it to the taste and the purse of the owner. Le Nôtre was invited by Charles II to come over in person to lay out Hampton Court gardens, but although he did not accept the invitation, he probably inspired the design, which was put into the hands of French gardeners. It is said that he also made plans for Greenwich and St. James' Parks. At any rate for the next half century his style was paramount in England, and his influence spread over the whole of Europe. His pupils became Court gardeners in Russia, Austria, and Germany, whilst his methods were even adopted in the Sultan's gardens at Constantinople. Amongst his pupils were his two nephews, Claude Desgots and Michel Le Bouteux; the former went to England as a young man and worked in the royal gardens, and, returning to France, designed the new gardens at Anet and the parks of Bagnolet and St. Maur.

The great pleasure houses of Meudon, Clagny, Marly and Sceaux, built as retreats from the etiquette of Versailles, have nearly all disappeared;

here and there remnants of the old avenues and bosquets remain with perhaps some moss-covered statue or fountain long past repair.

Elaborate and costly cascades were set up in every garden. They were by no means the ephemeral structures of rockwork and cement that contented the Italians, but fine architectural compositions of coursed ashlar stonework, very beautifully finished. At Saint Cloud the great cascade is a

THE CASCADE AT ST. CLOUD.

really fine conception; it consists of three central waterways and intervening stone channels and flights of stone steps; it is still in working order, and on the days of the *grandes eaux* presents a sight worth going far to see. Nearly every garden had its grotto intended to represent a wild cave; where it was impossible to excavate the natural rock, it was constructed beneath some artificial hillock, and ornamented with rustic work of spongy stone, rocks and rare pebbles, stalactites, and various kinds of shells. By means of water, engines and machines were set in motion by which figures worked, musical instruments were made to play and birds to sing.

The art of treillage was considerably developed towards the end of the seventeenth century, and Perelle's engravings of Clagny (illus., p. 137) and the *Trianon de Porcelaine* show the finest examples. The idea was handed down from classic times, but the French introduced an elaboration and refinement that transformed the rude carpentry of classic and mediaeval days into an important element of garden architecture. We can only translate *treillage* into English as trelliswork; this, however, does not suggest the same meaning to our minds as the French word, because it does not presuppose the existence of design of an architectural character.

The best account of eighteenth-century treillage in France is contained in Roubo's rare work *L'Art du Treillageur*, which appeared in Paris in 1775. "The Art of Treillage," says Roubo, "is one of the most modern, and its perfection, like that of *jardinage*, is due to the French. Like many another art it was simple in its origin and limited to utilitarian purposes, such as a support to the *treillis* or tendrils of the vine—whence its name." At first it was only used to train

A TREILLAGE DESIGN BY LE PAUTRE.

espalier branches, then to separate the paths of thickets and the different

PROMENADE DE JARDIN DU PALAIS-ROYAL, PARIS, SHOWING A TREILLAGE PAVILION, AFTER AN ENGRAVING BY DEBUCOURT.

parts of the vegetable garden; these were its principal uses until the days of Louis XIV, when under the guidance of Le Nôtre and J. H. Mansart *treillage* began to form a distinct and separate part of garden craft. Its execution was entrusted to workmen who made it their sole occupation and assumed the title of *treillageurs,* working under architects, or from their own designs, until in 1769 they were united to the *Corps des Menuisiers.* The use of *treillage* became very popular. It was a material particularly suited to the period when gardens often had to be designed and carried out within the space of a few months, and gave a finished effect long before the tree backgrounds had time to grow up. It was and is still especially used in town gardens, and often provides a most effective covering to an unsightly wall. Summer-houses, salons, gateways, galleries, and indeed any architectural feature could be easily imitated in *treillage,* and from its lightness of construction and cheapness it is often more suitable than solid stone or stucco.

" LE MOULINET," BY WATTEAU.

The Parterres of Le Nôtre's gardens are lighter and more refined than those of the previous century, animal forms being omitted and an attempt made to imitate embroidery patterns. Parterres were divided into four kinds:—*Parterres de broderie,* in which the box lines imitated embroidery,—these were considered the finest; *Parterres de Compartiment,* which consisted of a combination of scrolls, grass plots, knots, and borders for flowers; *Parterres à l'anglaise,* consisting of grass plots all in one piece or cut into shapes, and surrounded by a border of flowers; this was considered the most unattractive kind of parterre; *Parterres de Pièces coupées,* differing from the

GARDEN CRAFT IN EUROPE

Portique de treillage au milieu du petit Bois et en face du Parterre de l'Orangerie à Chantilly

A TREILLAGE ARCHWAY AT CHANTILLY.

others in that all the parts composing them were in symmetrical shapes of box-work and that they admitted neither grass nor embroidery.

The Grand Trianon at Versailles (illus., p. 127), which was so called after the Petit Trianon came into existence, was built by Louis XIV for Madame de Montespan during 1670 and occupied the site of a village named Trianon, which was removed to make way for the gardens. The building, which is not the one now existing, was entirely decorated with porcelain and was known as the *Trianon de Porcelaine*. It

A TREILLAGE SCREEN.

VUE DU CHÂTEAU DE TRIANON DU COTÉ DU PARTERRE.

THE GRAND TRIANON, FROM RIGAUDS' ENGRAVING.

was pulled down after seven years and the present *Trianon de Marbre* was built from Mansart's design in its place. *The Trianon de Porcelaine*, says a contemporary writer, " was regarded at first by every one as a work of magic, for it was begun only at the end of the winter and was finished by the spring, as though it had sprung from the

TREILLAGE OBELISKS AT THE ENTRANCE TO L'ILE D'AMOUR, CHANTILLY.

AN ELABORATE EXAMPLE OF TREILLAGE—THE TEMPLE D'AMOUR AT CHANTILLY.

earth with the flowers of the gardens that came into being with it." The garden of the first Trianon was designed by Michel Le Bouteux, who was given *carte blanche* to do as he pleased, the only stipulation being that there should be an abundance of flowers, for which a greater craving now became apparent, owing to the improvements made by the Dutch in their cultivation. Colbert, who was now in charge of all the royal palaces, wrote to his agent at Marseilles : " You know that for the ornamentation of the royal gardens we must have a large quantity of flowers. As there are so many varieties in Provence I beg you to buy all the jonquils and tuberoses that you can find, and also any other curious flowers that would contribute to the ornamentation of the gardens." Rare flowers were sent from all parts and Le Bouteux was so successful in propagating them that he was considered the first florist of his day. He established an open-air orangery, which was a great novelty. On the demolition of the *Trianon de Porcelaine* the orange garden gave place to the *parterre de broderie*. According to Dangeau the *soirées de Trianon* were conducted on a magnificent scale, the flowers in the parterres were changed almost every

THE GRAND TRIANON.

day, and on one occasion the King and the entire court were obliged to leave the gardens owing to the overpowering scent of the tuberoses. The glory of the Trianon de Marbre lasted only for a short time, and with Louis XIV its brilliant history came to an end; under the regency Trianon and Versailles were alike deserted, the former until the year 1741, when Louis XV gave it to his queen. Thanks to Madame de Pompadour in 1749, the Grand Trianon received a new lease of life, when in order to amuse the King, amongst other attractions, a completely equipped model dairy was started. The gardens of the Grand Trianon have been so well restored and kept up that they may still be seen at their best, with their cool bosquets and retreats and

A LEAD FOUNTAIN AT THE GRAND TRIANON.

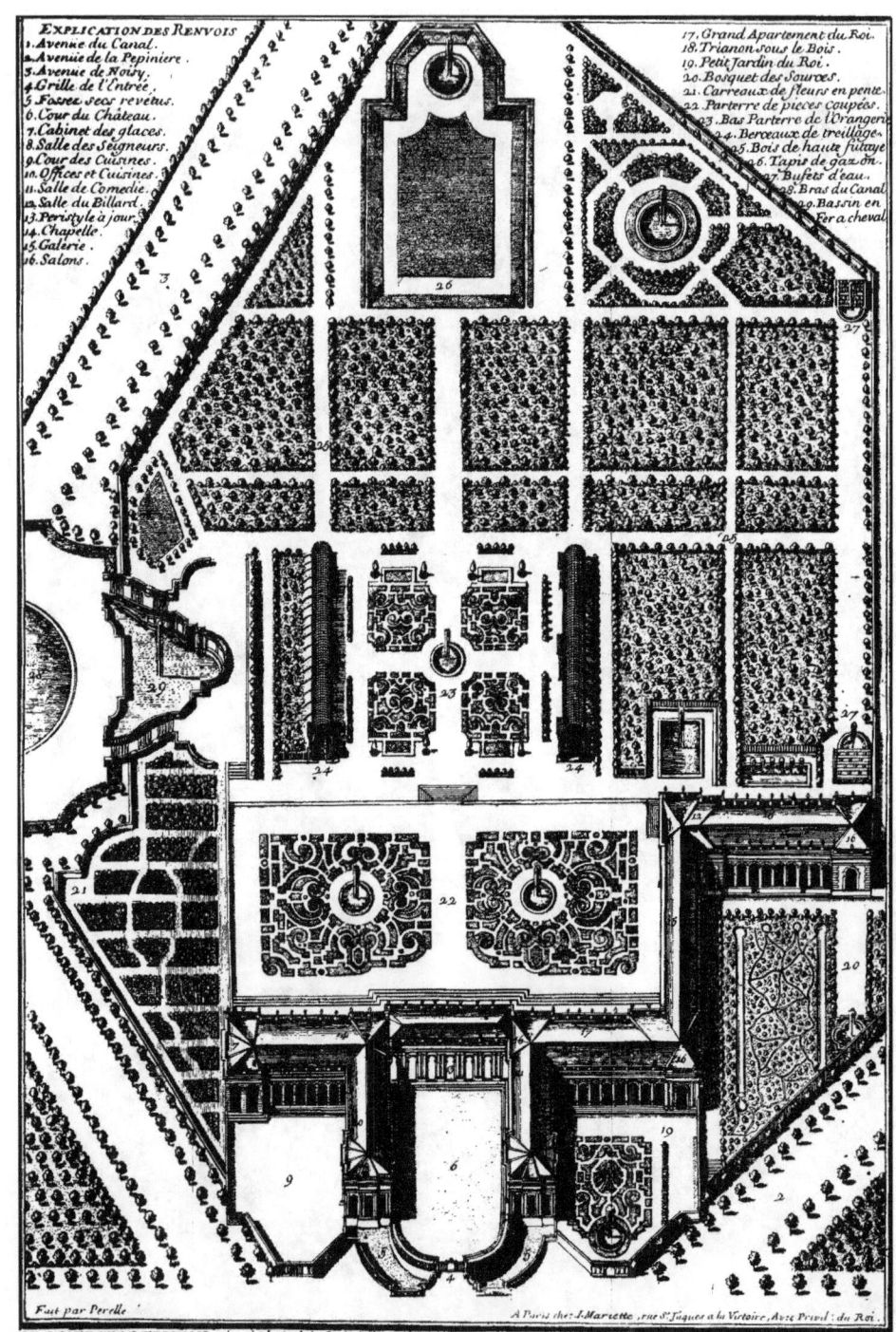

PLAN OF THE GRAND TRIANON AND ITS GARDENS.

FRENCH GARDENS: LATER 17TH AND 18TH CENTURIES

fountain basins bordered with little gilded cupids. The principal basin, known as the *Plafond*, lies in front of the château and is guarded by marine monsters. But the chief water feature is the *buffet d'eau*, designed by Mansart, consisting of steps of variously coloured marble with gilt figures and reliefs.

THE GRAND TRIANON.

Considerably more than half the environs of Paris within fifteen miles of the city, comprising all the finest sites, were given up to the immense parks and gardens of Louis XIV and XV and their courts. Delagrive's map of the environs of Paris, published in 1754, gives an excellent idea of the vast

GARDEN HOUSE IN THE PETIT TRIANON.

extent of these estates. The parks of St. Germain, Marly, Versailles, St. Cloud, Meudon and Sceaux occupied the greater part of an area 300 square miles in extent to the west of Paris; whilst to the east were the immense parks of Vaux-le-Vicomte and Fontainebleau, with the smaller estates of Gros-bois, St. Maur, Choisy, Vincennes, Raincy, Bois-le-Vicomte and others.

The original Château of Meudon (illus. opposite) was built for Cardinal Charles of Lorraine by Philibert de l'Orme, in the reign of Henri II, and eventually became the property of the Marquis de Louvois, when large additions were made to the château. Louis XIV purchased the property in 1694 and presented it to the Dauphin. After the death of the Dauphin in

THE PARTERRE AT THE GRAND TRIANON.

1711 the château, though occasionally occupied, was much neglected, and its ruin was finally completed during the Franco-Prussian war. Le Nôtre worked here, both under Louvois and also for the Dauphin.

In laying out the gardens, he was helped by their wonderful situation upon the heights overlooking the windings of the Seine. The Cardinal's garden had been quite small, but Le Nôtre made large additions; for the water decoration he worked in conjunction with the *maître fontainier*, Loppin, who published a volume of designs for the fountains here. A principal feature was an elaborate double terrace with ramps on either side, recalling that of the villa Mondragone at Frascati. The great orangery, with its

LE BASSIN DE TRIANON.

square parterre and terrace walls, is illustrated in several of Silvestre's engravings and remains almost the last vestige of the once famous gardens. Much of Le Nôtre's work in the park may still be admired; a broad green *tapis vert* leads from the terraces into the woods ascending the hillside, and superb vistas alternate with alleys and formal pieces of water. One of the remarkable features of this park was a large cluster of oaks (illus., p. 136), surrounding an octagonal space, with a large pool.

THE CHATEAU OF MEUDON.

Clagny was bought by Louis XIV in 1665 and presented to Madame de Montespan (illus., p. 137). The adjoining estate of Glatigny having been acquired, the gardens were laid out by Le Nôtre at a total cost, it is said, of three million livres. Some ten years later the *Mercure de France*, describing the garden soon after its completion, says " it derives its chief ornamentation from a wood of high trees, several *parterres en broderie* and bowling greens of various shapes. There are beautiful palisades of myrtle arranged to hide the tubs, which hold oranges in such a way as to make it appear that the orange trees are planted in the palisades." "We were at Clagny," wrote Madame de Sévigné in 1675. "How can I describe it? It is a veritable palace of Armida; the building is growing visibly; the gardens are made. You know the manner of Le Nôtre; he has left a little dark wood which does very well. There is a grove of orange trees in great tubs; you walk there; and they form alleys in the shade; and to hide the tubs there are rows of pallisades high enough to lean on, all aflower with tuberoses, roses, jasmines,

FOUNTAINS IN A BOSQUET AT MEUDON.

and carnations; it is surely the most beautiful, the most surprising, and the most enchanted novelty imaginable." According to a writer in the *Mercure Galant* the garden was celebrated for its bosquets of forest trees, parterres and grass walks, horn-beam bosquets and its treillage.

The cost of Clagny was a mere bagatelle to that of Marly, where between 1677 and 1684 Mansart and Durusé spent immense sums[1] in creating the

---

[1] Between 1679 and 1715 the money spent on Marly in pavilions and gardens amounted to 11,686,979 liv., or nearly 50 million francs in modern money. C. Pitou, *Histoire de Marly.*

CLAGNY.

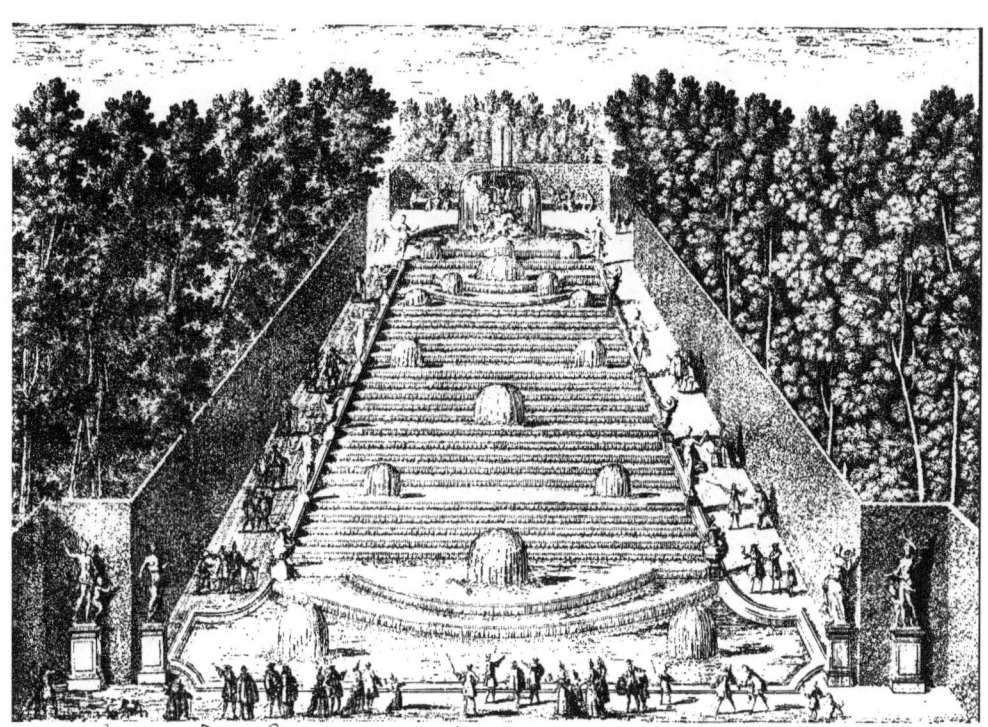

THE RIVIERE D'EAU AT MARLY.

FRENCH GARDENS: LATER 17TH AND 18TH CENTURIES 139

superb "Hermitage" that De Brosses thought finer than any of the villas in Rome. Saint Simon says the site was a narrow deep valley, without any view, solely chosen in order to spend money, such was the King's "superb pleasure in forcing nature." The "Hermitage" was rarely used and never for more than a few nights at a time, but in spite of this it was continually being enlarged; the hills were cut away to make space for building, and those which stood in the way of the view were bodily removed. Marly was in one respect preferable to Versailles —there was much more shade. The central pavilion was shaded on the south by dense bosquets ascending the hillside. The great cascade or *Rivière d'eau* (illus., p. 137) was planned on the

IN THE MARLY GARDENS, AFTER MOREAU LE JEUNE (1773).

central axial line of the garden. It was an entirely new and ingenious idea composed of sixty-three steps so evenly adjusted that the water flowing from one to the other gave the impression of a single sheet of water when viewed from below. The pool into which the water fell was decorated by magnificent groups of sculpture by Coustou. The park of Marly adjoined that of Versailles, and the two châteaux were connected by a broad avenue. The design of the park and gardens has been erroneously attributed to Le Nôtre, but they were entirely due to Mansart during the absence of Le Nôtre in Italy. Under Louis XV many changes were made with a view to decreasing the enormous expenses of Marly, and in 1728 the *Rivière d'eau* was replaced by a *Tapis vert*. The opening years of Louis XVI's reign saw the decline of Marly as a royal resort, and after 1784 Marie Antoinette's influence caused the King

SCEAUX.

to weary of the place. Just before the Revolution much of the park had been let for agricultural purposes, and subsequently all that remained of Marly was sold. Nowadays it is difficult to trace the outlines of what was once a famous pleasure house, the only architectural feature remaining is the *abreuvoir*, where from a gilded balcony the Court amused itself by watching the horses being watered. The balcony was flanked by the famous groups of horses, Coysevox's masterpieces, now adorning the entrance to the Champs Elysées. All was destroyed in 1793, and Le Brun's series of pavilions where Louis lodged his guests are now only shapeless ruins.

FRENCH GARDENS: LATER 17TH AND 18TH CENTURIES 141

The château of Sceaux, about four miles from Paris, on the road to Orleans, was bought by Colbert in 1670. Le Nôtre was employed to lay out the gardens, whilst Le Brun and Claude Perrault were engaged upon the alterations to the building (illus., p. 140). Colbert, possibly warned by the sad fate of Fouquet, decided to exercise a greater economy, and instead of entirely rebuilding the old château contented himself with remodelling. Le Nôtre, wishing to retain as much of the existing garden as possible, confined his alteration to the creation of two main axial lines; one formed the approach by a double avenue and passed through the château to the *parterres* beyond, the other, at right angles, took the form of a canal 1,000

THE PARTERRE DU TIBRE AT FONTAINEBLEAU (PRESENT DAY).

yards in length. The illustration (p. 140) shows the garden front with the *parterre de broderie* as planned by Le Nôtre. Colbert died in 1684 and Sceaux passed to his eldest son, the Marquis de Seignelay, who entertained here upon a lavish scale. The *Mercure Galant*, describing a fête at Sceaux in 1685 in honour of Louis XIV and Madame de Maintenon, relates how the royal party after reposing an hour in the Pavillon de l'Aurore, proceeded through the Salle des Marroniers to a little wood *fait en labyrinthe* and sparkling with fountains. From here they passed to the *allée d'eau*, a shady spot with terraces ranged on both sides, and a water jet between each—the water flowed through tiny channels to four large shells. High treillage covered with verdure formed a pleasing enclosure to the alley. In 1699 the property was sold to the Duc de Maine. The park and a few alleys still remain, but the château and gardens have been much changed. The *Pavillon de l'Aurore* still exists and is a delightful specimen of the seventeenth century garden-house at its best.

An immense sum of money was spent upon the gardens of Saint Germain. At one time Louis XIV thought of rebuilding the whole palace upon a much more magnificent scale; as it was, he added five pavilions and employed Le Nôtre to re-design the gardens. The parterres were

THE PARTERRE OF THE TUILERIES IN 1730.

entirely transformed, chiefly to please the *spirituelle* Henriette d'Orléans. A large bowling alley was laid out and three small terraces thrown into one great lime-planted promenade, one of the finest walks in Europe, extending nearly a mile and a half with a beautiful view overlooking the valley of the Seine. James II in his exile used to take his daily walks here, and often declared that the view from the terrace of Saint Germain was only equalled by that from Richmond Hill. The length of the terrace is most impressive, and the effect of distance is rendered even greater by a slight change of angle towards the middle.

Le Nôtre made considerable alterations to the gardens at Fontaine-

THE ORANGERY AT FONTAINEBLEAU IN 1679.

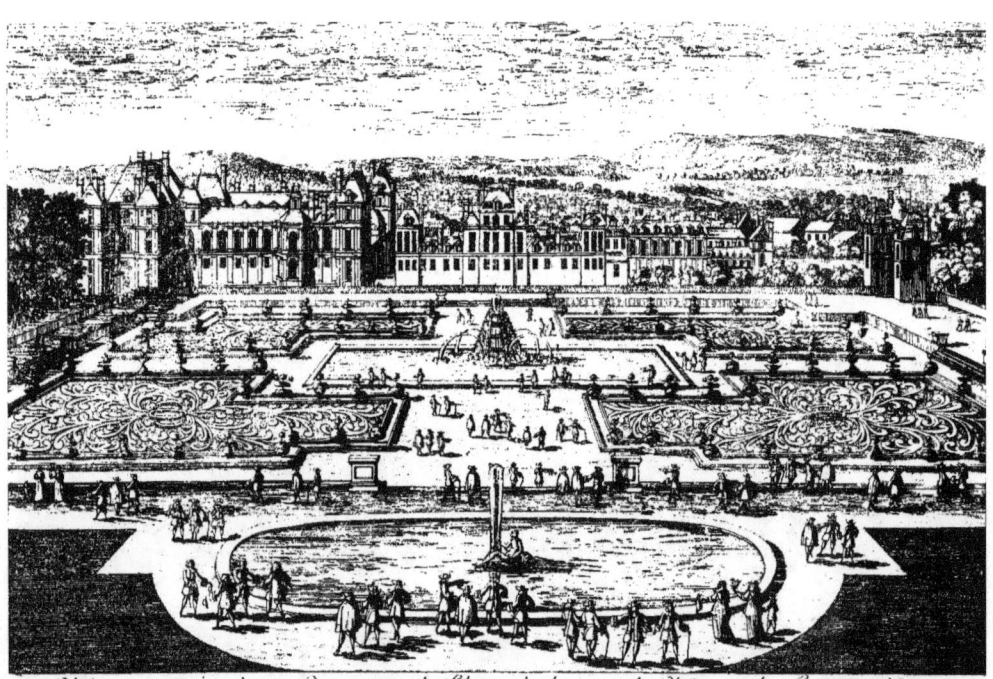

THE PARTERRE DU TIBRE, FONTAINEBLEAU.

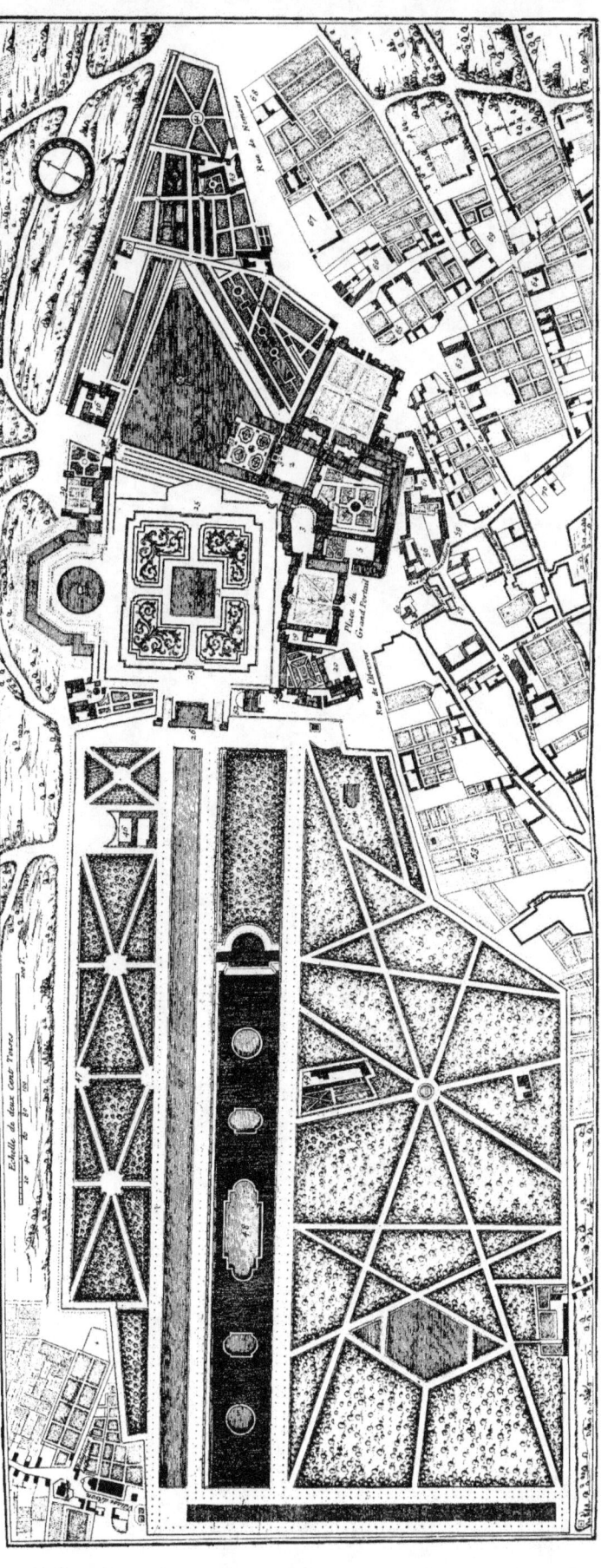

FONTAINEBLEAU IN THE EIGHTEENTH CENTURY, SHOWING THE DESIGN OF LE NÔTRE.

FRENCH GARDENS: LATER 17TH AND 18TH CENTURIES

bleau; his work consisted chiefly in bringing the garden up to date in obedience to the King's never-ceasing desire for change. The stiff square and intersecting canals of the grand parterre as they were designed for François I were all demolished, and in their place a large square *parterre de broderie*, known as the Parterre du Tibre (illus. opposite), was planned with a square pool in the middle. The grand canal was already cut, and Le Nôtre's work was confined to laying out the bosquets and re-arranging the parterre, which is shown in Perelle's view. Nowadays the elaborate embroideries have disappeared and grass plots take their place; in size this parterre

THE CANAL AT FONTAINEBLEAU.

will compare with anything of its kind ever laid out. At the head of the grand canal is a *théâtre d'eau*, which, although not so imposing as those of Versailles or St. Cloud, is decorated with some remarkably fine bronzes.

The gardens of the Tuileries in their present form are also due to Le Nôtre. He entirely re-modelled the designs of Regnard and D'Orbay and made great changes in the levels. The land had an inconvenient fall of some few feet towards the Seine, and in order to overcome this defect Le Nôtre raised the lateral terraces, and also extended the garden by enclosing the site of the Rue des Tuileries and a piece of ground known as Renard's garden, retaining the main division of the old garden; he enlarged the parterres in order to provide a greater space in front of the palace, at the same time doing away with the grotto, maze and other toys then out of fashion. The remainder of the garden he divided into quincunxes and bosquets, in the midst of which was an open air theatre. Le Nôtre made the terrace of the Cours la Reine overlooking the Seine, and planted the great central avenue which was later continued into the present Champs Elysées, and put in the two central fountains with their high single jets of water, which are still the delight of small children who sail boats in their large basins. Louis XIV made little use of the palace, preferring the life at Versailles, and after 1722 royal visits were restricted to rare ceremonial occasions.

DETAIL OF THE CASCADE AT ST. CLOUD.
(*For a general view see page* 122.)

Saint Cloud has suffered much; the palace was burnt down in 1870 and very little remains of its elaborate gardens and waterworks, while the park, with its straight avenues, is a desolate place save on fine Sundays, when it is generally gay with the population of Paris. It was bought by Louis XIV in 1658 and was rebuilt from Mansart's designs; the gardens were at once taken in hand and Le Nôtre worked in conjunction with Mansart. Being upon a hillside it was possible to make terraces without accumulating vast quantities of earth. The great *parterre de Trianon* is shown in Fragonard's delightful picture, " Fête at St. Cloud," and has been often engraved. In the midst was the *fontaine de Vénus* surrounded by *compartiments de*

From a drawing by C. A. Peixotto.
THE GARDENS AT ST. CLOUD.

A GARDEN SCENE BY MOREAU LE JEUNE.
From a Painting in the Victoria and Albert Museum.

FRENCH GARDENS: LATER 17TH AND 18TH CENTURIES 149

broderie, with here and there the wonderful vases of Le Brun. The greatest feature of St. Cloud is the cascade (illus., pp. 122 and 146), which was designed upon the hillside overlooking the Seine, and which when fully working, can hardly be matched in Europe. The cascade shows the distinct influence of those at the Villas Torlonia and Aldobrandini at Frascati; it is divided into two parts by a wide terrace; the upper part is an earlier work by

VUE DU GRAND JET D'EAU DU PARC DE St CLOUD
prise dans le Bosquet

THE GREAT "JET D'EAU" AT ST. CLOUD.

Le Pautre, the lower was afterwards cleverly added by Mansart. The water, spurting from an urn flanked on either side by recumbent figures of the Seine and Loire, falls down a series of steps and water buffets, through masks, shells, and dolphins into a big basin, and thence beneath the terrace to the second cascade shaped in horseshoe form. The wonderful series of statues by Coysevox and other great French sculptors has been removed, and now only poor copies remain. There is still the delightfully cool *allée d'eau* with its central water channel broken by alternate round and octagonal pools, where the water, issuing from a fountain, gaily sparkles from pool to pool. "Water," says Boyceau, "is necessary to a garden for its irrigation and refreshment during drought, but it also serves to embellish, especially running water in streams. Its vivacity and movement are the living spirit of the garden." Le Blond, in his work *La Théorie et la Pratique du Jardinage*, devotes a chapter to its treatment and illustrates several designs. Where the fall of the ground permitted, the water from the first basin was conducted by underground pipes to the third and fifth, forming a series of small water jets. Sometimes the channels were lined with coloured tiles and pebble work.

The Château de Maisons was designed by François Mansart, and in later years was the scene of the sumptuous entertainments which were offered by the Comte d'Artois to Louis XVI and Marie Antoinette. Saint Simon tells us that the château garden was celebrated for its rare

VUE DU CANAL DU CHATEAU DE RAMBOUILLET PRISE DU BALCON DU ROY.

THE ALLEE D'EAU AT St. CLOUD

FRENCH GARDENS: LATER 17TH AND 18TH CENTURIES

botanical collections, and that the gardeners here grew the only coffee that was successfully matured in France. The Château of Rambouillet (illus., p. 150) is situated some twenty miles south of Versailles; it was one of the favourite residences of Louis XVI and the gardens, which are now quite destroyed, were laid out by Le Nôtre. They were famous in their day for their beautiful parterres of roses which were grown in very great variety. Great canals were cut after the prevalent fashion of the day, to allow the ladies of the Court to be rowed in their gilded barges to all parts of the grounds. In 1780 an experimental farm was laid out with small farmhouse and dairies; flocks of sheep with their shepherds were brought from Spain. There is an immense park where the President of the Republic now hunts, though in less grand style than did the courtiers of Louis XVI.

Ses yeux font fermés au jour
Comme son cœur à L'amour.

A GARDEN SCENE, AFTER MOREAU LE JEUNE (1774).

Another famous eighteenth-century garden laid out by a pupil of Le Nôtre was at Rochefoucauld's Château at Liancourt. The waterworks were renowned in their day, and Silvestre's engravings show the *parterre des cascades*, and long alleys of fountains, each connected by a series of channels and small pools. The *Grand parterre* was surrounded by *berceaux* of lattice work, terminating in pavilions. Upon the eastern side of the château was the flower garden and orangery, a combined arrangement often to be met with in French eighteenth-century gardens, where the parterre was generally reserved for bedding out. Amongst other curiosities of these gardens was a large *cabinet de verdure*, or summer-house, in the midst of a square pool; this was quite surrounded by a series of green arcades each containing a tiny fountain jet. Another feature at Liancourt were the avenues of poplars, trees which found little favour with horticulturists of the seventeenth century.

A good insight into the smaller town gardens of the period may be obtained from the exhaustive collections of plans that exist, showing them in detail. They generally include a small forecourt set back from the street; behind the house, terraces led to trim parterres; the odd angles of the sites were often filled in with bosquets or cut trees, forming walls of verdure. Blondel, in his *Architecture à la Mode*, gives many examples of the larger town gardens. The Palais Royal, as laid out by Le Nôtre with little *parterres de broderie*, and planted with bosquets of chestnuts, limes, and hundreds of cut yews, is a good example of the palatial town gardens of Paris.

There are two manuscript volumes preserved in the *Bibliothèque Nationale* which give minute plans of scores of beautiful country seats existing round Paris in the middle of the century; these volumes are quite a study of eighteenth-century garden planning. The Châteaux were mostly planned with an avenue leading to the *cour d'honneur* which was frequently protected by a broad moat. The parterre is usually placed upon the opposite side, terminating in a formal *pièce d'eau*, and every garden, even of a few acres, had its *bosquet*. At Nogent and along the banks of the Marne were many large gardens, while Fromont, on the way to Fontainebleau, Ecouen, where the Condé property lay, and the Forest of Bondy were all favourite districts.

La Meutte was one of the smaller villas built for the Court of Louis XV,

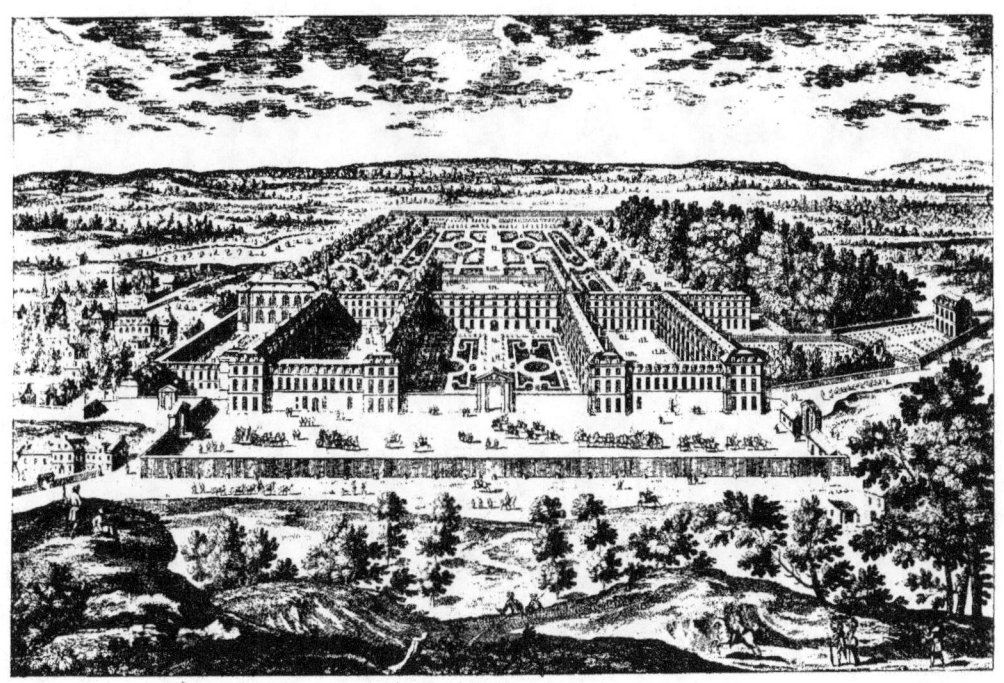

La Maison Royale de St Cyr à Paris chez J. Mariette aux Colonnes d'hercules.

ST. CYR.

VUE DU CHATEAU DE LA MEUTTE ET D'UNE PARTIE DU PARTERRE

THE CHÂTEAU DE LA MEUTTE.

FRENCH GARDENS: LATER 17TH AND 18TH CENTURIES

where an existing country house was adapted; the château was completed under Louis XVI, when the gardens were laid out.

At Lunéville, the Duke of Lorraine laid out immense garden schemes, which involved the destruction of whole villages and the removal of a monastery. Between the years 1711 and 1718 the colossal work was directed by Yves des Hours, who aspired to rival Le Nôtre, and in 1724

THE GROTTO AT LUNEVILLE.

the gardens were placed under the control of Louis Gervais, the future designer of Schönbrunn, then a youth fresh from studying at Meudon and Vienna. Voltaire wrote in 1738: "One can hardly think one has changed places when one comes from Versailles to Lunéville." A *théâtre de verdure* with grass seats, perfumed by numbers of orange trees and surrounded by varieties of water jets, was the scene of a famous *bal rustique* in 1739 upon the occasion of the marriage of Madame Louise Elizabeth with the Infante Don Philip. But the most wonderful feature of the garden was the *Rocher*

COLONNADE HYDRAULIQUE AT THE CHATEAU DE COMMERCY.

constructed by the architect, Emmanuel Héré (illus., p. 155); it was a grotto nearly 300 yards in length, attempting to reproduce a village grouped upon a mountainous site with an extraordinary collection of water devices.

For the same patron Héré laid out the gardens of the Château de Commercy, where there was a curious bridge crossing a canal with a colonnade upon both sides, known as a *colonnade hydraulique*; the shafts consisted of an outer framework of gilt metal with numerous tiny water-jets producing a sparkling column of falling water.

The style of Le Nôtre spread rapidly, and at every court in Europe garden designers, steeped in his traditions, found ample employment. In England and Holland the French gardens were imitated only upon a small scale, but in Italy, Germany, Austria and Sweden a number of extensive schemes were carried out.

JAN VREDEMAN DE VRIES.

CHAPTER VII

GARDEN DESIGN IN THE NETHERLANDS

HE influence of the Italian Renaissance in architecture penetrated to the Netherlands at about the same period as it did to France, that is, in the early years of the sixteenth century. The Dutch had already a European reputation for their cultivation of flowers. As early as the end of the fifteenth century we read of the *vermakhoven*, or pleasure yards, and of the dwellers in towns laying out their gardens. In Amsterdam a certain Sheriff Benning laid out the gardens at his country seat at Brillenburg on the Amstel. Such gardens were of very simple design, and quite small, only consisting of one or more courts, each serving a special domestic purpose.

Erasmus in his *Colloquies* draws a vivid picture of the square walled enclosures " neatly kept and in perfect order " that might as well have applied to his own native Holland as to either Italy or England. " Designed for the entertainment of the Sight, the Smell, and the Refreshment of the very Mind," it consisted of a series of walled enclosures, one containing nothing but sweet herbs " and those only choice ones too;" and every kind had its bed by itself. From the Fountain basin, cunningly contrived in imitation of marble, small channels run to every corner of the garden, reflecting the bordering flowers in their surface. The garden walls are painted with trees and flowers as " one piece of ground will not hold all sorts of plants " and " 'tis a double pleasure to compare painted Flowers with the Life, moreover, the Painting holds fresh and green all the Winter when the Flowers are dead and wither'd." Beyond the Herb-garden was " an indifferent fair garden cut into two: the one's for the Kitchin, and that's my Wife's; the other is a *Physick Garden*! Upon the left hand, you have an open green Meadow enclosed with a Quickset Hedge. There do I take the Air sometimes, and divert myself with good Company. Upon the right hand there's a Nursery of foreign Plants, which I have brought by degrees to endure this Climate. At the end of the upper Walk, there's an *Aviary*: at the further end of the Orchard I have my *Bees,* which is a sight worth your curiosity." [1]

The earliest Dutch book on garden craft that gives definite instructions for laying out gardens was published in Antwerp in 1582. It is a

A CASTLE GARDEN OF THE LATE SIXTEENTH CENTURY, FROM A PAINTING OF DIVES AND LAZARUS ASCRIBED TO VREDEMAN DE VRIES.

translation from the *Praedium rusticum* of Charles Estienne, which had appeared in Paris some thirty years earlier. According to this work the gardens of that time were mostly used for the cultivation of vegetables. The herb garden was considered the pleasantest of all. As in most horticultural books of this period, besides the description of each plant, there is

[1] *Colloquia:* "*Convivium Religiosum*" (Translated by Sir Roger L'Estrange, Kt.).

an account of its healing properties, and directions showing how it should be used in sickness.

The most famous garden designer of the sixteenth century was Jan Vredeman de Vries, the Dutch "Du Cerceau," born at Leeuwarden in 1527. His designs were published in Antwerp in 1583.[1] Amongst many books

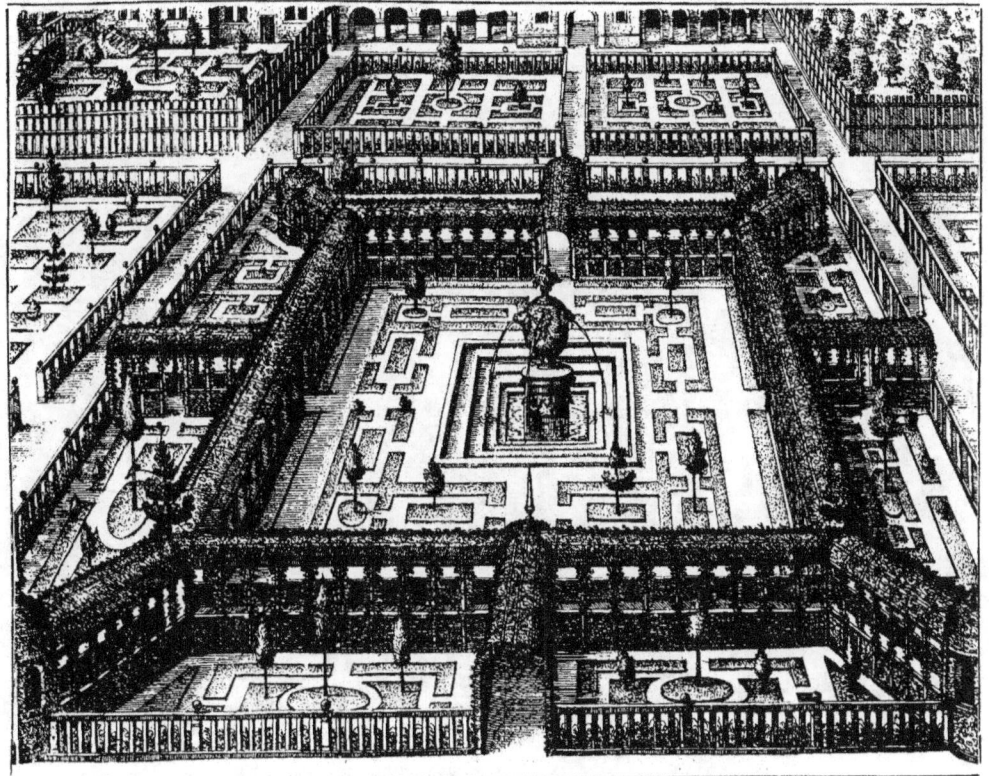

A GARDEN DESIGN BY DE VRIES ABOUT 1585, WITH GREEN ARBOURS AND PARTERRE.

dealing with architectural design, he published one volume entitled *Hortorum viridariorumque* together with many designs for fountains and grottos. His drawings give us almost as great an insight into the château life of the period as do those of his famous French contemporary, and taken in conjunc-

[1] Under the title of *Hortorum viridariorumque elegantes et multiplicis formae architectonicae, artis normam affabre delineatae a Johanne Vredemanno Frisio, Phillipus Gallaeus executebat Antwerpiae* 1583.

tion with the translation of Charles Estienne enable us to form a very complete idea of the gardens of that time. Here we see ladies being rowed in gaily-painted barges and luncheon served in richly decorated arbours, amidst the garden parterres. Even the bleaching ground is not forgotten " where should stand nothing but green grass or herbs and the fountain in the centre or with some platane or lime trees, the branches of which have been led

A DUTCH GARDEN IN THE SEVENTEENTH CENTURY.

and shaped to a bower, as may be seen at Basel and elsewhere, serving as an amusement to the Lady and her guests." In his engravings De Vries divides garden designs into various styles named after the orders of Architecture.

Though it is probable that few gardens were actually laid out from the designs of Vredeman de Vries, yet they set the style which was generally followed. This new Dutch style was largely followed both in England and in Germany.

For many years the region in which the principal châteaux of the Nether-

GARDEN DESIGN IN THE NETHERLANDS

lands were situated was the battleground of Europe, and during these troublous times most of the noble families to whom the estates belonged were ruined by revolution, their houses pillaged and burnt. As a result, it is hardly possible to find a château of the seventeenth century in the Netherlands that retains its garden surroundings unaltered; here and there the remains of some arbour, or perhaps a moss-covered fountain, long past repair, serve to mark what might once have been a gay pleasaunce, but we may search in vain for any complete scheme.

Fortunately we are able to know the châteaux as they existed in the first half of the seventeenth century by the splendid engravings of such artists as Wenceslaus Hollar, Peeters, Bruyn, Harrewyn, Vanweerden and others, collected in several comprehensive volumes. Chief among these are: A. Sandremius' *Flandria Illustrata*, 1641; *Brabantia Sacra et Profana*; the very early work Artzinger's *De Leone Belgico*, and *Castellorum et Praediorum Nobilium Brabantiae*.

A CASTLE GARDEN, 1568.

The last deals exhaustively with the provinces of Louvain, Brussels, Antwerp and Bois-le-Duc and gives quaintly-executed bird's-eye views of châteaux and their gardens that enable us to restore, mentally at least, these beautiful homes of the old Dutch and Flemish nobility.

A survey of these volumes must fill us with regret for all the fine châteaux that have been destroyed. We can hardly peruse them without realizing to what an extent the artistic influence of the Netherlands made itself felt in the sixteenth and seventeenth centuries in England, Germany, and Austria, and how fully the country gentleman of this period understood the art of beautifying the surroundings of his home.

The architecture of these châteaux is always picturesque, with varied outlines of gable and turret, twisted chimneys and elaborately-wrought vanes; delightful buildings that it would be a pleasure to surround with quaint gardens, thoroughly comfortable and cheerful old homes with none of the ostentation and pompous discomfort of the dwellings that succeeded them.

A FOUNTAIN AND BOSQUET, LATE SIXTEENTH CENTURY.

The principal buildings were grouped round an internal courtyard and were approached by a drawbridge across the moat, which usually came right up to the castle walls. The upper part of the portcullis tower was sometimes treated as a dovecot. The *basse-cour* was planned in close proximity and conveniently arranged for stables, farm buildings and granaries. The orchards, kitchen gardens, herbaries, and the pleasaunce consisted of a series

GARDEN DESIGN IN THE NETHERLANDS

of small islands, divided by canals and each approached by its little bridge. Occasionally, though very rarely, the pleasaunce is planned upon the same island as the dwelling house.

In all these châteaux the parterre was planned upon an elaborate scale, with an infinite variety of designs worked in cut box, and planted with flowers. An illustration is given of a garden which forms the frontispiece to Crispin

A CASTLE GARDEN OF THE LATE SIXTEENTH CENTURY.

de Passe's *Hortus Floridus*, published at Arnhem in 1614 (p. 166). There was an English edition published in 1616, and described as containing "Rarer and less Vulgar flowers accurately drawn by the incredible labour and diligence of Crispin de Passe, Jun." The garden is surrounded by architectural wooden galleries such as may be seen in Du Cerceau's drawings of the princely gardens of France in the sixteenth century. A cavalier rests on the balustrade and a lady is gathering tulips, of which there are four beds. The tulips do not appear in the earlier print, and in the later edition there are eleven additional plates giving new varieties, mostly named after Dutchmen; this addendum marks the beginning of the tulip mania and roughly fixes its date. The use of coloured earths and sands, an expedient invented by the Italians rather than by the Dutch, became more prevalent; in some cases the paths and alleys were covered over with fine sand or marble dust or

A FLOWER GARDEN FROM CRISPIN DE PASSE'S HORTUS FLORIDUS, 1614.

paved with bricks, tiles, or cut stones. Sometimes when the parterre is large it is divided into four parts by miniature canals. Fountains occupy an important part in the design, and they were frequently elaborate structures of bronze, marble or lead.

The storks' nests, provided by the owners of the houses, are always shown in these old illustrations, and may still be met with in any country house in the Netherlands. They are constructed about twenty or thirty feet above the ground, and unfortunate is the house that fails to secure a tenant for its nest.

In Holland, which Butler sarcastically describes as

"A land that rides at anchor and is moored
In which they do not live, but go aboard,"

the *vyvers*, or fish ponds, were important accessories in all country houses. They often covered a considerable area and had a system of dams, water-wheels, and sluices to prevent the water from becoming stagnant. The arrangement of moats and canals, with their varying levels, was of the utmost importance, and as a sanitary precaution great care and attention were required to regulate the levels of the water courses and to prevent the accumulation of weeds.

GALLERIES IN THE GARDEN OF ADRIAAN VAN DE VENNE AT MIDDLEBURG, SEVENTEENTH CENTURY.

The edges of the canals were carefully trimmed and kept in position either by lattice work or by an edging of stone. When these precautions were neglected and the sluices and dams allowed to fall into disrepair they were soon liable to become plague spots, and Alderman Beckford, who toured in Holland in 1780, must have suffered considerably, for he notes in his diary that although "Every flower that wealth can purchase diffuses its perfume on the one side, every stench a canal can exhale poisons the air on the other. Who knows, but their odour is congenial to a Dutch constitution? One should be inclined to this supposition by the numerous banqueting rooms and pleasure houses which hang directly over their surface and seem calculated on purpose to enjoy them."

There is an immense variety shown in the designs for arbours and summer houses (illus., pp. 169, 170), which, with their quaintly-shaped roofs, gilt vanes and gaily-painted shutters added greatly to the attraction of the gardens. The principal arbours were comfortable retreats, solidly built of brick and

SPRINGTIME, FROM AN ENGRAVING BY P. VAN DER HEYDE, 1570.

stone to withstand rough weather, the less important constructed of light woodwork and often of topiary. Green tunnels frequently surround the parterre; the quaint example illustrated shows an oblong island surrounded by a crenellated wall and divided into two circular parterres with surrounding tunnels of verdure and cone-shaped arbours.

GARDEN DESIGN IN THE NETHERLANDS

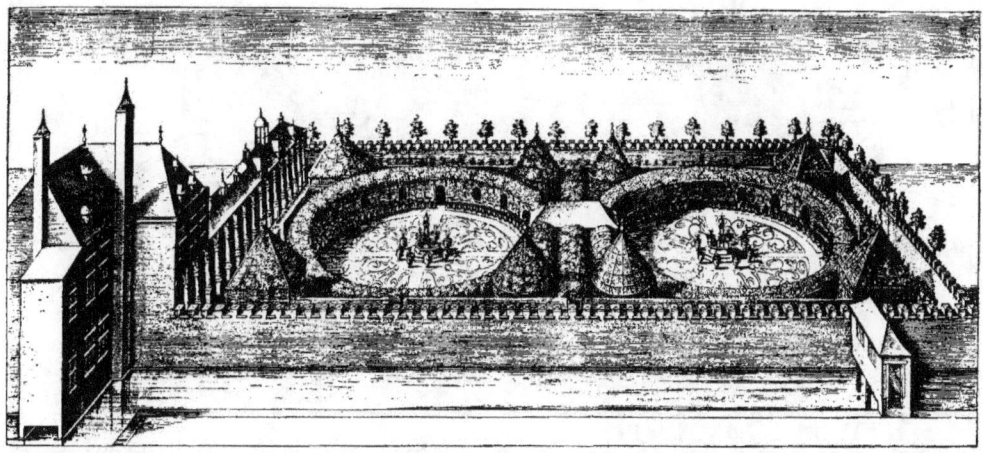

SEVENTEENTH-CENTURY WALLED GARDEN, WITH TWO CIRCULAR PARTERRES.

Terraces are not often to be met with in Holland, and it is this which principally gives individuality to the Dutch garden, for nowhere is the country sufficiently hilly to allow of their natural construction. Even in Guelderland and Overyssel, where the ground is partly hilly, the incline are too small to allow of terracing. Instead we sometimes find an artificial mount placed in a position commanding a view or as the central feature to a maze. Any want of variety which in other countries would have been overcome by a change in the levels of the garden, was, in Holland, provided by a profusion of flowers that the smallness of the gardens and the

AN EIGHTEENTH-CENTURY GARDEN HOUSE.

DUTCH GAZEBOS

high state of cultivation of the land permitted. In all the larger gardens the vast parterre unrelieved by any difference in level appears dull and uninteresting.

Later gardens are well illustrated in De Cantillon's work *Vermakelykheden van Brabant*, containing a variety of garden designs in quaint perspective views. The characteristics of the gardens we have already noticed are not to any extent changed and the influence of Le Nôtre is not yet felt. Although the work was published in 1770, the probability is that these engravings are much earlier, for another work, *Les délices de Brabant*, which was published in 1757, shows into what a state of disrepair the châteaux of this district had then fallen.

KASTEEL-VAN-TERVUEREN

The influence of Versailles and Le Nôtre did not immediately spread to Holland, and garden books that appeared a quarter of a century after Versailles reached the height of its glory, do not even mention the new style that Le Nôtre had introduced. It was not until William III had laid out his royal gardens, that the great French gardens were imitated on a much smaller scale. The reasons are not far to seek, for in Holland, which at this date was thickly populated, the land was mostly in small lots and in the hands of the middle classes, and though there were many among the wealthy Amsterdam merchants who could have afforded to lay out large estates, their democratic spirit prevented them doing

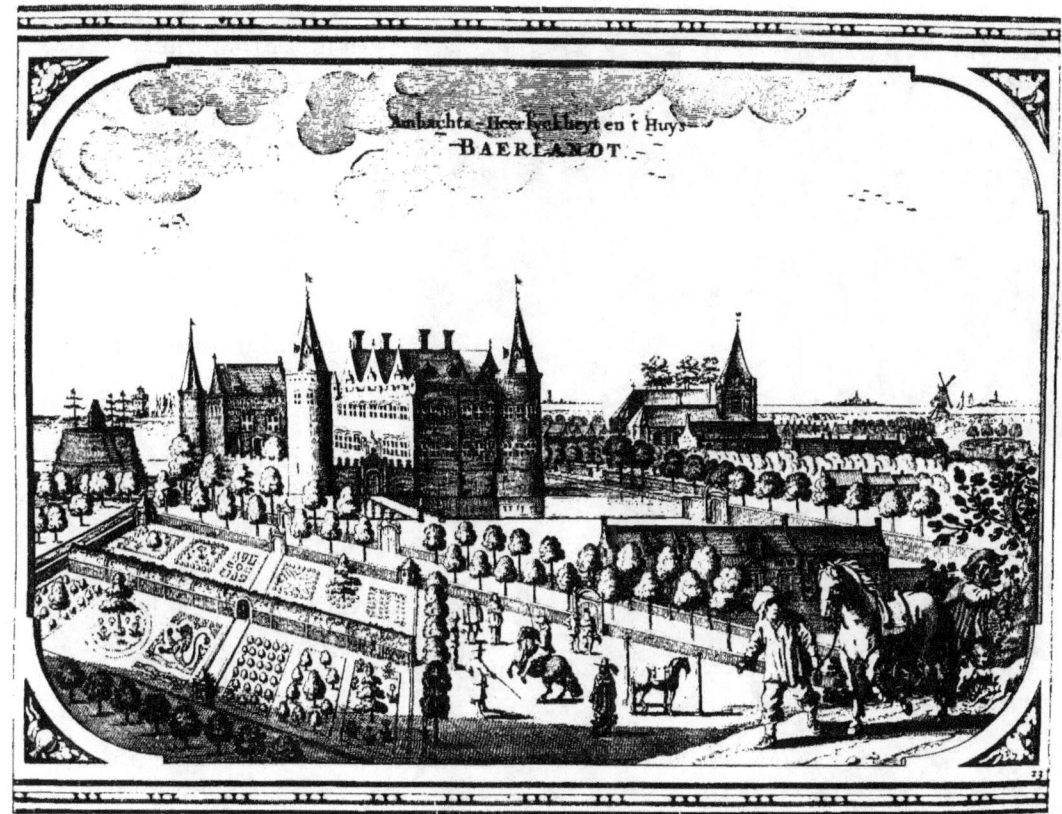

THE CASTLE OF BAERLANDT.

so. Le Nôtre is sometimes reputed to have designed the gardens at Het Loo, but we are unable to find any evidence that he worked there or anywhere else in Holland.

Another reason why the style of Le Nôtre was not considerably followed lies in the fact that the French gardens relied largely for their effect upon the treatment of bosquets and woods. In most parts of Holland the growth of large trees was prevented by heavy winds, and because the roots were unable to penetrate into the ground to any depth without coming to water.

One of the most interesting Flemish gardens was that of the Castle of the Duc d'Enghien, eighteen miles from Brussels, destroyed during the French Revolution. From the engravings of Romain de Hooghe we see it illustrated when the gardens were at their best, and as they appeared at the period when Voltaire and the Marquise de Châtelet stayed here in 1739. "The gardens were so attractive that they almost reconciled Voltaire to a house where there was not a single book except those which he had brought himself." De Hooghe's plan shows a broad alley leading directly from the castle to a kind of fort with seven bastions overlooking shooting ranges. There was a mount known as "Parnas" planned in three tiers, each connected by ramps enclosed with hedges. The *Vyver* was near the castle and contained a square island known as "la Motte," surrounded by hedges, with a tremendous water-jet in the middle. Another feature was the Mall (p. 174), an alley some three

SIMON SCHYNVOET.

hundred yards long enclosed within high hedges and terminating in a fountain and pavilion. It had side walks, slightly raised, from which spectators might witness the game. A labyrinth, an orange garden and an ingenious mechanical island were also among the attractions of Enghien. The Park still existed in the early years of the nineteenth century, and

THE ORANGE GARDEN AT ENGHIEN.

Loudon describes the famous temple and the *grande étoile*. The temple was of a heptangular shape and at every angle were two parallel columns placed about a foot apart. "From the seven large sides proceed as many broad, straight and long avenues of noble trees affording rich prospects of the distant country in all these directions; and from the seven angles, and seen between the columns, proceed an equal number of small and narrow alleys, each terminated by some statue, vase, bust, or other ornament. The temple is surrounded by a moat lined with polished marble. The old orange-grove is situated at the end of the avenue, and contains one hundred and eight orange trees in tubs, many of them, as is the case in different old family seats in the Netherlands, presents from the Kings of Spain 200 years and more ago. The trees show straight stems of six and eight feet, and

THE MALL AT ENGHIEN.

globular heads, from which, according to continental practice, protruding shoots and blossoms are pinched off as soon as they appear, for culinary and perfumery purposes."

Among the better-known garden designers were Simon Schynvoet (1652–1727), Daniel Marot, and Jacques Roman. All three followed closely the traditions of Le Nôtre. Schynvoet designed the gardens of Soelen and had a large Court connection; he was responsible for most of the import-

GARDEN DESIGN IN THE NETHERLANDS

ant gardens round the Hague, and many villas along the banks of the Amstel and the Vecht. His portrait, engraved by Schenck, might almost be taken for a likeness of the King himself. Daniel Marot was a pupil of Le Nôtre, and while still a young man left Versailles and went to The Hague, where he was soon afterwards appointed Court gardener to William III, whom he accompanied to England. He is said to have been partly responsible for the gardens at Hampton Court. He published a large number of his schemes, together with many designs for treillage, garden ornament, etc. Besides

RUPELMONDE ON THE VECHT.

working at The Hague he laid out the Huis-te-Dieren for William III and Voorst near Zutphen for the Count of Albemarle. Jacques Roman was also employed by William III; the most important of his gardens was that of "Het Loo." Jan van Call was another famous Dutch designer; he was born at The Hague in 1689, and he laid out a number of gardens in that neighbourhood, including Clingendaal.

In 1669 J. van de Groen published *De Nederlandsche Hovenier* (The Dutch Gardener). The work was issued in both French and German, and up to the middle of the eighteenth century held the field as the most popular

THE ORANGERY AT GUNTERSTEIN.

treatise on garden craft. The quaint illustrations of Ryswyck, Honsholredyk and the Huis 'ten Bosch near The Hague show these gardens before they had been remodelled on French lines. Van de Groen gives a dissertation on country life in general, on fountains, the cultivation of flowers, trees, vines, and oranges. He deals with the laying out of simple parterres and the construction of treillage, which he illustrates by a quaint collection of designs for pyramids, doorways, galleries, and arbours. Finally, he instructs his readers on dials, and illustrates a curious example laid out upon the ground, its gnomon formed by a tree and the figures cut out in box.

A more elaborate work appeared in 1676, entitled *De Koninglycke Hovenier* (The Royal Gardener), with a variety of more extensive parterres. This work was in great repute in England, and no doubt many of our best gardens were laid out from its designs. It consists of two parts, the first devoted to fruits and flowers, and the second to garden design.

There was a great similarity between the Dutch house of the late seventeenth and eighteenth centuries

A SEVENTEENTH-CENTURY ORANGE TUB.

and the English country house of the same period. Almost invariably of classic type, solidly built of brick with a sparing use of stone, they lack the variety of outline that characterized the châteaux of Germany and Flanders. Until the beginning of the nineteenth century it was still necessary to surround the house by a deep moat, which was also put to good use as the fish-pond. The garden generally followed the earlier French taste of Marot and was laid out in symmetrical and regular forms. But as the style of Le Nôtre spread over the Continent after his death, many gardens were laid out for the rich merchants of Amsterdam, furnished with bosquets, allées and canals, but lacking the profusion of sculpture that was such an important feature in the French garden. What is usually spoken of as the Dutch style hardly differs from the French, except in the more extended use of canals, and in the fact that the Dutch gardens are more enclosed.

A ROADSIDE GAZEBO NEAR HAARLEM.

The *clairvoyée* is a purely Dutch invention. Placed at the end of an alley, it consists of two or more brick piers with an ornamental iron grille between, to extend the garden view to the country beyond, perhaps to some church steeple or other feature of the landscape.

The orange was much cultivated in Holland in the seventeenth and eighteenth centuries, and every garden of importance had its orangery. The cultivation was brought to great perfection, and Dutch oranges are said to have been not inferior to those of Spain. There are many works treating of the cultivation of oranges in Holland, but the most important is Jan Commelyn's *Nederlantze Hesperides*, published in 1676, which was translated into English in 1683 as "the Belgick or Netherlandish Hesperides"; it has a collection of engravings of the many varieties of oranges, lemons and citrons in cultivation. Dutch methods soon spread to England, and until recent years, some of the orange trees brought from the Loo were flourishing at Hampton Court.

AN EIGHTEENTH-CENTURY GAZEBO.

The Dutch summer house (*zomerhuis*), or gazebo (illus., pp. 170, 177), is a characteristic feature in every garden, and great variety is shown in its design. It is usually built of brick or stone, panelled in wood, and often with a fireplace. Whenever the house is situated near the high road or canal it is sure to be placed in a position from whence the passing coach or post-boat may be easily hailed. In the long summer evenings the men bring their pipes here and the ladies their needlework. Often in the neighbourhood of large towns the citizens would erect such gazebos upon some little patch of ground outside the town, to which they could retire with their families after the business of the day and criticise the passers-by. These little buildings are quite a characteristic feature, and often have quaint names or mottoes inscribed over their doors, bespeaking content or comfort on the part of the owner. Thus amongst others we read *Lust en rust*, Pleasure and ease ; *Wel tevreden*, Well content ; *Nood gedacht*,

A COUNTRY HOUSE NEAR HAARLEM.

Never expected; *Vriendschap en gezelschap,* Friendship and sociability; *Het vermaak is in t'hovenieren,* There is pleasure in gardening. In the early Dutch gardens, aviaries were provided for domestic purposes, but by the seventeenth century they had become decorative accessories.

LAYING OUT THE PARTERRE, SEVENTEENTH CENTURY.

The elaborate example from Westerhof dates from the early eighteenth century; an octagonal aviary for smaller birds is placed within a sunken square court. During the landscape period a great variety of aviaries were designed, in the shape of Classic temples and Chinese pagodas, Gothic ruins and Turkish Mosques, but they do not compare with the more appropriate structures of the seventeenth century.

AVIARY AT WESTERHOF, FROM AN ENGRAVING BY J. MOUCHERON.

The cultivation of flowers, and especially of tulips, has always been a considerable industry in Holland, and according to Loudon is believed to have originated as early as the twelfth century. Lotel, in his preface to his *Histoire des Plantes*, 1756, states that the taste for plants existed among the Flemings during the Crusades, and under the Dukes of Burgundy; that plants were brought home from the Levant, and the two Indies; that exotics were more cultivated in the Netherlands than anywhere else; and that the Dutch gardens contained more rarities than all the rest of Europe, until, during the desolating civil wars of the sixteenth century, many of the finest gardens were abandoned or destroyed. To-day a traveller by rail from The Hague to Haarlem in springtime will pass field upon field of gorgeous colour. In the seventeenth century the competition to obtain the rarer bulbs was very remarkable and became quite a mania, thousands of florins being lost in tulip speculation. In 1637 the registers of Alkmaar show that at a public sale for the profit of the Orphanage 120 bulbs were sold for 9,000 florins, a single bulb fetching upwards of 4,000 florins. The writer of a letter in 1780 says: "Yesterday I was in a garden where they showed me The Emperor and Empress of Russia, the King of Peru, the Comte d'Œyras, Madame du Bari, Donne Margarite, la Comtesse de Wassenaer, le Baron de Cranendonc, the Prince Charles Frederic, and a quantity of other most illustrious personages, which together they offered me for 100 sous. However, I refused them, for all these grand persons were only *oignons* (bulbs). Thus they honour here the different flowers and distinguish them from each other [apparently at this date it was unusual to call flowers by other than their generic names]. I bought a catalogue of flowers of one of these gardeners, which is a thing very curious for a foreigner, for it contains the names of more than 6,000 bulbs of different kinds. The first sort is the double hyacinth, amongst which is one, the *beauté tendre*, of which the price is 100 florins, the 'chrysolora,' 60 florins; the Prince Guillaume Frederic,

A SMALL AVIARY, EIGHTEENTH CENTURY, FROM AN ENGRAVING BY D. A. CLEMENS.

of 80 florins; the 'Nimrot,' of 45; the 'Flossanguines,' of 60. There are many others even more costly, and some as cheap as 5, 3 or 2 sous each. Hyacinths were the most sought after, first the double, then the single, and tulips only came third; after tulips came renoncules, anemones, narcisses, oreilles d'ours, and violets last of all. Haarlem is of all the seven provinces the most celebrated centre for the cultivation of flowers. The gardeners have a quarter in one of the fauxbourgs of the city, and in the season the fashionable world comes from all the seven provinces to see these gardens. There are also professional gardeners at other places, but principally at Alkmaar and Leyden." The cultivation of the hyacinth and tulip probably started the idea of the use of flowers for table and household decoration. In Hampton Court may still be seen fine specimens of Delft vases specially designed for the effective display of these flowers, and as a *motif* for decorative schemes they are frequently to be met with in the textiles and furniture of the period. This love of flowers acted upon the design of both English and French gardens, and the French parterre was never popular with the Dutch, who wisely preferred their simple square flower beds to the elaborate display of a *parterre de broderie*. In the *Koniglyck Hovenier*, published in 1676, the designs of the most palatial gardens retained the old-fashioned square beds of the previous century.

PARTERRE BORDER.

The Dutch are often supposed to have revived the ancient topiary work, but there can be no doubt that the revival came from Italy to France. Both Palissy in 1564 and Olivier de Serres in 1604 give directions as to the best method of cutting trees. Mérian in 1631 gives further information, together with many illustrations, and mentions France and England (especially Hampton Court) as the countries where the fashion was in vogue.

Topiary work was still fashionable in the eighteenth century, though not carried to its former excesses. Low hedges of box and rosemary were often cut into fanciful lines to border the parterres, the angles being accentuated in the forms of obelisks. The example illustrated (p. 183) is from Bosch-en-Hoven, near Haarlem, where the whole parterre was surrounded by a topiary border.

Most of the country seats were in the neighbourhood of Amsterdam, the largest commercial city, The Hague, the seat of Government, Haarlem,

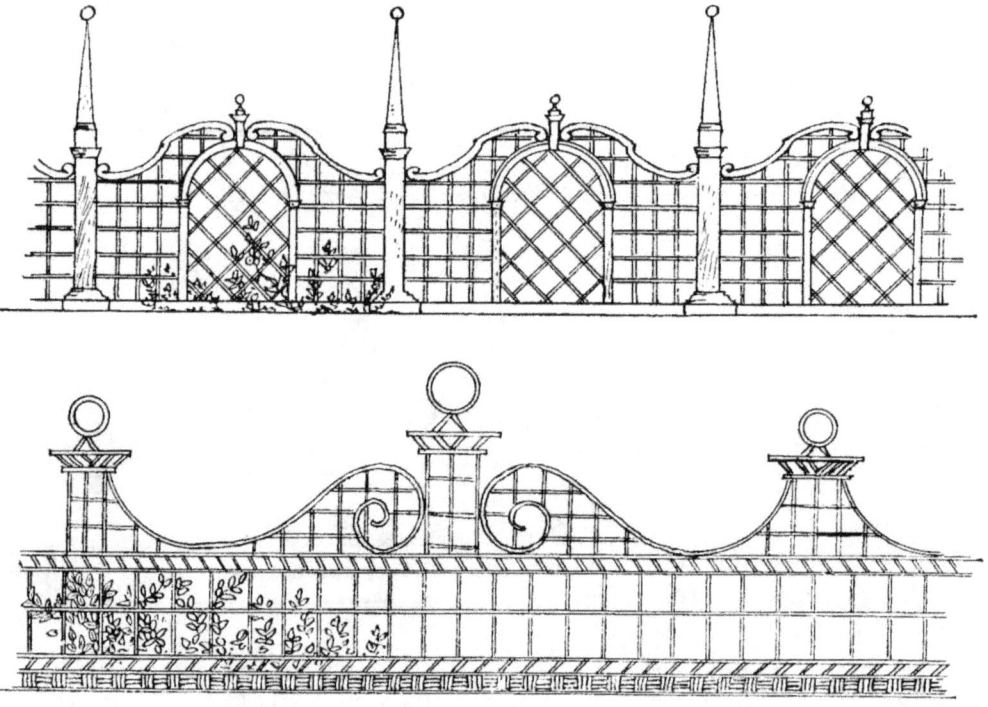

SEVENTEENTH-CENTURY DESIGNS FOR TREILLAGE FENCES.

Leyden and Utrecht. Travelling by road was neither safe nor easy, and as both the Amstel and Vecht offered fine opportunities for transport to and fro by yacht, the whole district between Utrecht and Amsterdam became one vast garden. Mr. Wortley Montagu writes in 1763 : " At every moment we passed a succession of these gardens with their labyrinth, parterres and hedges cut out in all manner of fantastic designs. Sometimes the gardens are divided from each other by a tiny canal, sometimes by a little field. They extended without interruption as far as Brenkelm during more than

BOENDERMAKER ON THE VECHT.

BOENDERMAKER ON THE VECHT.

an hour, each garden touching its neighbour, then came a break of a few miles, only to be continued again for several hours." Haarlem was connected with Amsterdam by a line of small country seats, and from Alkmaar to The Hague stretched a long string of picturesque estates.

It seems to have been the ambition of every owner to have his garden engraved, and these engravings, together with the surveys prepared to show the drainage of the polders, enable us to study the plans of practically every country seat in the North of Holland.

In 1732 Rademaker published a delightful series of engravings of the Dutch *Maison de plaisance*,[1] each surrounded by its canal, crossed by little bridges variously treated in design and flanked by massive gate piers. A forecourt generally leads to the plain severe brick house, or in its absence, an alley of limes serves the same purpose. There are many quaint gazebos with an endless variety in the shape of their roofs. The hedges are invariably cut low to permit a good look-out over the surrounding scenery, and very pleasant it must have been to survey the long panorama of quaint little country places on the canal banks from the deck of a gaily-painted yacht.

To the north of Haarlem, in a district known as the "Kennemerlant," a number of wealthy merchants from Amsterdam had their country seats during the prosperous times of the eighteenth century. Many of these still remain, but few of their gardens escaped the general spoliation of the early nineteenth century. They were mostly laid out in the style of Le Nôtre, though of necessity upon a very modified scale. Their plans and a splendid series of small engravings were published at Amsterdam by Hendrik de Leth.[2] The houses as a rule are not large, but are often beautifully decorated and are built with an air of comfort, although they were only intended for summer use. Here and there we may come across some remnant of a scheme of avenues, some forecourt, or oftener still a gazebo or orangery that has escaped the general destruction. A mile beyond Haarlem, at Mannepall, is a typical small country seat. Here the house is approached by a short drive, through a quincunx of limes, flanked upon either side by out-buildings, one the orangery, the other used as stables; an ornamental bridge leads to the square built house surrounded by a broad moat, and beyond and on either side are parterres.

[1] *Rhynlands Fraaiste Gezichsten.* Abraham Rademaker, Amsterdam, 1732.
[2] *Het zegepralent Kennemerlant.* Hendrik de Leth, Amsterdam, 1730.

At Marquette, near Haarlem, many of the old avenues remain; the château was placed upon an island with a broad surrounding moat. At Merestein the house is protected by no less than three moats. The Dutch always had a predilection for avenues, and almost every house was approached from the high road by an avenue of limes, sometimes, as at Watervleit, so closely planted as to form a dense tunnel of verdure. At Waterland, near Velsen, there is little or no parterre, and the whole effect is concentrated upon a magnificent central water piece from which a series of lime avenues radiate, each terminating in a summer house or temple.

The neighbouring house of "Velsenbeck" had formerly one of the most interesting garden schemes in the neighbourhood, but all was unfortunately changed in the early nineteenth century. The house was of quite small dimensions, but was approached by several superb lime avenues. Here, as at Waterland, the parterre was small, for the frugal Dutchman never favoured the large and expensive French parterre, preferring rather to lay out his bosquets in positions where they could always be turned to good account in affording an occasional day's shooting. The old orangery is still in perfect condition, and scattered about the grounds are many little buildings, including a hermitage upon an island, an inn and a children's play-house, completely furnished.

EIGHTEENTH-CENTURY SEAT IN A GARDEN AT VELSEN.

Garden theatres were frequently to be met with. That at Westerwyk was quite elaborate with a proscenium of hornbeam arranged as a big arch, behind which the orchestra sat in a sunken oval arena adjoining the stage. The wings were of hedges closely trimmed and formed backgrounds to a series of leaden statues. The back of the stage was a permanent architectural composition. These theatres were often constructed of treillage, but naturally, none so made are now in existence. An ephemeral element such as treillage is particularly suited for a garden theatre.

The hedges were invariably of hornbeam, which seems to thrive well in the light, sandy soil of Holland; they were kept well trimmed and occa-

SOETENDAEL ON THE VECHT.

sionally cut into fanciful forms. Sometimes the fruit gardens were surrounded by brick walls, their plan consisting of a series of concave and convex curves for the better protection of the fruit. The Dutch may be said to have introduced the hot-house, and early examples of such buildings with their heating arrangements are still to be met with.

A Haarlem country seat is thus described in 1748 in a letter. The writer, after expatiating on the number of villas round the town, says: " I walked to Madame Redelyk's country seat, situated quite close to the mooring place of the *trekschuyt*. The name of the house was Tulpenburg, the first owner having bought it from the winnings gained in gambling; the late proprietors have considerably enlarged it. After having been originally designed upon the system of Le Nôtre—now condemned as stiff—the garden has just been improved according to the principles of d'Argenville. I must confess to have nowhere seen a garden where those principles had

A PLEACHED ALLEY AT ZEYST.

been followed and carried out in a prettier and better way. The many ornaments of box alternated in a pleasant way with coloured stones, coloured glass, sand, and the refuse of smithies. A so-called English parterre had been arranged of curiously cut grass beds enclosed within wide borders ornamented by flowers. Low hedges, clipped into different shapes, divide the various parts of the garden, whilst a maze with countless turns and corners, arranged so as to mislead the visitor, forms the centre of the

garden. A part of the garden has been laid out as a bosquet through which a few alleys have been cut, but these are so narrow that a lady dressed in a stylish farthingale could with difficulty traverse them."

The Palace of the Loo (*v.* annexed illus.) had fine formal gardens until the end of the eighteenth century, but these have now all given place to landscape gardens. The palace originally consisted of a central block of buildings with wings, enclosing small square parterres on either side, one known as the King's parterre, or *Koningstuin*, and the other the Queen's garden, or *Koninginnetuin*;

THE FOUNTAIN OF VENUS AT "HET LOO."

the latter was a *cabinet de verdure*, with pleached alleys or tunnels disposed in serpentine winding walks, and in the centre a gilt leaden fountain. The bowling green was surrounded by a low box hedge, and near by was the *Doolhof*, or Labyrinth. There was a famous orangery that supplied most of the plants to Hampton Court when William III took up his residence there. From a detailed description of the Loo in 1699, by Dr. W. Harris, we learn that " the hedges are chiefly of Dutch elms, and the avenues of oaks, elms, and limes. The figures into which the trees and shrubs are cut are, for the most part, pyramids. On the walls fresco paintings are introduced in various places between the trees. In the arbour walks of the queen's garden are seats, and opposite to them windows through which views can be had of the fountains, statues, and other objects in the open garden. The parterres in the queen's garden are surrounded by hedges of Dutch elms about four feet high. The seats and prop-work of all the arbours, and the trellis work on the fruit tree walk, are painted green. All along the gravel walks and round the middle fountain are placed orange trees and lemon trees in portable wooden frames and flower pots about them."

At The Hague the most important garden was that of the Royal Palace; it was laid out in the seventeenth century, but in later years the formal *vyver* was converted into an "English" lake and the gardens were entirely remodelled and spoiled. The plan engraved by Jacob de Remier in 1730 shows the garden parterres unspoiled, and is also quite a study in itself of the smaller town gardens of the court officials. In the neighbourhood of The Hague were several important palaces with gardens upon a large scale; Ryswick, Honslaerdyck, Sorgvliet and the "Huis t'en Bosch," or House in the Wood (illus., p. 194), were all designed upon a very large scale, but with the exception of the last have all disappeared. Honslaerdyck, between The Hague and the Hook, was one of the finest seats in the Low Countries, and the favourite palace of William III, who replanned it upon the foundations of an old manor house, and fitted it up with great magnificence. Behind the palace was an extensive bosquet regularly planted, and beyond was a menagerie where foreign birds and beasts were kept in large numbers. An engraving in the *Nederlandsche Hovenier* shows the gardens as they existed in the seventeenth century, and they have also been engraved by Vischer.

The Château of Sorgvliet, on the road to Schevening, was another important country seat near The Hague; it belonged to the Duke of Portland, was often visited by William and Mary and was the scene of many famous fêtes in the early eighteenth century. The great feature of these gardens was an immense orangery planned as a semicircle with pavilions in the centre and at both ends. There was also a mount known as *Parnassus-berg*, a grotto with rockworks, cascades, *berceaux*, fish ponds, a labyrinth, aviaries for cranes and a series of fountains, which last are rarely to be met with in Holland. All these features have long since disappeared, but a part of the low one-story building still remains. In 1780, when Alderman Beckford

HONSLAERDYCK.

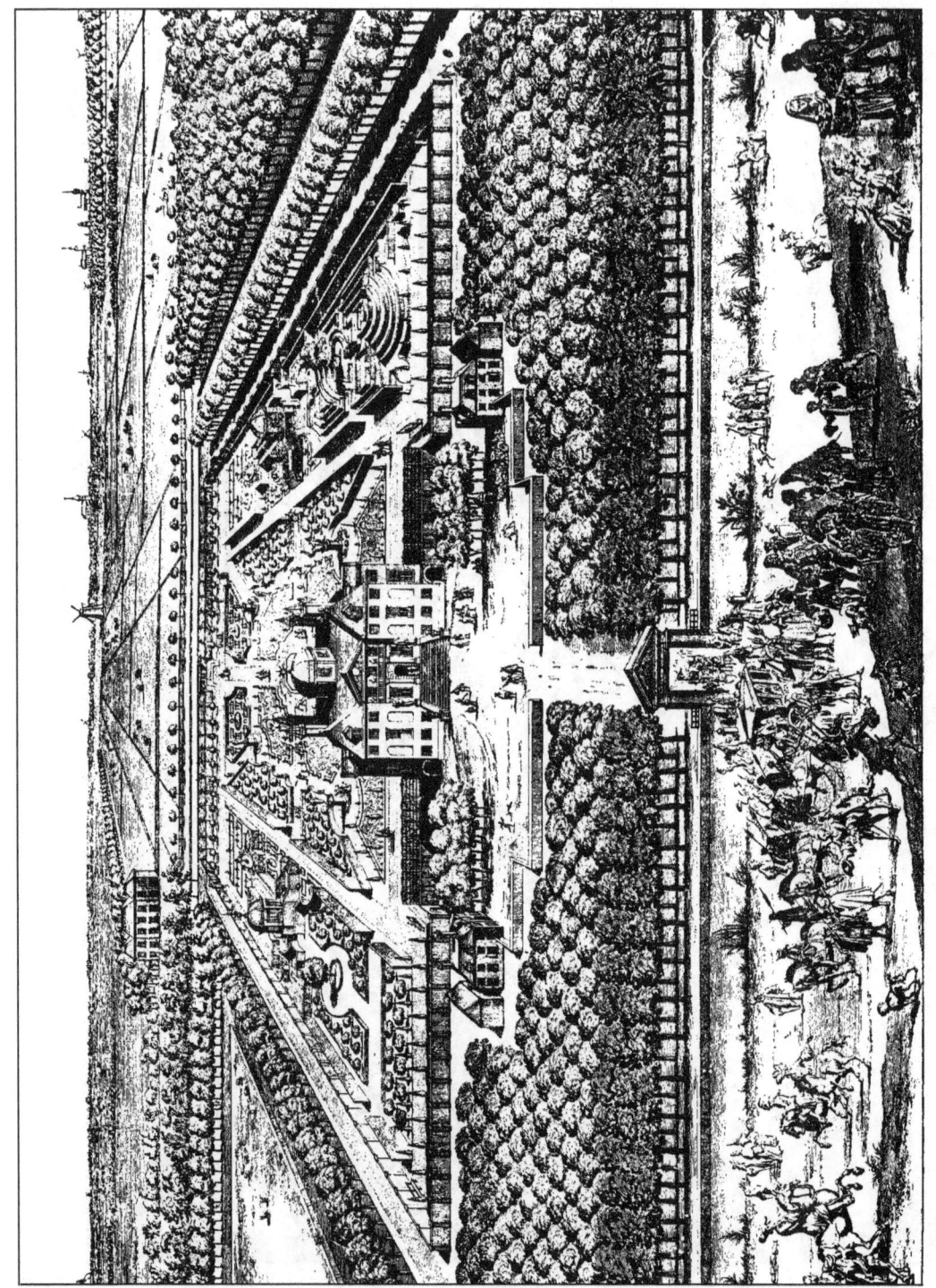

"THE HOUSE IN THE WOOD," AT THE HAGUE.

visited the garden, it had been already replanned in accordance with the ideas that had recently been introduced from England. "I returned towards The Hague," he writes, "and looked into the country house of the late Count Bentinck, with parterres and bosquets by no means resembling, one should conjecture, the gardens of the Hesperides. But, considering that the whole group of trees, terraces and verdure were in a manner created out of hills of sand, the place may claim some portion of merit. The walks and alleys have all the stiffness and formality which our ancestors admired, but the intermediate spaces, being dotted with clumps and sprinkled with flowers, are imagined in Holland to be in the English style. An Englishman ought certainly to behold it with partial eyes, since every possible attempt has been made to twist it into the taste of his country.

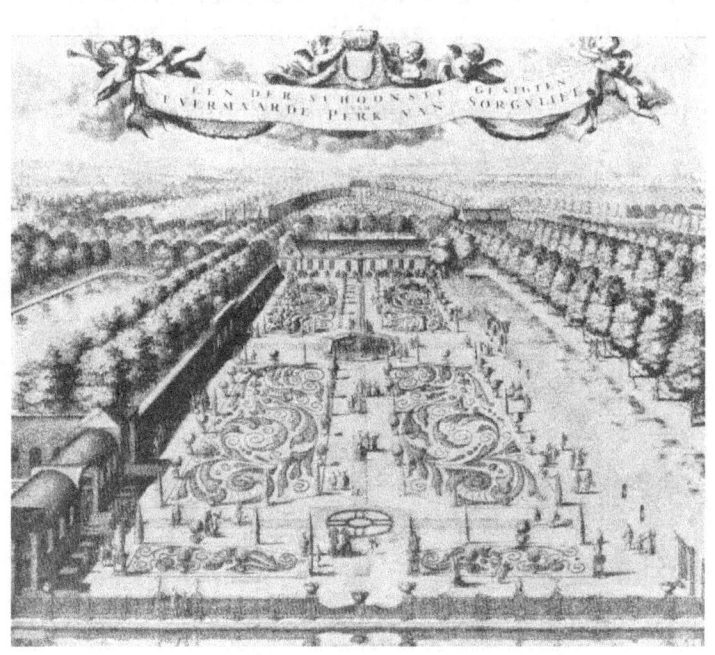

SORGVLIET.

"I need hardly say how liberally I bestowed my encomiums on Count Bentinck's tasteful invention; nor how happy I was, when I had duly serpentized over his garden, to find myself once more in the grand avenue.

"All the way home I reflected upon the unyielding perseverance of the Dutch, who raise gardens from heaps of sand, and cities out of the bosom of the waters."

"The House in the Wood" was originally built as a dower house by Amelia of Solms, the widow of Frederick Henry, Prince of Orange. About the year 1645 the Princess, dissatisfied with the old dower houses at The Hague and Ryswick, conceived a wish to build a country house in part of the beautiful wood which still forms the entrance to The Hague on the north side. In building the house she was imbued with the idea of making it a monument to the House of Orange, an idea, no doubt, supplied by Marie de Medicis, Luxembourg Palace. The illustration shows the palace as it was originally laid out, upon a large square plot of land surrounded by a moat, which is the only part of the old gardens still remaining, for the grounds have been completely changed and hardly a vestige of their original design is left. Many engravings exist which show the palace as it was in the sixteenth and seventeenth centuries, and the plans were published by the architect, Pierre Post, in 1715,[1] and later in 1758 by Bescot, showing the great alterations in the design that had taken place then.

A TOPIARY PARTERRE AT "THE HOUSE IN THE WOOD."

Other famous gardens in the neighbourhood of The Hague were those of Swanenburg, Ryxdorp, and Vredenburg, plans of all of which have been engraved by Pierre Post.

At Ryswyck (illus., p. 197), belonging to the House of Nassau, the gardens occupied an oblong piece of ground surrounded by a moat. The palace was famous as the scene of the signing of the Treaty of Peace in 1697, and the gardens were laid out in formal lines, which in their design suggest those of Herrenhausen, near Hanover. The palace was destroyed by the French, but parts of the gardens still exist.

[1] *Le Sale d'Orange. Bâtie par son altesse Amalia Princesse Douairiere d'Orange* par Pierre Post, 1715.

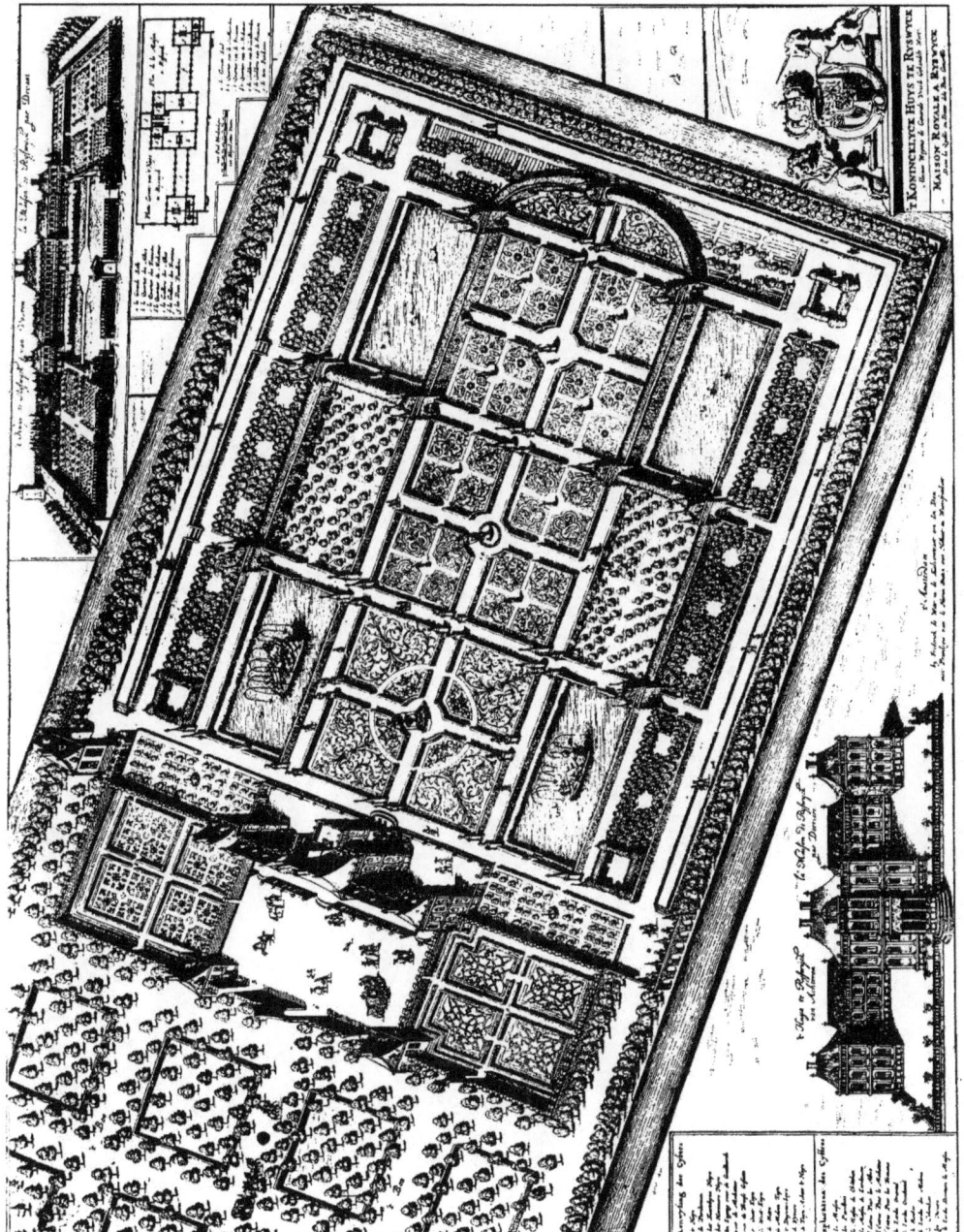

PERSPECTIVE PLAN OF THE GARDENS AT RYSWYCK.

The gardens at Rosendaal, Twickel near Delden, Zuylesteyn, Ameringen, Middachten near Dieren, all retain some of their original features.

Magnificent gardens were designed at Clingendaal and also at Gunterstein. The former occupied an immense oblong piece of land divided into square plots by numerous canals. The *Bloemenpark* terminated in a large *Vyver* crossed by bridges which led to a bosquet, and beyond were extensive fruit gardens and more fishponds. Gunterstein was planned upon a triangular piece of land and had a large bosquet and labyrinth some little distance from the house. Here the orangery had a courtyard enclosed within high walls, the piers of which were decorated with full size leaden statues (p. 176). Both of these gardens have entirely disappeared, but complete monographs with delightful little illustrations were published by Nicholas Vischer.

In their smallness of scale the old Dutch gardens resemble those of Japan, though in all their other characteristics they are entirely different. Kaempfer, who whilst in the service of the Dutch East Indian Company visited Japan in 1690, gives a quaint description of the smaller gardens, many of which were laid out upon a space no more than 30 feet square. " If there be not room enough for a garden," he writes, " they have at least an old ingrotted plane or cherry tree. The older, the more crooked and monstrous this tree is, the greater value they put upon it." Similarly, in the Dutch garden, no tree could be admitted until its growth had been stunted, and only those flowers like the tulip could be allowed to engross the space without danger of spoiling the composition. It was for this reason that topiary work became so important a feature in every small garden, that it came to be looked upon as a purely Dutch invention.

In many of the smaller towns of North Holland, where the houses are closely packed together, gardens were designed upon the smallest scale, always surrounded by a moat and in most cases approached by a drawbridge. The Dutchman is even more than the Englishman master of his own castle. The approaches to these miniature fortresses are sometimes by fixed bridges, but more often by draw or swing bridges which are designed in a variety of ingenious ways, and, painted in tones of green and black or white, they impart a most picturesque aspect to the village streets. The little gardens themselves are full of quaint ideas and seem to have been made for children. The paths are scarcely wide enough to walk upon, and the

LIME TREE ARBOUR: KLEEF

arbours often hardly large enough for two persons. Silver balls reflect and magnify the tiny flower beds and gaily painted statues of lead and wood. Houses and gardens are surrounded by trees cut into fantastic forms, and occasionally the artistic owner goes so far as to paint their trunks in shades of blue and white. At Zaandyck the angles of a small parterre have leaden figures of Night, Morning, Midday and Evening with Bacchus in the middle.

At Zaandam some of these Lilliputian gardens may still be found, and for an extreme instance we cannot do better than quote De Amicis's description of the gardens at Broek: "The gardens are not less odd than the houses. They seem made for dwarfs. The paths are scarcely wide enough for the feet, the arbours can contain two very small persons standing close together, the box borders would not reach the knee of a child of four years old. Between the arbours and the tiny flower beds there are little canals, apparently made for toy boats, which are spanned here and there by superfluous bridges with little painted railings and columns; basins about as large as an ordinary sitz-bath contain a Lilliputian boat tied by a red cord to a sky-blue post; tiny steps, paths, gates and lattices abound, each of which can be measured with the hand, or knocked down

A TOWN GARDEN IN THE EIGHTEENTH CENTURY.

GARDEN DESIGN IN THE NETHERLANDS

with a blow of the fist, or jumped over with ease. Around houses and gardens stand trees cut in the shape of fans, plumes, discs, etc., with their trunks painted white and blue, and there appears a little wooden house for a domestic animal, painted, gilded and carved like a house in a puppet show."[1]

Some of the earliest and most famous botanical gardens in Europe are

THE BOTANIC GARDEN AT LEYDEN, SEVENTEENTH CENTURY.

to be found in Holland. The garden at Leyden was founded as early as 1577, only thirty-one years after that of Padua. It was confided to Cluyt, a celebrated botanist, afterwards to Bontius, and in 1592 L'Ecluse from Frankfort, was appointed professor of Botany. In 1633 the catalogue of the garden contained 1,104 species. At this time the magistrates, the

[1] *Holland,* translated from the Italian by Caroline Tilton, 1880.

learned men and the wealthier citizens, all gave their attention to facilitating the progress of botany. "A ship never left the port of Holland," says Deleuze, "the captain of which was not instructed to procure seeds and plants wherever possible." The most distinguished citizens filled their gardens at great expense and had a pleasure in communicating those plants to the garden at Leyden. This garden in the early eighteenth century contained upwards of 6,000 plants. Sir J. E. Smith, who visited the garden in 1786, says, "that it has been much enlarged within the last forty years and is now about as large as the Chelsea garden." By 1814 it appears to have already been much neglected, though it still contained many curious old specimens of exotics, such as Cluyt's palm, twenty feet high and upwards of 225 years old, a curious ash and various other trees and shrubs planted by Cluyt. A merchant, Pierre de la Court, had famous gardens at Dreihock, near Leyden, where he was the first to introduce and cultivate with success the pineapple and the tuberose. It was more than fifty years before the example of Leyden was followed in other cities, but by the middle of the seventeenth century Botanic Gardens were established in all the provinces. That of Amsterdam was under the direction of Jan Commelyn, who did much for the advance of botany and spared neither pains nor money to let the treasures of his garden be known among savants. He was succeeded by his nephew Gaspard, who was the author of *Hortus Amstelodamus*, 1678—a superb collection of engravings of plants, the greater part until then unknown, and derived largely from the Dutch colonies. This volume contains the earliest representation of the sweet pea. Amsterdam was the first garden in Europe that procured a specimen of the coffee tree. A seedling of this tree was sent to Paris in 1714. Two seedlings from this plant were sent to Martinique in 1726; from them were produced all the coffee trees afterwards cultivated in the French colonies. According to Loudon, the botanic garden at Groningen was begun by Henry Munting, a zealous botanist and man of learning who had spent eight years travelling in the different countries of Europe, establishing correspondence between botanists and cultivators. He spent the greatest part of his fortune upon his garden; but in 1641 the States of Groningen, thinking so useful an establishment ought to be under the protection of the republic, purchased it and appointed him professor. The catalogue of this garden, published in 1646, contained about 1,500 plants.

THE GARDENS AT CANONS ASHBY, NORTHAMPTONSHIRE.

CHAPTER VIII

ENGLISH GARDENS OF THE SIXTEENTH, SEVENTEENTH & EIGHTEENTH CENTURIES

THE England of the Tudors was wealthier and more secure than that of the Plantagenets, and it was also better informed; more in touch with the new learning which had taken such hold upon the Continent; and with the beginning of the Tudor age we reach a point when great changes came over English domestic architecture. The destruction of the old nobility during the Wars of the Roses, the magnificence of the Court, and the dissolution of the monasteries were all powerful incentives to the remarkable activity of housebuilding that characterized the period. Of these three causes the dissolution of the monasteries exercised the greatest influence; for, during the three years 1536–1539, nearly one-third of the land in the country changed hands, and large fortunes were quickly made. Inevitably, a large part of this land given, or granted on very easy terms, to royal favourites, found its way into the market and was sold at relatively low prices. The opportunity thus afforded was eagerly seized by countrymen and townsmen alike. The former, landed proprietors already, had amassed wealth by turning their land into sheep runs; the latter by a rapidly developing commerce. Thus a new class of landowners was created, and with the possession of land came the necessity of building; for the modest granges that sufficed for the monks were quite inadequate to the needs of the new owners. The mediaeval castle too, with its confined garden enclosures, was eventually succeeded by the more comfortable type of house, and in this development of building gardening had its share. Those Englishmen who had travelled in Italy and France must have been struck by the enormous development in Italian and French gardens, and on their return home they determined to imitate what they had seen abroad.

As in the Dutch and German gardens of this period, the moat often enclosed an area sufficient for the formation of a fair-sized kitchen and herb garden, whilst the orchards and vineyards were more usually planned beyond. As the sense of security increased and the necessity of keeping all property within the protecting lines of a moat was thereby lessened, a much greater scope was afforded for the development of the pleasure garden. The love of our Tudor monarchs for flowers and gardens was very pronounced, and Henry VIII, like François I, delighted in surrounding all his palaces with splendid pleasaunces. In the portraits, too, of Queen Elizabeth we often see her decked with blossoms, and she evidently shared her father's love of flowers. By her influence she did very much to encourage her nobles

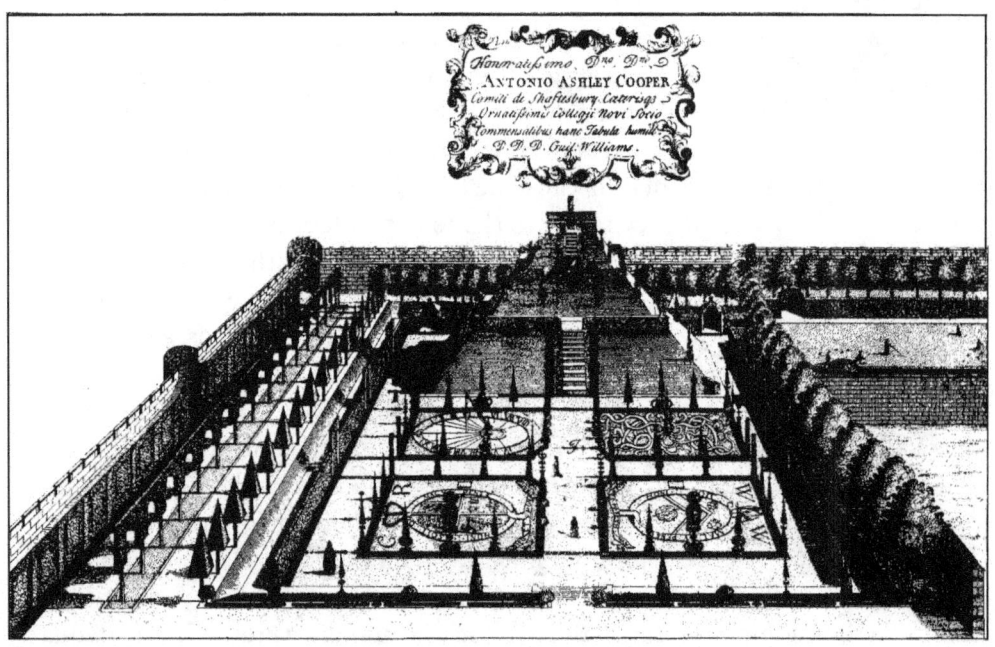

ENCLOSED GARDEN AND MOUNT AT NEW COLLEGE, OXFORD, ABOUT 1733.

to live at their country seats; and the fine houses and gardens laid out in her reign have not often been equalled for good taste and beauty.

One of the first innovations in garden design was the flower bed, separated and enclosed within a railing of trellis, or raised from the ground by a low wall of brick or stone. Another important feature was the introduction of topiary work. The more sober tastes of the English gardeners restrained them from the excesses of their Continental neighbours, neither were water surprises and hydraulic jokes to the liking of the gentleman of Tudor days. The mount, often, as Leland says, "writhen

THE 'TWELVE APOSTLES' YEW HEDGE,
CLEEVE PRIOR MANOR HOUSE, WORCESTERSHIRE.

about with degrees like the turnings of cockil shelles to come to the top without payn," is very frequently to be found in Tudor gardens, and is in all probability a feature of great antiquity; it was planned principally in flat situations and was a favourite expedient for getting a view beyond the confines of the high walled gardens, and it did not die out until the *clairvoyée* and the ha-ha began to take the place of the wall in the seventeenth century. William Lawson, writing in 1618, suggests that mounts might be placed near the stewpond, so that from within a shady arbour " you might sit and angle a peckled trout, or a sleightie Eele." Old mounts still remain in many English gardens. At Rockingham, in Northamptonshire, the great terraced mount is raised against a high wall surrounding the garden, and an even finer example may be seen at Boscobel, near Wolverhampton. Another Tudor innovation was the knot or knotted bed, which corresponded to the French parterre.

The most characteristic and original feature of Tudor gardens was, however, the gallery. These were often constructions of considerable solidity completely surrounding the gardens, and gave access to the various outlying buildings, which could thus be reached under shelter from the main building. The pond garden at Hampton Court was designed in this manner.

By far the most famous Tudor gardens were those of Hampton Court, where Cardinal Wolsey laid out a park with gardens and orchards covering an area of close upon two thousand acres. When the Cardinal was disgraced in 1529 and Henry VIII entered into possession, the pleasure gardens were still further enlarged between the palace and the river. The King's new garden was laid out in 1533 and occupied the space now known as the Privy Garden. There is preserved a drawing of the garden in the Bodleian Library which gives an idea of its appearance with its little knots and dividing gravel walks, its alleys, arbours and banqueting houses; its heraldic beasts on gaily painted pedestals, distributed about the gardens and orchards, or placed at intervals on posts round the parterre or on the stone copings of the terrace, holding vanes with the King's arms and badges, or supporting curious dials of brass.

Another important Tudor palace was Nonsuch, near Ewell in Surrey, which Henry VIII built towards the end of his reign. Hentzner, who visited the palace in 1591, says " it is so encompassed with parks full of deer, delicious gardens, groves ornamented with trellis work, cabinets of verdure, and walks that it seems to be a place pitched upon by pleasure herself to dwell in along with health. In the pleasure and artificial gardens are many columns and pyramids of marble, two fountains that spout water, one round, the other like a pyramid upon which are perched small birds that stream water out of their bills. There is besides another pyramid of marble full

PAVILION IN THE FORECOURT AT MONTACUTE, SOMERSETSHIRE.

of concealed pipes, which spirt upon all who come within their reach." The palace and gardens have been entirely destroyed, and it would be difficult now to trace even the outlines of what was one of the most famous Tudor palaces.

A similar fate befell the palace at Theobalds which Cecil exchanged with James I for Hatfield House. The great garden here is described in the Parliamentary Survey of 1650 as having "nine compleat squares or knotts lyinge upon a levell in ye middle of ye garden whereof one is sett forth with box borders in ye likenesse of ye Kinges arms; one other plott is planted with choice flowers; the other seven knotts are all grass knotts handsomely turfed, a quicksett hedge of white Thorne and Privett cut into a handsome fashion at every angle."

The Elizabethan garden combined much of what was best in the older English garden, with the new fashions which travelled country gentlemen were beginning to introduce from Italy, France, and the Netherlands. Although the designs of these countries were copied, the men employed to carry them out were generally English, and we do not find any evidence of foreigners being employed in England until the beginning of the seventeenth century.

ST. JOHN'S COLLEGE, OXFORD, ABOUT 1733.

THE TERRACE, POWIS CASTLE, WALES.

The chief point of difference between English and continental gardens at this period was in the desire that the English showed for a greater cultivation of flowers. Under the influence of a more gloomy atmosphere the English gardeners sought to supply a note of gaiety by bright flower parterres rather than by the use of coloured earths, sculpture and vases. In the

DETAIL OF THE TERRACE, POWIS CASTLE, WALES.

sixteenth and seventeenth centuries the houses of the upper classes must have been very fragrant, for in addition to placing flowers about the rooms, the floors were often strewn with herbs. Levimus Leminius, a Dutchman travelling in this country in 1560, writes of the English people that " their chambers and parlours strawed over with sweet herbes refreshed mee ; their nosegays finely intermingled with sundry sorts of fragraunte floures, in their bed chambers and privy rooms, with comfortable smell cheered me up, and entirely delyghted all my senses."

The most important rooms of the manor houses generally faced the flower plots massed with bright colours. "What more delightful than an infinite varietie of sweet smelling flowers ?" writes William Lawson, the Isaac Walton of Gardeners, " colouring not onely the earth, but decking the ayre, and sweetning every breath and spirit."

The plan, subject to much variety in the treatment of detail, was usually drawn up on somewhat similar lines to that of Montacute, in Somersetshire, with a walled forecourt in front of the house, which unlike the continental châteaux was rarely moated, sometimes paved with stone, but more often laid out in turf with a fountain pool. Occasionally there was also a second or ante-court which seems to have been designed more for the sake of dignity than utility. On one side of the forecourt lay the base or bass-court surrounded by the kitchens, stables, and other domestic offices which it was intended to serve, and on the other sides the more ornamental pleasure gardens and parterres.

Overlooking the garden and next to the house would be the terrace, usually some twenty to thirty feet wide. In Tudor gardens these were often placed in a position next to the enclosing walls where a view of the surrounding country might be obtained, as well as affording a convenient point of vantage from which to see the arrangement of the garden plots. Such a terrace may still be found in the Privy Garden at Hampton Court, where it rises to within a few feet of the top of the wall.

The parterre was divided into square plots edged with knots and compartments. Much attention was devoted to the edgings or borders, and for this purpose strongly perfumed plants were usually chosen ; lavender, sage, rosemary, marjoram and thyme, with a fountain in the middle with pipes and open conduits carrying the water to all parts of the garden. Arbours of trellis were placed at convenient places at the angles or elsewhere.

Parkinson advises that the walks may be made of sufficient breadth, "for the fairer and larger your allies and walks be, the more grace your Garden shall have, the lesse harm the herbs and flowers shall receive, by passing by them that grow next unto the allies sides, and the better shall your Weeders cleanse both the beds and the allies."[1]

JOHN GERARDE, FROM TITLE-PAGE OF HIS "HERBAL," 1597.

Any account of Tudor and Elizabethan garden craft must be somewhat fragmentary from the scantiness of surviving specimens or of written record. The garden literature of the period helps us little, the writers being mostly agricultural or medical. Amongst others, Fitzherbert and Tusser wrote on husbandry, Thomas Hill and Leonard Mascall on plant raising, growing, and grafting.

The first English writer who gave directions upon the planning of gardens was Dr. Andrew Boorde, who published about 1540 *The boke for to Lerne a man to be wyse in buylding of his howse*; he gives much practical advice which was, however, borrowed wholesale from Italian writers. Boorde was followed by Thomas Tusser, who wrote a curious poem, *A hundreth*

[1] *Paradisi in Sole Paradisus Terrestris (The Earthly Paradise of Park-in-Sun) or a Garden of all sorts of pleasant flowers, etc.,* 1629.

good pointes of husbanderie, which appeared in 1557. Tusser's advice is practical and simple-minded. Thomas Hill was another author, whose two works, *The proffitable Arte of Gardening* (1563) and *The Gardeners Labyrinth: containing a discourse of the Gardener's life* (1577), also add to our information concerning the gardens of this period. The voyages of Raleigh and Cavendish in 1580 and 1588 immensely stimulated the growing interest in botanical study and research. The return of Raleigh and the fame of his collections brought over from the continent the celebrated Clusius, translator of Dodoeus' *History of Plants*. John Gerarde's Herbal, published in 1597, is founded entirely on that of Dodoeus. Gerarde was born in 1546, cultivated his physic garden at Holborn, and for twenty years superintended the garden of Lord Burleigh.

Bacon's essay upon Gardening is too well known to need transcribing here. Whether the garden which he described was ideal and wholly imaginary, or whether it was the picture of an actual garden, we cannot tell, but there can be no doubt that the essay fairly represented the ideal of a nobleman of the Elizabethan and early Jacobean period. It is interesting to note, as the late J. D. Sedding pointed out,[1] that in spite of its lofty

JOHN PARKINSON, FROM THE ENGRAVED PORTRAIT IN THE "THEATRUM BOTANICUM."

dreaming, "it treats of the hard and dry side of gardening as a science and exhibits the rational attitude of Bacon and his school towards external nature, with no trace of the mawkish sentimentality of the modern landscape gardener, proud of his discoveries, bursting to show how condescending he can be towards nature."

John Parkinson was the first English gardener who seriously encouraged the cultivation of flowers for other than medicinal purposes; he was appointed

[1] *Garden Craft, Old and New.* J. D. Sedding.

apothecary to James I, and in the course of a life of travel he collected many rare plants at his gardens in Long Acre. He divides the country gentleman's garden into four separate parts, namely that of pleasant and delightful flowers, of kitchen herbs and roots, of simples, and of fruit trees. He is the first writer who appears to have had regard for the flower garden as a

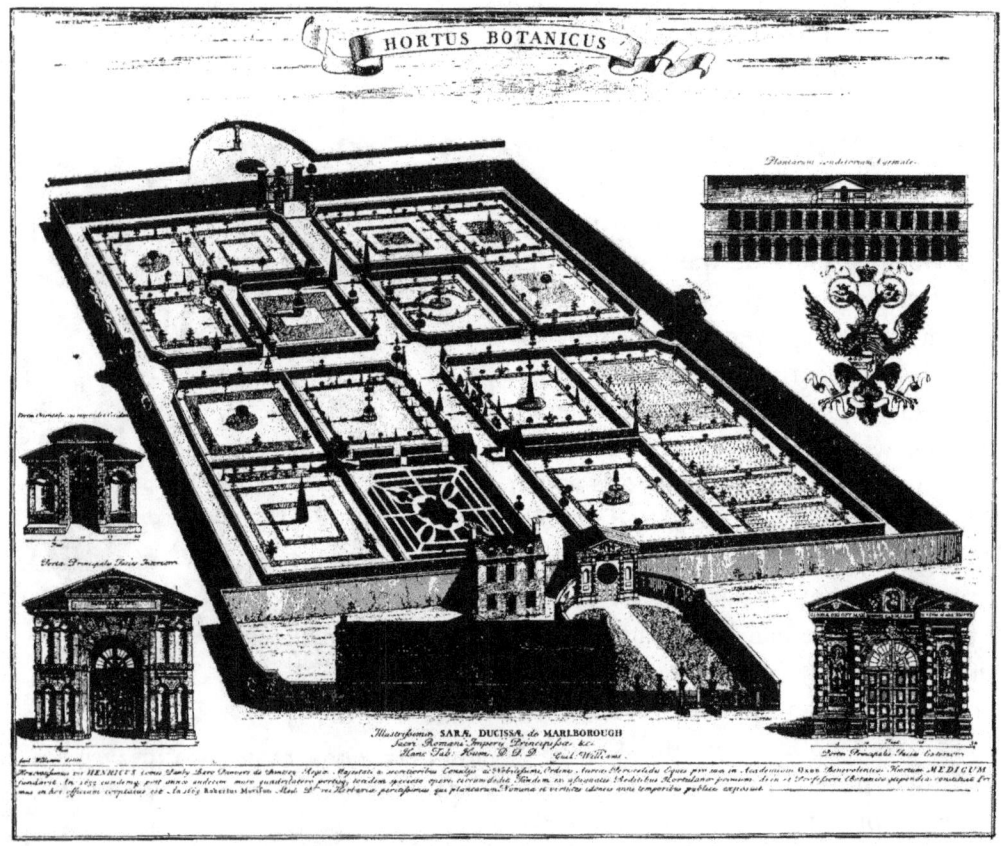

THE BOTANIC GARDEN, OXFORD, 1633, FROM AN ENGRAVING OF 1733.

pleasaunce and not only for the growth of medicinal plants, and he gives many designs for setting out parterres.

In the reign of Charles I the first Botanical Garden in England was laid out from the designs of Inigo Jones in 1632 at Oxford, just one hundred years after the establishment of that at Padua. The Oxford Garden was founded by Henry, Earl of Danby, who gave five acres of land

and endowed the institution, and built greenhouses for the reception of tender plants. These houses were among the earliest of their kind to be constructed. The garden still flourishes, and during its long career has done much useful work in furthering the study of botany.

Fountains and pools were largely in use as decorative features and were sometimes used for practical joking, when the water from hidden jets, being made to play upon unsuspecting visitors, caused much merriment to the

STEW-POND AT BRICKWALL, SUSSEX.

onlookers. In the gardens of Whitehall Palace was a fountain with a sundial which, whilst being inspected by strangers, suddenly sprinkled them well with water, turned on by a gardener from a distance. These practical jokes were not, however, carried to such an excess in England as they were in France and Italy

Bacon speaks of bathing pools as being frequently found in gardens of his day and says they should be thirty to forty feet square. Every garden had its fishpond or stewpond. There are good examples of these at

Penshurst Place, in Kent, and at Brickwall (illus., p. 213), a charming Sussex house built towards the close of the sixteenth century. Here the stewpond—75 feet long by 25 feet wide—is placed upon one side of the flower garden.

A maze or labyrinth was an almost indispensable adjunct to the Renaissance garden. The hedges were not always planted high enough to conceal

THE BOWLING GREEN, ST. CATHERINE'S COURT, SOMERSET.

the intricacies of the paths, as we are accustomed to see them nowadays, but they were more often mere borderings of lavender, rosemary or some other low-growing plant. The central feature of the maze was generally an arbour or some fancifully clipped tree. Long covered walks and pleached alleys of lime or of hornbeam formed another important feature in every garden, and were so woven together as to make a complete enclosure. They were often solidly constructed of wooden posts and trellis work covered with creeping plants. The pond garden at Hampton Court was originally so enclosed.

Bowling greens and greens for practising archery were considered essential in the gardens of every important country house. They are still to be met with throughout England; carefully levelled and shaded stretches of turf generally overlooked by some pleasant gazebo.

A TERRACE AT ST. CATHERINE'S COURT.

The English garden authors of the seventeenth century relied almost entirely upon the French writers of the sixteenth, for though Richard Surflet brought out his edition of Estienne's *Maison Rustique* towards the latter years of the sixteenth century, it did not attain any great popularity until Gervase Markham re-edited the work in 1616. Markham had travelled much on the Continent, having also served as a soldier in the Low Countries. He was a practical agriculturist, an intelligent reformer in matters connected with horse-breeding and racing, and almost the first importer of Arab horses, of which he sold one to James I for £500. He was, moreover, a poet and a playwright.

Among the best sources of information about English Renaissance gardens is a work called *The Country Housewife's Garden,* published by Gervase Markham in 1617, and also William Lawson's *A new orchard and garden* (1618). These two authors were friends and sometimes collaborators, and both wrote from their own experience. Lawson in his preface tells us that his work was the result of forty-eight years' experience. Gervase Markham affects a supreme contempt for those garden authors who contented themselves with merely translating the works of foreigners. " Contrary to all other authors," he writes, " I am neither beholding to Pliny, Virgil, Columella, etc., according to the plaine true Englishe fashion, thus I pursue my purpose." But nevertheless in the title page of his *Country House* he tells us that it is a " translation from Estienne and Liebault by Rd. Surflet Practitioner in Physicke " but " reviewed and augmented with additions out of Serres, Vinet, and others Spanish and Italian, by G. M." The work is composed of five books ; book II deals with gardens. A situation is recommended where the owner can enjoy the garden from his windows : " Some plaine plot of ground, which is, as it were, a little hanging and thereby at the foot receiving the stream of some pleasant water." It must be hedged, or better, walled " if the revenues of the house will beare it."

William Lawson treats more of orchards and fruit trees ; he writes in a delightful style of country life and deals with one of the most charming sides of the English Renaissance, its delight in flowers and birds. " One chiefe grace," he writes, " that adorns an Orcharde I cannot let slippe. A brood of nightingales, who with their several notes and tunes with a strong delightsome voyce, out of a weake body, will beare you company night and day."

It was not until the early years of the seventeenth century that the English gardeners seriously devoted themselves to the collection of foreign plants. Amongst others the three generations of the Tradescant family stand pre-eminent for their zeal and knowledge, and under their influence gardening rose to be a more exact art than it had hitherto been. The family originated in

Holland and came over to England in the reign of James I. John Tradescant was employed at Hatfield by the first Lord Salisbury and soon made the gardens famous for the many new varieties of fruit trees and other plants he introduced from abroad. We are told that he travelled much in Europe, Barbary and Virginia. It is curious that so many of the most famous gardens of this period were to be found in London, though Parkinson complains bitterly that "neither herb nor tree will prosper since the use of sea-coal." The Tradescant garden in South Lambeth was the resort of the learned, and was even honoured by a visit from the King and Queen. In its day it was said to be the finest in England, but it had retained a good deal of the old herbalist character. All the English botanists looked up to Mathias de Lobel as their master in the art of horticulture. He was one of the first to attempt the scientific classification of plants, and the *lobelia* was so named in his honour. For many years he had charge of the gardens belonging to Lord Zouche, in Hackney, and he was made botanist to James I.

JOHN TRADESCANT.

During the reign of Charles I no great progress was made in gardening, but during the Commonwealth much was done to improve horticulture. The Puritan did not wish for anything so frivolous as a parterre, and considered the garden from a purely practical point of view—what would pay best to cultivate, and how the fertility of his garden could be increased. Not many pleasure gardens were laid out in consequence, and during the Civil War nearly all the finest Tudor and Elizabethan examples were destroyed. Nonsuch and Wimbledon were sold, and the fate of Hampton Court itself hung in the balance, but it was eventually left untouched.

A good type of the seventeenth-century garden, devoid of such exaggeration as Pope afterwards effectually ridiculed, was that at Moor Park in Hertfordshire, of which Sir William Temple has left so delightful a description. He considered it "The perfectest Figure of a garden" he ever saw, either at home or abroad.

Charles II, during his sojourn abroad, acquired much of the taste for stately gardens with which Le Nôtre and his followers were imbuing the whole of France and Holland. He remarks on "Ye improvement of gardens and buildings now very rare in England comparatively to other countries," and one of his first cares after his accession was the improvement and renovation of his gardens at Hampton Court, for which purpose he sent to Versailles for gardeners. Of the alterations made by Charles II the most important was the laying out of the Home Park in its present form, the planting of the great avenues of limes with the semi-circular avenue enclosing the great parterre of nine and a half acres, and the digging of the great canal, three-quarters of a mile in length. These radiating avenues are probably the earliest instances of the introduction of that French taste which was afterwards copied all over the country, for though the planting of single avenues of approach was customary as early as the reign of Queen Elizabeth, nothing had been attempted in planting avenues as part of the garden scheme.

When William and Mary made the alterations to the palace from Sir Christopher Wren's design they carried to completion the works begun by Charles II. They appointed George London to the post of Royal Gardener, who, acting in conjunction with his partner, laid out the gardens as we see it in the engraving of Kip. There can be no doubt that much of the actual design for the gardens emanated from the master mind of Sir Christopher Wren, and there is a plan by him which shows the Privy Garden exactly as in Kip's view (illus., p. 219). Under William III the avenues surrounding the great parterre were set back, and many changes made in the design of the parterre itself. When Queen Anne came into possession of the palace the gardens were again remodelled, alterations were made to the fountain garden and all the box scrollwork of William and Mary was rooted up, plain lawns being substituted. The gardens were again altered under William Kent about 1736, in the early days of the landscape garden movement.

With the accession of William and Mary came further changes in the fashion of gardens, and the Dutch manner as practised in the great gardens at Honslaerdyk, the Hague, and the Loo was mingled with the more stately principles of Le Nôtre's school. The old Dutch garden at Levens Hall

THE GREAT PARTERRE AT HAMPTON COURT PALACE, FROM AN ENGRAVING BY J. KIP.

THE PARTERRE AT KENSINGTON PALACE, FROM AN ENGRAVING BY SUTTON NICHOLLS.

ENGLISH GARDENS OF 16TH, 17TH AND 18TH CENTURIES

is probably the most perfect example remaining in England of a garden designed under the Dutch influence, although curiously enough the designer happened to be a Frenchman. It is a particularly valuable example, because in all its main features the garden has been handed down to the present day exactly as it was originally designed. The property belonged to Colonel James Grahme, Keeper of the Privy Purse to James II, who, soon after becoming possessed of the estate, called in the assistance of M. Beaumont, a pupil of Le Nôtre who had previously worked at Hampton Court. The garden was begun about the year 1700, and there is fortunately preserved in the house a plan made in 1720, which shows that, with the exception of

VIEW IN THE TOPIARY GARDEN, LEVENS HALL.

a few alterations, every path and hedge remain as originally planned; this is probably a unique instance in England.

Amongst the gardeners sent to France to study under Le Nôtre was John Rose, reputed to be the best English gardener of his time. On his return from Versailles he became chief gardener to Charles II, at the royal gardens in St. James's Park. He had an extensive connection, and laid out a number of gardens for the larger country houses. Another who by his writings did much for gardens was John Evelyn, the author of the well known Diary. Besides his great work on Forest Trees he intended to write a book on garden design, but unfortunately never got further than a list of the chapters. He laid out the gardens at Wooton in Surrey and Albury near Guildford, and is believed also to have designed the delightful little garden at the moated manor house of Groombridge in Kent.

The early years of the eighteenth century saw the creation of many garden schemes, principally under the direction of London and Wise. In 1706 they jointly published *The Retired Gardener*, which is a translation of *Le Jardinier Solitaire* by the Sieur Louis Liger of Auxerre. London

WESTBURY COURT, GLOUCESTERSHIRE.

died in 1713. The firm carried out many gardens separately and in partnership; few, especially of the smaller class, are now remaining. Melbourne Hall in Derbyshire may be considered a good example on a comparatively small scale of the manner of Le Nôtre as developed in England. The gardens were remodelled for Thomas Coke, afterwards Vice-Chamberlain to George I, from designs by Henry Wise, between the years 1704 and 1711. They have been altered since this date, but many of the alleys and the great fishpond still remain.

ENGLISH GARDENS OF 16TH, 17TH AND 18TH CENTURIES

The charming formal water garden at Westbury Court in Gloucestershire (illus., p. 222) is a good example of a smaller garden of this period, and preserves its original character in a marked degree. It is situated amid pleasant surroundings, somewhat reminiscent of Holland. A long narrow canal runs through the garden. Beyond the canal the outlook is extended to the surrounding country

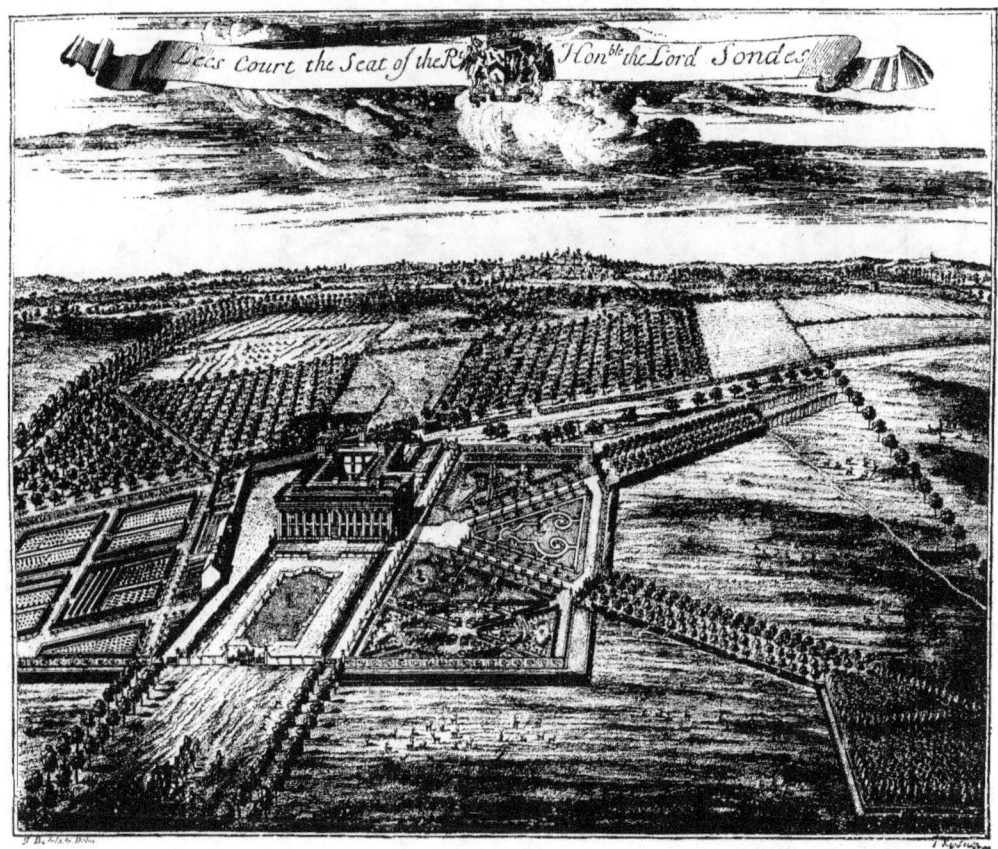

LEES COURT, KENT, A GARDEN LAID OUT IN THE STYLE OF LE NOTRE.

through a *clairvoyée* or open iron grille, which was a favourite device for carrying the view beyond the garden enclosure. On the south side of the house were the bowling green and parterre, beyond which a pleached alley divided the kitchen garden, which was surrounded by a quincunx of fruit trees. Beyond, and occupying the greater part of the ground, is the water garden.

Following London and Wise as garden designers came Stephen Switzer, the author of *Ichnographia Rustica* and other important works in gardening, and later on Bridgeman, who laid out Stowe in Buckinghamshire for Lord Cobham about 1714. Bridgeman, amongst other changes, almost discarded topiary work and, says Horace Walpole, " introduced a little gentle disorder into the plantation of his trees and bushes." What great changes were

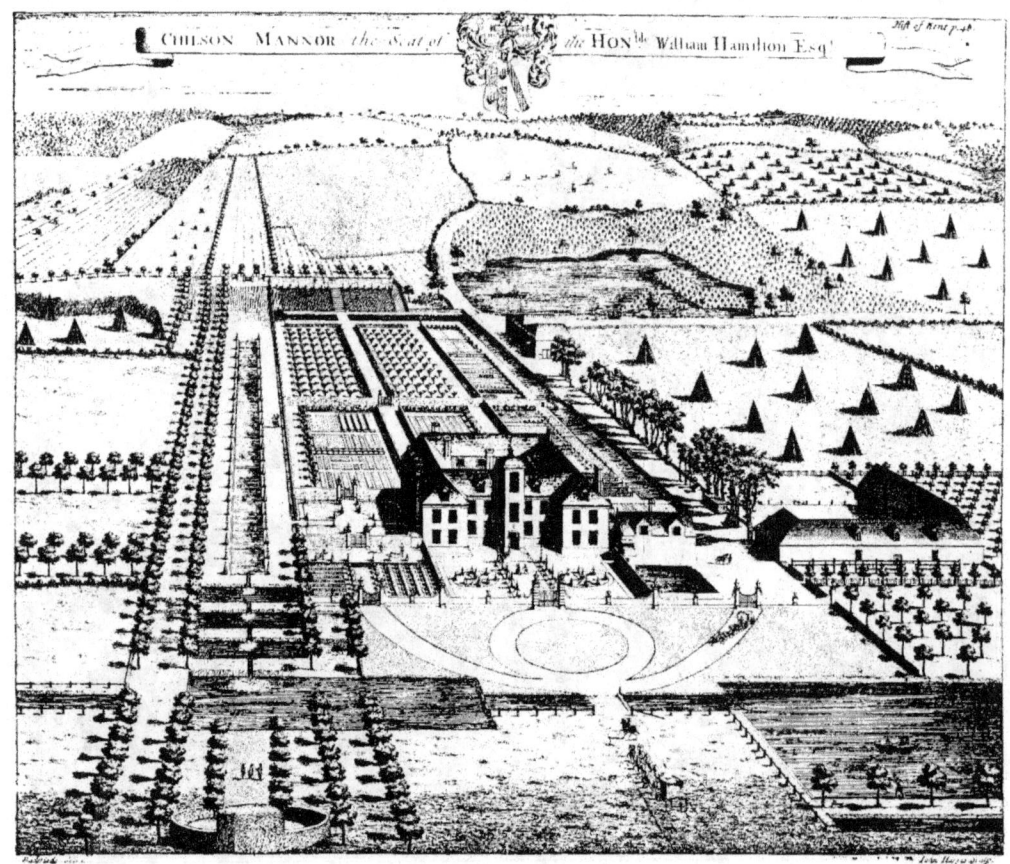

CHILSON MANOR HOUSE, KENT.

to result from this " little gentle disorder ! " Soon after this the reaction began to set in. A taste for specimen trees, or " trees of curiosity " as they were called, was fostered by the nurserymen gardeners ; the employment of variegated foliage became more usual, and some difficulty having arisen in accommodating the old fashions in garden craft to the new fashion in specimen plants, the only solution of the problem that presented itself was

ENGLISH GARDENS OF 16TH, 17TH AND 18TH CENTURIES

the abolition of the formal garden altogether. A bitter attack was made by those who declared that the formal garden was opposed to nature, which they proposed not to leave untouched but to " improve." " Nor is there anything more ridiculous and forbidding than a garden which is regular," says Batty Langley, and this was the opinion generally held by garden designers for a century, as far as the more ambitious schemes were concerned, but in the quiet country places the older tradition was never entirely obliterated.

The eighteenth-century country gentleman took a keen delight in erecting here and there a good, substantial garden house and realized that besides being an ornamental feature it should be able to withstand the vagaries of our climate. Generally speaking they seem to have been of two types, those that closed a vista in a garden at the end of a long walk and those that were placed in the corner of a bowling green or court. These were raised a few steps above the terrace on which they stood, which in its turn sloped down to the bowling

GAZEBO AT OXENHOATH.

green below. There is a good example of this type at Clifton Maubank in Somerset, and another is illustrated in an old view of Oxenhoath in Kent with elaborate pilasters and gabled roof. With the dilettantism of the latter half of the eighteenth century the substantial summer house gave place to *the Greek temple and Chinese pagoda.*

Banqueting houses, gazebos, and garden houses mean very much the same thing in an old English garden. As we have already seen, the word gazebo is of Dutch origin, and signifies particularly the type of summer house built at the corner of a terrace, or angle of a moated garden, whence from its position it could command a widespread view. Such a garden house was frequently used as a waiting-room for

THE GARDEN HOUSE AT POKESWELL, DORSET.

the coach, and this is no doubt the reason why a fireplace was sometimes provided. At the little village of Beckington, in Somerset, there is a small square brick building with stone quoins and a handsome pedimented doorway, with one window overlooking the roadway, and others the bowling, green and garden. At Nun Moncton near York, there is a gazebo with an ogee-shaped lead roof. It is placed at the end of a walk lined with lead figures and clipped yews. The windows on one side overlook the trim bowling green, and on the other the picturesque windings of the River Ouse.

In some cases garden houses were used as retreats, but instances are not often to be found. A two-storied

GARDEN HOUSE IN THE MOAT, LONG MELFORD HALL, SUFFOLK.

AN OLD GARDEN HOUSE, SUTTON PLACE, SURREY.

ENGLISH GARDENS OF 16TH, 17TH AND 18TH CENTURIES 227

example exists at Severn End, erected in 1661 by Judge Lechmere as a place for retirement and quiet contemplation amongst the flowers. Another prominent feature which might have been seen in many of the larger country houses after the time of William III was the orangery. Kip's views show many examples; the largest were at Windsor and Chatsworth. At Chiswick House the small orangery still remains overlooking

A SMALL PAVILION AT KINROSS HOUSE.

a little amphitheatre of grass terraces on which the trees were placed in the summer. At Bredby in Derbyshire the orangery overlooked a semi-circular pool with a series of terraces, and at Swanstead in Sussex it was planned along one side of a grass court, well protected by high walls. In summer time arrangements could be made for placing the trees in a separate orange garden in the park. These orange trees were used only for purposes of decoration, for placing round the margins of pools, on terraces, etc.

The bowling green was to be found in every garden of any size.

Markham distinguishes between three sorts of bowling greens: The bowling alley; "open grounds of advantage," that is bowling greens with a fall one way; and level bowling greens. They were generally placed where they could be overlooked by the windows of the house, but where this was impossible they were planned in other convenient parts of the garden, either as a central feature as at Chatsworth, or in the angles of the parterre as at Staunton Harold in Leicestershire and at Grimsthorp. The shape was either oblong, or oval as at Knole in Kent. Occasionally, as at Guisborough in Yorkshire, or Esher Place in Surrey, the green was placed at some little distance from the house; at Cassiobury the circular bowling green was in the midst of a wood, approached from the house by an avenue.

A LEADEN FIGURE.

One of the most characteristic features of English gardens is the Gate Pier, frequently surmounted by heraldic animals or stone balls. The use of wrought-iron gates did not become general until the end of the XVIIth century, and many of the finest examples perished in the era of landscape gardening. Frequently handsome wrought-iron screens were erected, as may be seen in XVIIIth century views, and in some remaining examples, such as those illustrated from Belton House. English wrought ironwork possesses, according to Mr. Starkie Gardner, a simple dignity and fitness which harmonizes admirably with the national temperament, and which expresses itself in well knitted and graceful lines.

A LEADEN CISTERN.

THE MAIN GATES.

THE WILDERNESS GATE.

IRONWORK SCREENS AT BELTON HOUSE. LINCOLNSHIRE.

Among the many delightful ornaments that go to make up the charm of the eighteenth century garden the most satisfactory were the figures, vases, and other ornaments formed of lead. The adaptability of this material and the delicacy of its colouring make it eminently suitable for such objects, and one can readily recall many instances of the fine effect produced by the soft silvery-gray colour of a leaden figure against the rich green background of an old yew hedge. Throughout the eighteenth century, lead-work was very much used in the large gardens of the nobility as well as in those of the smaller manor-houses, and there is no lack of good examples still to be found in excellent preservation, showing both how extensive its use in gardens has been, and its lasting value in the English climate. The making of leaden statues was largely undertaken by such workers as Cheere and a Dutch modeller Van Nost, who towards the middle of the century established himself in St. Martin's Lane and seems to have had a flourishing business. His stock principally consisted of classic subjects; Flora and Bacchus, Venus, Juno, Neptune, Minerva, were all represented, as well as little leaden Amorini, such as those at Wilton known as "Lady Pembroke's boys," and the fine series of groups at Melbourne Hall. Portrait statues in lead are also frequently to be met with, as for example those at Wilton and Wrest and of William III in the courtyard of Hoghton in Lancashire and at Petersfield. These statues were sometimes picked out in colours or

LEADEN AMORINI AT WILTON HOUSE.

A LEAD VASE AT CHISWICK HOUSE.

painted to imitate stone, and where this was the case, in order to carry the imitation even further, sand was thrown on the paint when wet.

In addition to the vases and statues, sundials occupied a foremost place among the ornamental adjuncts of the eighteenth century garden. It is curious that sundials should be so much more frequently found in England than on the Continent. They are sometimes seen in Holland, but rarely in Italy, France or Spain. They seem to take the place of the fountain of warmer climes in supplying the central *motif* of a garden scheme. Although, of course, they were originally regarded entirely from the utilitarian standpoint, it was not long before it became the custom to devote considerable attention and skill to their design, for which reason they have often survived in their position when all other trace of the garden has disappeared. The example from Belton in Lincolnshire, dating from about the middle of the eighteenth century, is particularly pleasing; the dial is supported by a figure of Father Time assisted by a Cupid. In Scotland, sundials were much more elaborate and monumental than in England; one situated in the grounds of Holyrood Palace stands on a high wide-spreading base, consisting of three moulded and panelled steps; the dial support is hexagonal, delicately carved and moulded.

5' 1" HIGH
SUNDIAL AT BELTON HOUSE.

ENGLISH GARDENS OF 16TH, 17TH AND 18TH CENTURIES

It belongs to a type known as "facet-headed dials," and has about twenty different facets or sides, some ornamented with heart-shaped sinkings, others hollowed out and with gnomons, others again containing the royal arms with the collar and badge of the thistle.

A comprehensive record of English gardens of the seventeenth and eighteenth centuries may be found in the engravings of Kip, Badeslade, Atkyns, Dugdale, Switzer and others. In these realistic bird's-eye views of country seats we are able to form a good idea of the number of important gardens that existed during this period, and get a vivid impression of the care and intelligent interest then being taken in garden design. Unfortunately they also afford evidence of the losses this country has sustained owing to the vandalism of succeeding ages.

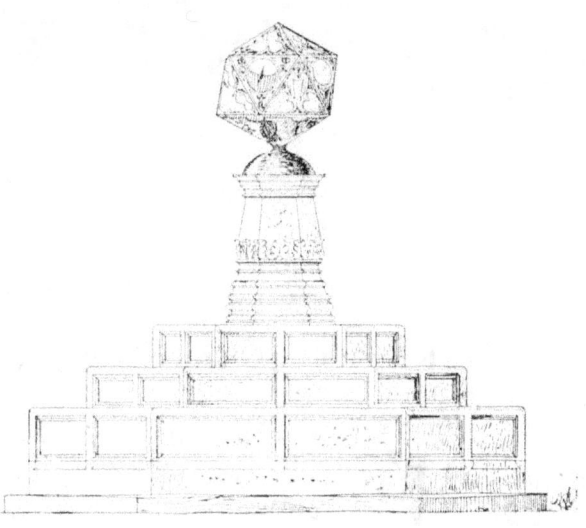

SUNDIAL AT HOLYROOD.

SUNDIAL AT WREST, BEDFORDSHIRE.

CHAPTER IX

GERMAN AND AUSTRIAN GARDENS

N garden-craft, as in architecture, we find that Germany has always been a follower rather than a leader. The great princely gardens of the sixteenth and seventeenth centuries were generally designed by Dutch artists; in the eighteenth century they closely followed the school of Le Nôtre, under the direction of designers who had served their apprenticeship at Versailles, and finally, towards the end of the eighteenth century, they eagerly took up the craze for the English garden then pervading the Continent.

But although Germany has never been distinguished by a school of her own she has produced in Hirschfeld a writer whose comprehensive work [1] played an important part in spreading theoretical knowledge. He deplores the Gallomania pervading his country in the eighteenth century, from the prince down to the peasant, "*ainsi font les françois ; voilà ce que j'ai vu en France ;* these words were sufficient to reduce the German to a mere copyist, and in consequence we had French gardens as we had Parisian fashions. Our nobles gave the first example of imitation, and everywhere laid out miniatures of Versailles, Marly and Trianon."

Botanic gardens were founded in Germany soon after those of Italy, and the earliest private one is said to have been formed by William, Landgrave of Hesse, early in the sixteenth century; his example was imitated by many of the nobility, and in 1580 the first public botanic garden was established at Leipzig by the Elector of Saxony, while those of Giessen, Ratisbon, Altdorf and Ulm soon followed. A famous writer on botany was the apothecary Basil Besler of Nuremberg (1561–1629). In 1613 he published his work,

---

[1] *Théorie de l'art des Jardins.* Leipzig, 1770. 5 vols.

Hortus Eystettensis, a description of the plants collected by Jean Conrad de Gemmingen, Bishop of Eichstätt, in the gardens of the monastery at Mount St. Willibald. It is a remarkable book as regards the engravings of flowers and plants, but its arrangement is not so scientific as the Dutch works of the period. Besler afterwards founded a museum and accumulated an important botanical collection.

The first great garden designer in Germany was Salomon de Caus; he was born in 1576 at Dieppe, and after spending his early years studying architec-

A GERMAN GARDEN IN THE SEVENTEENTH CENTURY, FROM A PAINTING BY VALKENBORCH.

ture in France, he crossed to England. We first hear of him in an important capacity in 1609, as mathematical tutor to Henry, Prince of Wales, for whom he made many designs for fountains, which he afterwards published. In his book *Des Grots et Fontaines pour l'ornement des Maisons de Plaisance et Jardins* are many designs, which he tells us were made for the adornment of Richmond and the amusement of the Prince who lived there. He, no doubt, is the "Frenche Gardiner" whom we find employed at Somerset House and at Greenwich. After the marriage of the Princess Elizabeth with the Elector

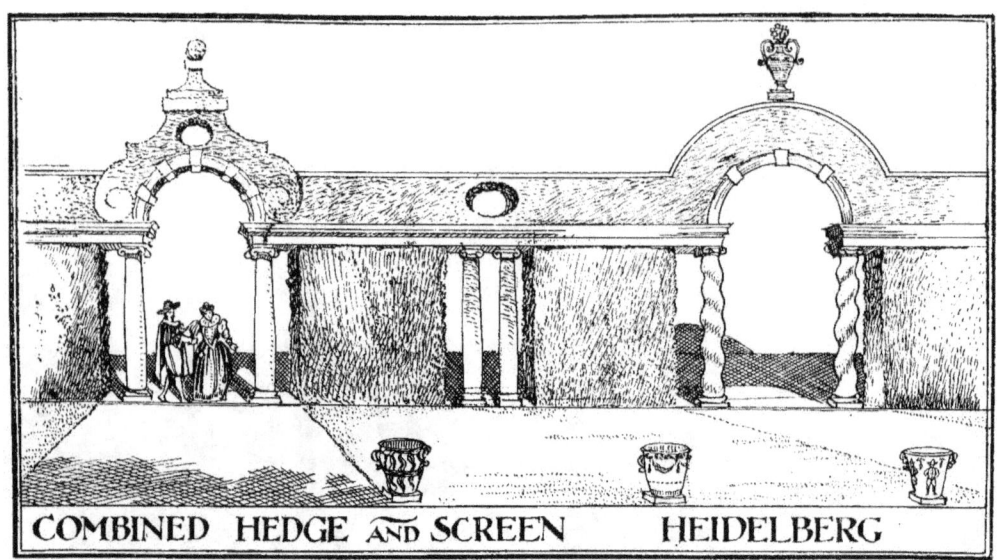

COMBINED HEDGE AND SCREEN — HEIDELBERG

Palatine, Frederic V, de Caus followed her to Germany, where about 1615 he was employed upon the great palace of Heidelberg (illus., p. 235), observing closely his master's instructions in laying out the gardens with "toutes les raretés que l'on y pourroit faire." These works were stopped in 1619, when they were almost finished, on account of the Thirty Years' War, and at the same time de Caus returned to France, where his fame had already preceded him, and was appointed to the Court of Louis XIII. De Caus was the author of an interesting work on hydraulics, *Les Raisons des Forces mouvvantes* (translated into English by Moxon), wherein he gives directions for making the hydraulic toys without which no garden was then complete. He shows how birds may be made to sing, owls to hoot, and illustrates a number of other quaint water devices. In one design for a grotto, Galatea, drawn by dolphins, glides round a pond to the accompaniment of a Cyclops playing upon a flute. In another, Neptune stands upon a shell, drawn by sea horses and attended by amorini riding dolphins. He describes the construction of water organs, musical wheels, trumpets which sound only when the sun reaches the meridian, etc. Many of these extraordinary water curiosities were constructed in the Heidelberg gardens, and de Caus published the designs in 1620,[1] in a quaint book full of interesting drawings. The

[1] *Hortus Palatinus a Frederico. . . . Electore. . . . Heidelbergae exstructus.* Frankfort, 1620. Also Pfnor, *Monographie du Château de Heidelberg*, 1857.

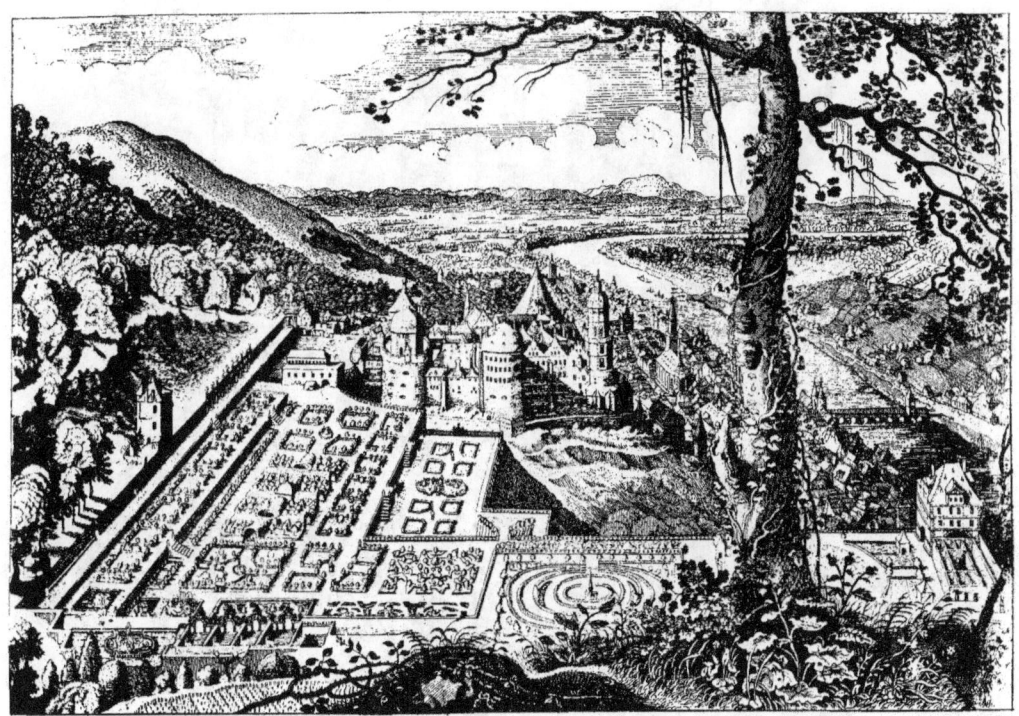

SCENOGRAPHIA HORTVS PALATINVS A FREDERICO V. ELECTORE PALATINO HEIDELBERGÆ EXSTRVCTVS

THE CASTLE OF HEIDELBERG IN THE SEVENTEENTH CENTURY.

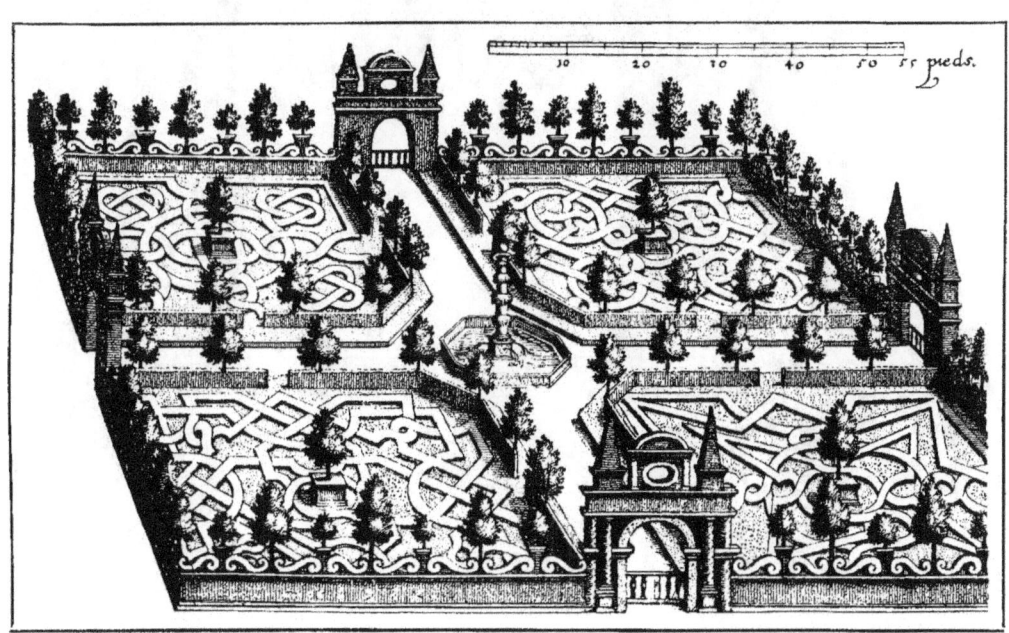

A KNOT-PARTERRE FROM HEIDELBERG, DESIGNED BY DE CAUS, 1620.

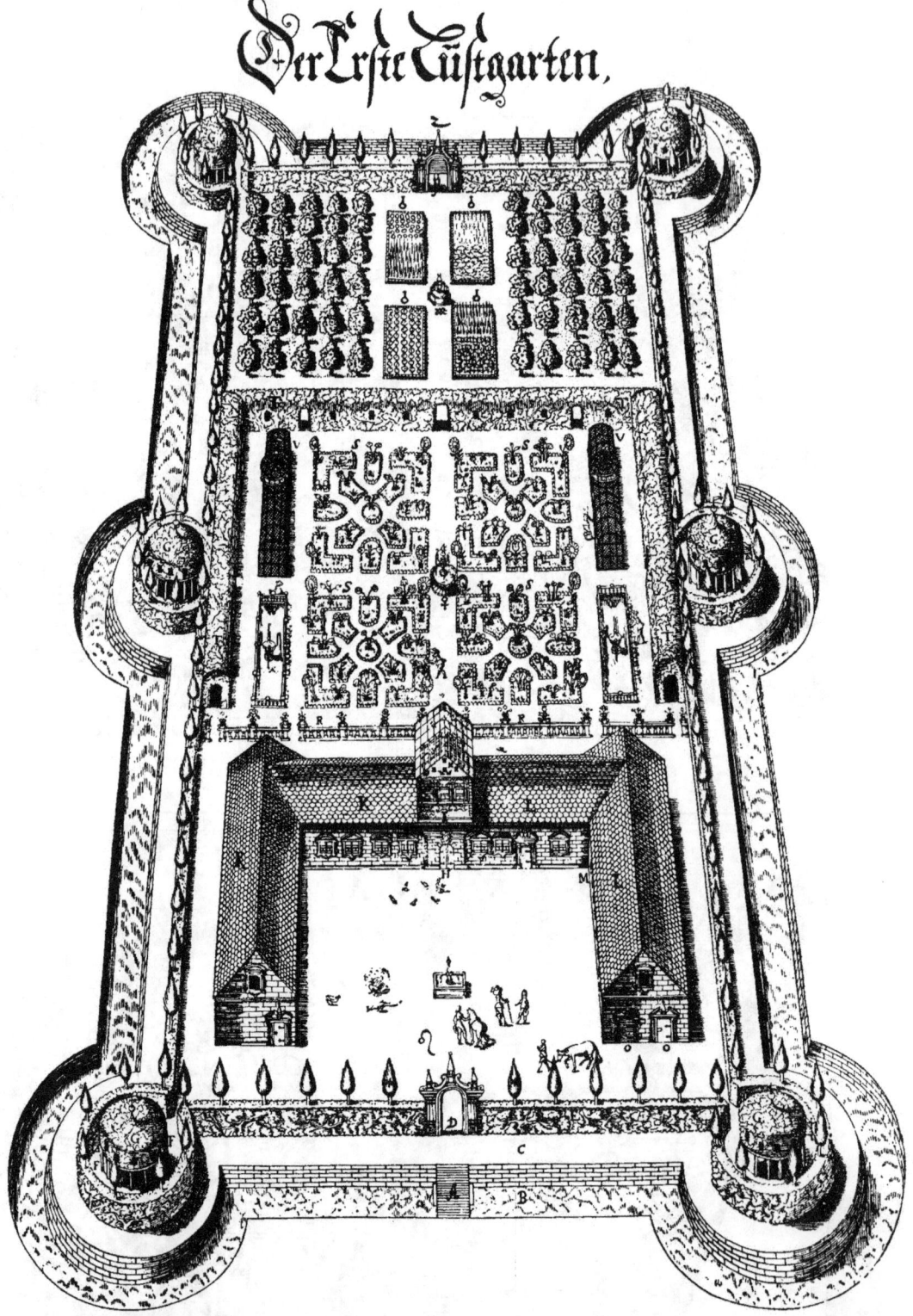

DESIGN FOR A PRINCELY GARDEN, BY FURTTENBACH, 1640.

GERMAN AND AUSTRIAN GARDENS

Heidelberg gardens were planned in a series of terraces adjoining the old castle and overlooking the Neckar, and the situation, with an abundant water supply from the mountain behind, was particularly advantageous for hydraulic displays. The gardens have long since disappeared and we know them only from drawings; there are several paintings on vellum in the *Biblio-*

DESIGN FOR A SMALL HOUSE AND GARDEN BY FURTTENBACH, 1641.

thèque Nationale of these gardens, in one of which is a series of the quaint painted vases that gave such an air of gaiety to all old German gardens.

Joseph Furttenbach, 1591–1667, published several important works on architecture. His *Architectura Recreationis* and *Architectura Privata* contain many designs for princely and private gardens. The illustration opposite shows a large garden enclosed within a moat. The entire space is divided into three parts: the first consists of the house and forecourt; the second is devoted to the parterre surrounded by pleached tunnels; the third is divided between the orchard and kitchen garden; six circular arbours project into the moat, and each arbour has an upper chamber formed by pleaching the branches of the trees. Smaller designs for town gardens are also illustrated.

The best general idea of German and Austrian gardens of the seventeenth century is to be had from the exhaustive collection of topographical prints published about 1650 by Matthew Merian.[1] His descriptive accounts are most instructive, and the engravings include all the principal German castles, together with a number of smaller houses and monasteries. In one of these gardens near Vienna we see a low orangery with dining halls at either end leading to two terraces and to the flower garden. The great parterre upon the other side of the orangery is surrounded by a stone-paved walk with picturesque angle towers rising to a height of three stories; beyond the walls that enclosed the parterre was a meadow separated by a canal from the deer park, which was enclosed within a high wall having ten large round pigeon towers.

A GERMAN SEVENTEENTH-CENTURY GARDEN, FROM AN ENGRAVING BY MATTHEW MERIAN.

Another garden known as *Der Kielmännische Garten* (illus., p. 241), also near Vienna, has both orchard and parterre enclosed within long tunnelled walks; part of the parterre is reserved for herbs, and the remaining part laid out in regular geometrical patterns.

---

[1] In addition to his topographical works he published a volume *Florilegium Renovatum et Auctum*, Frankfort, 1641, containing a series of garden designs.

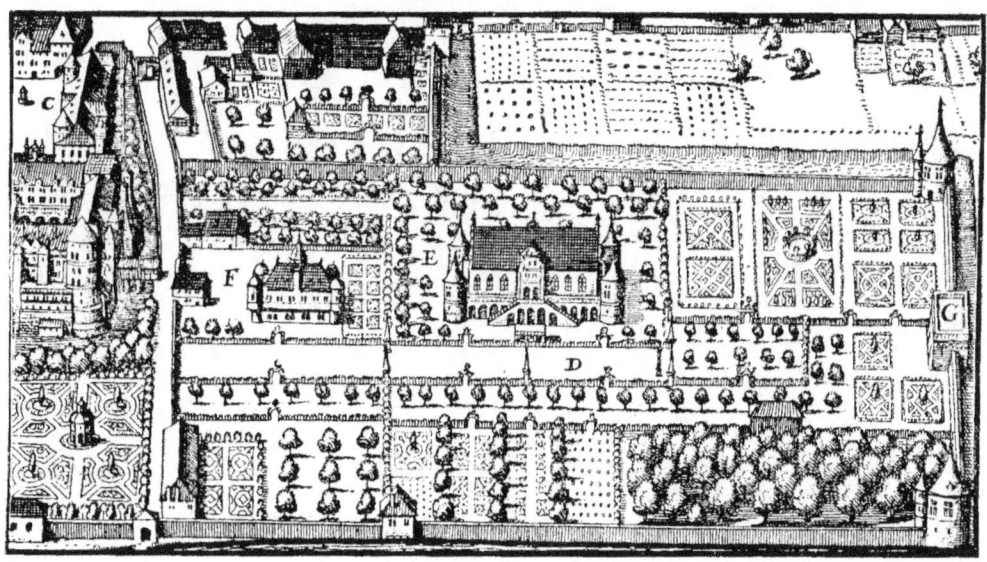

FURTTENBACH'S GARDEN AT ULM, 1641.

THE CASTLE GARDEN AT STUTTGART, 1643.

As in Holland, the moat survived as a means of protection well into the eighteenth century and the majority of castle gardens were moated, but where this was not possible for lack of water they are enclosed within strong walls with protective angle towers. Old engravings of the city of Brunswick show a collection of large and small gardens and parterres beyond the fortifications of the city, each with its little watch tower and gardener's

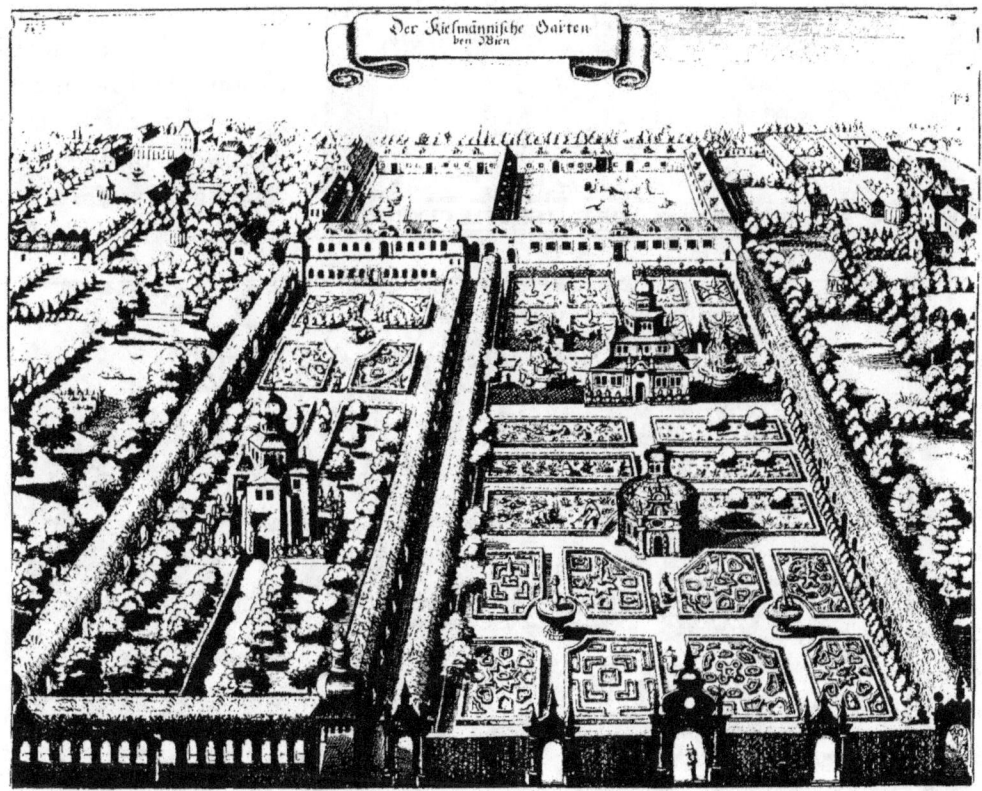

DER KIELMANNISCHE GARTEN, NEAR VIENNA.

house. The Castle of Zeillern had its gardens entirely within the moat. The Palace of the Kurfurst at Berlin had one of the finest gardens of the period, laid out upon an artificial island surrounded by an arm of the Spree. Here water forms the principal part of the design. It was pumped up from the river and traced out the design of the parterre in little running channels set within stone kerbs.

GARDEN CRAFT IN EUROPE

GERMAN SUMMER HOUSES SEVENTEENTH CENTURY

The pleasure garden of the Alte Residenz at Munich, laid out by Peter Candid for the Elector Maximilian I, 1600–1616, was planned upon part of the city fortifications, and connected with the castle by a covered bridge; the rectangular form resembles the idealistic

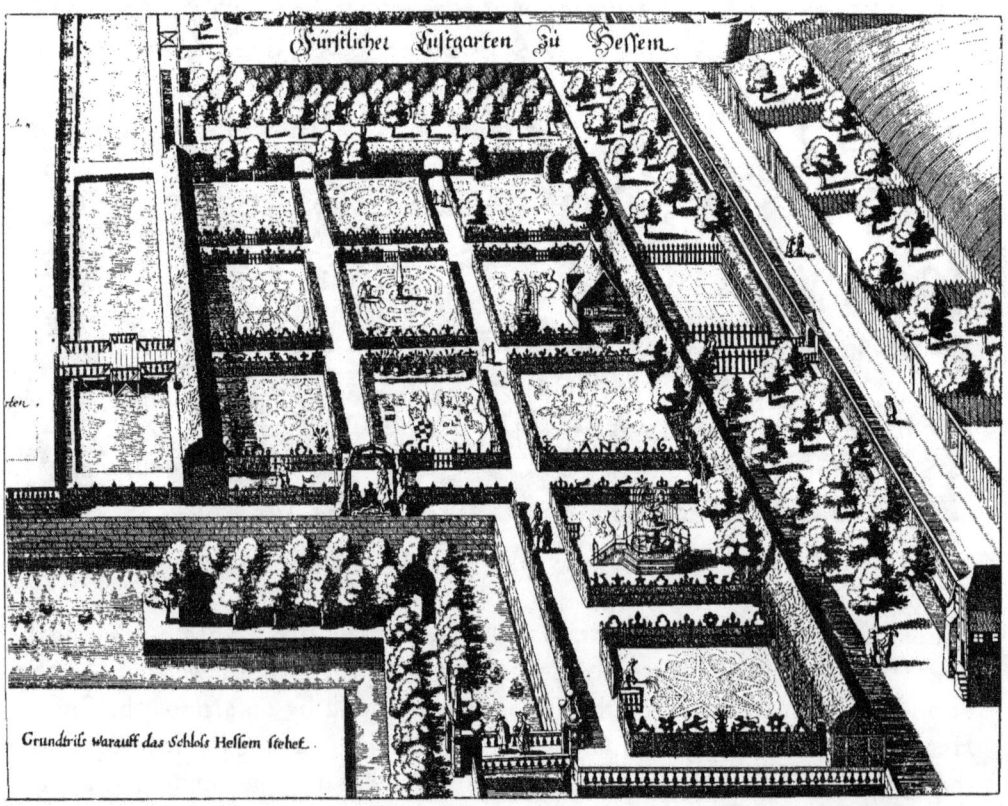

THE CASTLE OF HESSEN, 1631, FROM AN ENGRAVING BY MERIAN.

THE SWIND'SCHER GARTEN, FRANKFORT, 1641.

designs of Furttenbach. The parterre is divided by a number of walks, and at each intersection is a little arbour. At one end of the garden is a large banqueting house overlooking the fountain pool.

In the Castle of Hessen (illus., p. 242) a bridge across the moat leads from the castle to the garden, which is divided into squares, some with the family crest worked into the parterre, others with regular geometric patterns, while the tops of the hedges are quaintly cut into lions and crowns with the date— 1631. The Germans were particularly ingenious in their mechanical garden fountains, which were more generally of metal than stone; they were often arranged in tiers, approached by steps, and surrounded by balustrades. The well was made a very decorative feature and even the garden pump! In some gardens we find the parterre surrounded by long *berceaux*, or tunnels, which in other cases divide the parterre into four parts.

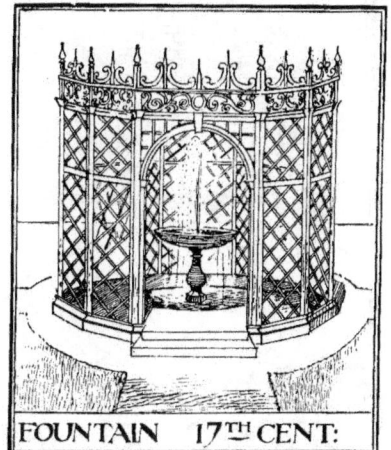

FOUNTAIN 17TH CENT:

Topiary work was to be found in every garden, hedges and trees being cut in all manner of quaint shapes. In the Count of Sachsen's garden at Schlaumwerth the entrance to the parterre was through the legs of a huge topiary Colossus. Every garden had a variety of arbours and summer houses, aviaries and pigeon towers, which were usually placed in the centre or at the angles of the parterre.

Another garden feature was the mount, a square mound of earth with a gazebo on the top, ascended by paths in easy stages, as at the Castle of Weimar, where a great circular mount known as Parnassus had corkscrew paths protected by low hedges.

Many castles had their tilt yards. At Schloss Lothen we find one in a very prominent position adjoining the castle and the stables, the space reserved for jousting being surrounded by a low wall. There was another fine example at the Castle of Gothen in Saxony.

The orchards, fruit and kitchen gardens were usually laid out apart from the pleasaunce, and protected by stout palisades or by moats.

The gardens of the early eighteenth century are illustrated in a curious volume by J. C. Volkamer, *Nürnbergische Hesperides*; a work that is especially instructive upon the subject of the smaller gardens, of which a number of examples are given with a variety of designs for summer houses, gazebos and treillage. Nearly every garden had its orangery, and in some cases, instead of this being a building, we find a substantial framework of columns, surmounted by little gilt leaden figures and so left that the plants could

GERMAN FOUNTAINS 17TH CENTURY

be protected in winter by a covering stretched over the framework. This arrangement added considerably to the architectural embellishment of the garden in the winter months.

In the eighteenth century the gardens of Heidelberg Castle fell a prey to the landscapist, and in their present form offer the greatest contrast to their original character, but the gardens of the summer palace of Schwetzingen, a few miles away, have been fortunately preserved and still retain a great deal of their former glory. The present garden occupies the site of one laid out in the first half of the seventeenth century, when the castle became the residence of the Counts Palatine, under whom the gardens were chiefly devoted to the cultivation of fruit and vegetables. Karl Ludwig, the hereditary Prince of Pfalz, who had spent his early youth in Holland, ordered the gardens to be laid out in close imitation of the Dutch, but his son in 1682 transformed his father's kitchen gardens into parterres, and denuded the Royal gardens of Mannheim of their lemon and orange trees. Its glories lasted but a short time, and Schwetzingen fell a victim to the desolation of war. The garden exists to-day as it was replanned in the early eighteenth century by Johann Belling, Court gardener of Düsseldorf, when a sum of 1,500 gulden was set apart every month for their upkeep. There was an immense parterre and in its centre a great fountain, afterwards presented to the town of Mannheim. In 1722 a number of statues were brought from the old Heidelberg gardens. Two years later, in the autumn of 1724, the whole of the Düsseldorf orangery, over

THE ORANGERY AT HERRENHAUSEN.

700 plants in all, was conveyed by ship down the Rhine, amongst them 447 orange trees, pomegranates, laurels and myrtles, with 100 Spanish jasmines. The parterres were planted with Dutch tulips, hyacinths, auriculas, stocks and pinks, the fashion of the day being to introduce more colour in the parterres and to impregnate them with the scent of orange blossom and flowers. In 1726 further land was added, and Schwetzingen became one of the most famous gardens of its day. In 1748 the gardens were again extended by the Elector Karl Theodor, and immense numbers of limes, planes, and elms were brought from the

nurseries of Haarlem and from Vitry-sur-Seine and most of the pomegranate, lemon and orange trees were despatched to Mannheim.

The Palace of Herrenhausen (illus., opposite) lies about 1½ miles from Hanover, being connected with it by a beautiful avenue of limes, known as the Herrenhausen Allee, which is believed to have been laid out by Le Nôtre. It was made the summer residence of Hanoverian royalty in 1665, when the Duke John Frederick began the broad low building that was designed by

THE GARDEN THEATRE AT MIRABELL.

an Italian, Quirini. The following year saw the commencement of the superb gardens, which are also said to have been designed by Le Nôtre. The probability is, however, that he only made the designs on paper and that the gardens were laid out by another Frenchman, Charbonnier, with his son. The plan very closely resembles a design for an imaginary garden by André Mollet, which is illustrated and described in that author's work, *Le Jardin de Plaisir*. The gardens were enlarged in 1692 and then comprised a large square *Luststuck*, or arrangement of parterres, bounded upon three sides by a broad moat,

GENERAL VIEW OF THE CASTLE AND GARDENS OF HERRENHAUSEN.

the fourth being enclosed by the Schloss; triple rows of limes bordered the moat and the angles were marked by pavilions in the form of small Roman temples. Large sandstone statues of ancient heroes and handsome stone

A TREILLAGE NICHE AND FOUNTAIN AT MIRABELL.

vases mark the intersecting points of the parterre, and at one side the old garden theatre still remains; with its *coulisses* of high hornbeam hedges and the inclined stage decorated with rows of statues; opposite rises the amphitheatre where the spectators were seated on a series of seven terraces. The vast waterworks of Herrenhausen were very famous in their day; the cascade partly remains, occupying a wall of the eastern wing of the palace, and consists of a series of rows of small basins, each overflowing in turn to that beneath; the extensive display of fountains involved a large plant for pumping.

At Salzburg the gardens of the Mirabell Schloss, laid out in the French

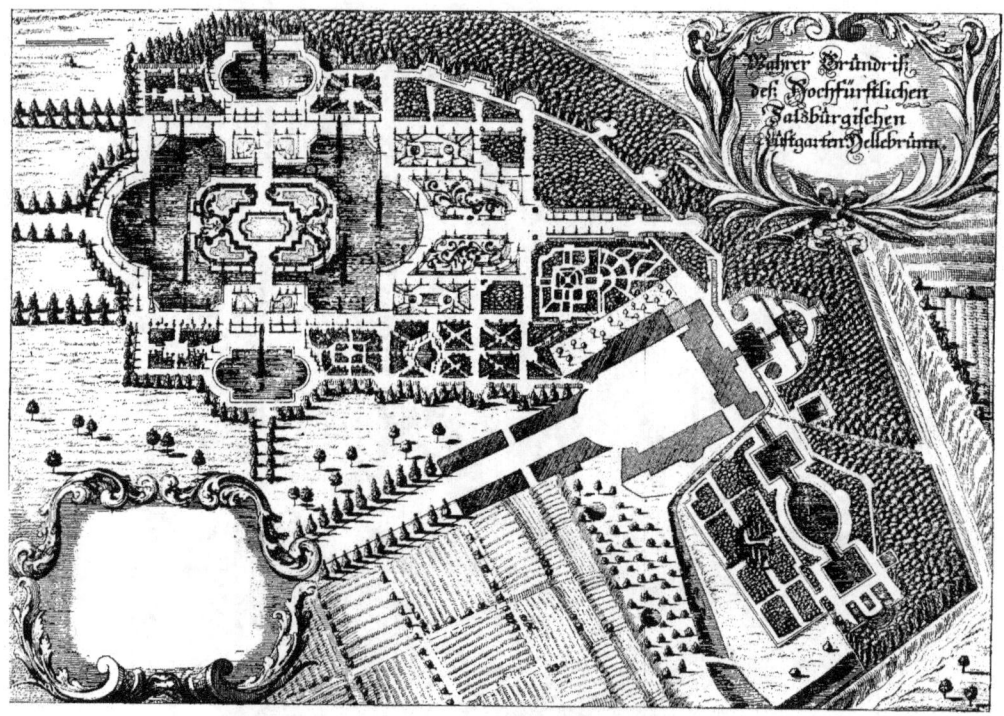

THE GARDEN AT HELLBRUNN IN THE SEVENTEENTH CENTURY.

style of the eighteenth century, may still be seen in something of their original state, but a more interesting garden is that of the Schloss Hellbrunn,[1] three miles to the south, laid out by Archbishop Marcus Sittich. Both were designed by M. Diesel,[2] who modelled them upon the lines of Versailles

[1] For engravings see *Die Garten Prospect von Hellbrün bei Salzburg.* F. A. Danreiter, 1740.
[2] *Fortsetzung erlustierenden Augenweide in vorstellung Herrlicher Garten und Lust gebaüde* n.d. I. Wolff.

and Saint Cloud. The gardens are full of curiosities; raised upon a hill is a casino known as the *Monats-schlösschen*, built within a single month, and a garden theatre and water garden combined, where pastorals and operas used to be performed before the archbishops, but the interest of Hellbrunn is centred in the wonderful waterworks and fountains, which are still preserved intact, and in working order. Water is made to accomplish

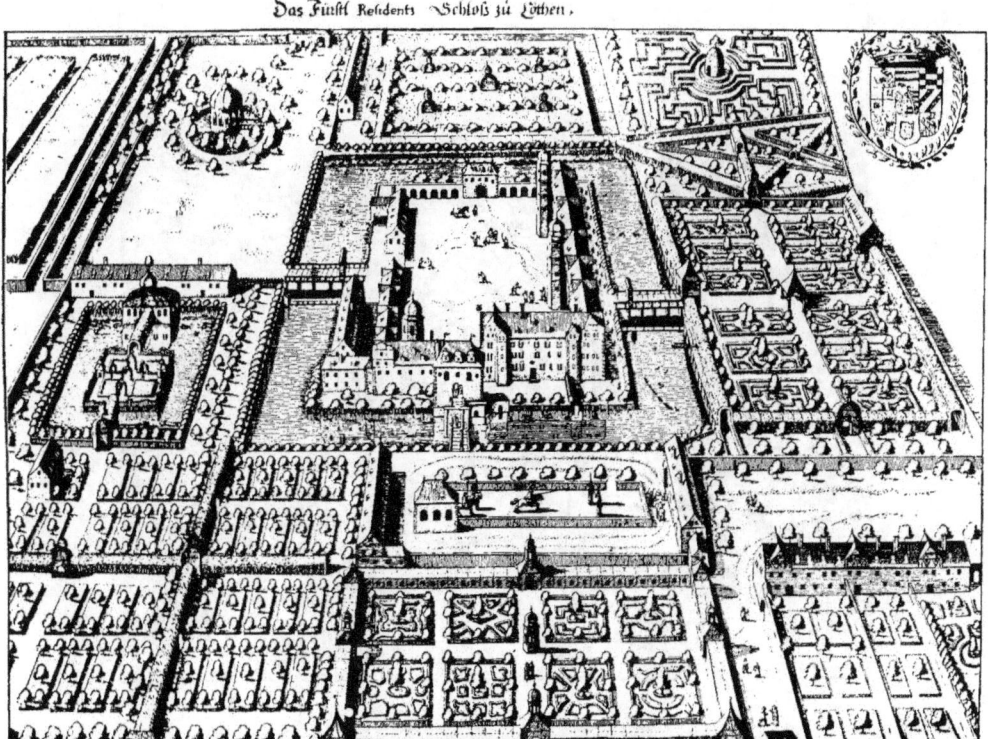

SCHLOSS LOTHEN, FROM AN ENGRAVING BY MERIAN.

every variety of purpose, and some of the contrivances are very curious. There is the representation of a town in all the bustle of daily life, the figures in it as well as the music being driven by water-power. Munich was formerly a city of beautiful gardens, but these have almost all disappeared, the Hof Garten, laid out in 1614, alone being kept up.

The Palace of Nymphenburg (illus., pp. 254, 255), three miles from

Munich, was built for the Elector Max Emanuel in 1663. The gardens were laid out upon a small scale some few years later, and in 1701 a Dutch garden-architect re-designed them upon the more elaborate scale as existing to-day. Imbued with the Dutch idea, he laid out long canals on both sides of the palace and round the gardens. In 1715 a Frenchman, le

THE SKITTLE SWING AT NYMPHENBURG.

Sieur Giraud from Paris, was appointed head gardener and *fontainier*. He constructed the elaborate scheme of waterworks and fountains for which Nymphenburg was so celebrated; one fountain threw up a jet of water 85 feet in height. The whole of the works were completed about 1722, when magnificent fêtes were given by the Court. In a bosquet to the left of the parterre a charming casino, known as the Amalienburg, still exists, but a corresponding building upon the opposite side, the " Hermitage," has long since gone. Perhaps the finest feature of these gardens was the magnificent

THE CANAL AND CASCADE AT NYMPHENBURG

THE MALL AT NYMPHENBURG.

GERMAN AND AUSTRIAN GARDENS

approach from Munich. A long lime-bordered canal, ending in a fine waterpiece, leads from the city to an immense semi-circular forecourt, 600 yards across, round which are grouped the white houses of various court functionaries.

Besides Nymphenburg there were several other Court gardens in

THE CASTLE OF LINDERHOF.

the neighbourhood of Munich, connected with each other by a network of canals. They were all in the height of their glory about the early years of the eighteenth century, and were designed by le Sieur Giraud and his assistants. Dachau was laid out upon a very irregular site upon sloping ground. Schleissheim and Lustheim were conceived upon such a gigantic plan that, although the two palaces stood nearly a mile apart, the whole of the intervening space was devoted to parterres and bosquets. Lustheim, which was intended only as a temporary residence, stood upon a huge circular island laid out as *parterres de broderie*; beyond was a semi-circular gallery, 400 yards in length, for the exhibition of paintings and sculpture. There seems no end to the vast parterres, long straight waterpieces and immense bosquets of these German Court gardens, laid out upon a scale of grandeur which their owners could hardly hope to keep up.

THE CASINO AT SANS SOUCI.

The German princes of the eighteenth century vied with each other in creating immense garden schemes. At Carlsruhe the Margrave of Baden conceived the stupendous idea of combining the palace and gardens in a huge circular plan that included the whole of the town itself. The Schloss, planned fanwise, was connected by a gallery, used for the *jeu de paume*, with a tower from which the Prince could look down thirty-two main avenues, twenty-three stretching across his park, and nine forming the streets of his town. The gardens of the Elector's Palace at Dresden were famous

GERMAN AND AUSTRIAN GARDENS

in the seventeenth and eighteenth centuries. Those which the Bishop of Würzburg laid out, adjoining the fortifications of the city, had a large rockwork cascade, with groups of huntsmen and dogs, and in the labyrinth were a series of small retreats or chapels. At Cassel the gardens of the Prince of Hesse were designed by a Frenchman, De Lisle, about 1761.

In the neighbourhood of Berlin the principal old gardens are those of Charlottenburg and Potsdam. The former have been engraved by Jeremias

SCHÖNBRUNN IN THE EIGHTEENTH CENTURY.

Wolff, who gives a good idea of their ancient grandeur. There is little left now except the orange garden and the great forecourt; the parterres have been made into lawns. Clean, quiet Potsdam stands on the River Havel, sixteen miles from Berlin. The gardens of the old Schloss have been modernized, but the little white, rococo Palace of Sans Souci (illus., p. 258), which the great Frederick built in 1745, has still its delightful terraced garden. He desired to be buried at the foot of a statue of Flora on one of the terraces—"when I am there I shall be *sans souci.*" Frederick's own design for laying out the gardens still exists in the library. Sans Souci is a kind of miniature Versailles, and was the King's favourite retreat; here it was that he first met Voltaire, July 10, 1750. The one-storied casino, decorated with a row of caryatides supporting the cornice, stands upon a hill with six formal terraces descending in concave form to a large circular fountain pool below. The terraces were intended for fruit cultivation, but the long rows of orange trees and glass-houses have now disappeared, and specimen shrubs have taken away much of the charm these terraces must have had when they were first laid out by the royal architect.

SCHLOSSHOF.

The largest and most important of the older Austrian gardens is that of the Palace of Schönbrunn (illus., p. 259), two miles east of Vienna, the summer residence of the Emperor of Austria. Like Versailles, the palace had its origin in a small hunting lodge, built by the Emperor Maximilian II, in 1570. It was rebuilt in 1619 and again after the Turkish siege of Vienna in 1696, this time from the designs of the Court architect, Fischer von Erlach. An English traveller who visited Schönbrunn in 1676 says that the gardens were neglected and ruinous; they consisted of two large square parterres about the size of the Palais Royal at Paris. He speaks of pavilions in the garden with roofs of copper so burnished " that the common people think them to be gold." The menagerie that was founded in these days still exists, the delight of the youth of Vienna on Sundays. The great parterre, shown in our illustration, was enlarged and re-laid out for the Emperor Francis I by Adrian Steckhoven, a Dutch gardener from Leyden. Steckhoven was assisted by Van der Schott of Delft, and together they constructed immense ranges of hothouses and formed the great botanic garden here, bringing from Holland all the plants they could collect. Expeditions were despatched to the West Indies and to South America to collect rare plants, which were shipped to Leghorn, whence they were transported on the backs of mules to Schönbrunn. Unfortunately in 1780 an accident caused the loss of most of the plants; the gardener forgot to light the stoves during a frosty night, and hoping to remedy the evil in the morning by making a brisk fire; the sudden change of temperature proved fatal to most of the trees. Joseph II engaged naturalists to undertake a new voyage to the West Indies and America to replenish the houses. Schönbrunn was celebrated for its beautiful sculpture; in the parterre were thirty-two marble statues by Beyer and others. There are still many fine fountains remaining in the gardens.

AN ALLEY AT SCHÖNBRUNN.

Just outside the fortifications of Vienna, but now quite within the city boundary, were the gardens of Princes Liechtenstein and Schwartzenberg; the latter were laid out in the French manner in about 1720 under the direction of le Sieur Giraud, whose work has been already noticed at Nymphenburg. Giraud was considerably assisted here in his fountain display by the slight fall in the land, of which he took full advantage. The garden walks are laid out everywhere for carriages, and upon both sides of the garden stairways are mosaic ramps for carriage traffic. The old Augarten is now in quite a ruinous condition; it was originally laid out as a public promenade.

The Count of Schönborn's gardens at Weissenstein and Genbach were both famous in the eighteenth century. The engravings of Salomon Kleiner show them laid out in the stiff French manner of the school that succeeded Le Nôtre, Weissenstein occupying a large oblong space with elaborate fountains. Genbach, surrounded by a moat, was the more inter-

A MODERN GERMAN GARDEN.

esting of the two, and had curious waterworks, a grotto and a very original circular parterre garden.

According to Loudon, gardening as an art of design was introduced into Poland by the electoral kings about the end of the seventeenth century, and especially by Stanislaus Augustus, the third elector. The palace of Lazienki was built by Stanislaus I at Ujasdow, and the garden, which was a poor imitation of the style of Le Nôtre, consisted of a number of broad green alleys crossing each other at right angles, and of smaller paths leading to open circles of turf for dancing and music, and for tents and booths. Pavilions and coffee houses with ice-cellars attached were placed in different parts of the garden, and the principal casinos were connected with the palace by trellis berceaux. The garden appears to have been wanting in statuary, but in order to overcome this scarcity, living figures, both male and female, were dressed in character and posed to represent mythological deities upon the occasion of any important fête.

CHAPTER X

GARDEN DESIGN IN SPAIN

SPAIN, "The Paradise of flowers," ought to be the land of gardens. The love of outdoor life amongst a people predisposed by climate to habits of indolence and indulgence, the fertility of the soil, and the necessity for shade from a scorching sun are all good reasons for the existence of beautiful gardens, and yet everywhere the traveller is struck by the scarcity of them.

For the golden age of Spanish garden design, we must go back to the time of the Moors, "nature's gentlemen," in whom, as we can easily imagine,

A MODERN MOORISH GARDEN.

a love of gardens, as of all other forms of beauty, was inherent. Having invaded Spain in the eighth century, they eventually spread their influence over the whole of the Peninsula and developed a luxury and refinement far in advance of anything known at the time; they cultivated the arts with a success which Western Europe might well have envied, had it better realized their immense value, and taken the trouble to reap the benefit of Moorish culture, when in the fifteenth century the great cities of Seville, Cordova, Segovia, Granada and Toledo were finally taken from the Moors.

FOUNTAIN IN A GARDEN FORMERLY ATTACHED TO THE PALACE AT CORDOVA.

The first Omeyyad Sultan, Abd-er-Rahman I, who ruled about the middle of the ninth century, took a peculiar delight in his gardens, and nothing was too precious for their enrichment. He was passionately fond of flowers, and caused all kinds of rare and exotic plants and fine trees to be brought from foreign lands. Agents were despatched to Syria, India and other countries, commissioned to procure at all cost rare plants and seeds for the royal gardens. By this means many new varieties were introduced from the Far East which were previously unknown even to cultivated Rome. To remind him of his old home, he im-

ORANGE PATIO, MOSQUE OF CORDOVA.

ported a date tree from Syria and planted it in a part of the gardens which he laid out in imitation of those of his grandfather at Damascus, where he had been brought up as a child. So skilful were the Sultan's gardeners that these foreign importations were speedily naturalized and spread from the palace throughout the land. The pomegranate, the emblem of Andalusia, was among the fruits introduced at this time by means of a tree brought from Damascus.

THE GENERALIFE, GRANADA.

Ebn-el-Avram, in his works on agriculture, gives the names of several renowned gardeners, and we read of the horticultural fame of Abu Zacharias, and Abu-el-Thair of Seville, of El-Hadj who flourished at Granada, and Abu-Xacer, who was famous for his profound knowledge of flowers. The work of El-Avram has been translated into Spanish,[1] and amongst much concerning the growth of plants contains some curious details on the culture of roses.

Cordova, says an old Arab writer, is the bride of Andalusia, and in the days of its greatest prosperity it must have been a capital to be proud of. The fairy palace of Abd-er-Rahman III, in the neighbourhood of Cordova, possessed beautiful gardens, abounding in jets of sparkling

[1] Josef Antonio Banqueri, *Libro de agricoltura traducido por Don J. A. B.* 1802, fol.

water with a marvellous central fountain of quicksilver, whose glitter in the sun is said to have been too dazzling for eyes to bear. There was also a menagerie of curious animals and aviaries of rare birds, while fruits and vegetables were cultivated in rare perfection and variety. Oriental eulogy is apt to be somewhat high flown, but Cordova really deserved the praise that has been lavished upon it. At the time of the Ommeyads the city measured twenty miles by six, the greater part of which area was covered by mosques and palaces, many of them standing in beautiful gardens. These houses were palaces of luxury, magnificently decorated and kept cool in summer by ingeniously arranged draughts of fresh air drawn from the garden over beds of flowers carefully chosen for their perfume; an idea which has been already noted in the gardens of ancient Greece.

FOUNTAIN AT THE GARDEN OF THE GENERALIFE, GRANADA.

The other cities of the Arabs in Spain were no less remarkable for their gardens. In one of the palaces of Toledo there was an artificial lake, in the centre of which stood a kiosk of stained glass adorned with gold. The architect so contrived this that water was made to ascend to the top of the pavilion, dropping at both sides in the form of a dome. In this room the Sultan could sit untouched by the water which fell everywhere around him and refreshed the air in the hot season. Sometimes wax taper were lighted within the room, producing an admirable effect on the transparent walls of the Kiosk.[1]

[1] Lady Lugard, *A Tropical Dependency*.

The Cordova palaces and pleasure grounds have vanished like a dream of the Arabian Nights, and the once splendid Alcazar is now a nursery garden with just a few pools and fountains to remind us of its past glory; but fortunately the Spanish kings had sufficient taste to spare some works of Moorish art. Even Ferdinand, who so despised the learning and literature of the Moors as to burn in an open square of Granada all the Arab books he could collect throughout Spain, refrained from destroying all their buildings, so we can still enjoy the Alhambra and the Generalife with their cool shady terraces and endless streams of water, and the sweetly scented court of oranges in front of the old mosques at Cordova and Seville. The feathery palms and fountains of the gardens of the Alcazar at Seville still remain to give some faint idea of what garden design has once been and might be again, if only the Spaniard could awaken to a sense of the beautiful in art, and consent to take a lesson from the beauty-loving Arab.

MARBLE TAZZA, PATIO DE LOS ARRAYANES, ALHAMBRA.

Granada, " the city of groves and mountains," rising 3,000 feet above the level of the sea, was compared by the old Arabian historians to a " goblet of silver full of emeralds " and considered by them far superior in extent and productiveness to the celebrated *ghauttah*, or meadow of Damascus.

The remains of the gardens are unfortunately very few, but there is quite enough left to enable the authorities to restore them to their original Moorish form at no very great expense, and thus add immensely to the charm of this wonderful palace. The Court of the Lions, which is now gravelled over, would be much finer if its original garden could be restored with its wealth of flowers; again the delightful little patio of Lindaraja, or the

A FOUNTAIN AT THE ALHAMBRA.

larger garden overlooked by the mosque, how exquisite could both be made by the restoration of their water courses, tiled benches and gay flower-beds! As you enter through the Gate of Justice a flight of steps leads to the beautiful little garden of *Los Adarves* on the way to the Torre de la Vela, laid out by Charles V on the bastions of the fortress wall as hanging gardens with fountains, busts and *cinquecento* sculpture, of which alas very little remains.

THE PATIO OF LINDARAJA, ALHAMBRA.

The entrance to the Alhambra is through the *Patio de los Arrayanes* (illus., p. 268) with its oblong pool used for ablutions by the Royal Family and all who were present at the *zalàh* held in the private mosque of the palace, which is close by. The pool is full of goldfish, and along the sides are broad hedges of myrtle, carefully trimmed and kept low. At each end is a great white marble *tazza*, where the water oozes rather than flows through a bronze pipe and trickles into the reservoir. Near by is the famous Court of the Lions, built by the architect Abu Concind in 1377. In the centre is an alabaster fountain with its great basin resting on the backs of twelve rudely carved heraldic lions, each with a water pipe stuck into its mouth, hardly adding to its dignity.

MOORISH FOUNTAIN AT THE ALHAMBRA

Just beyond the Court of the Lions, a balcony overlooks the garden of Lindaraja (illus., p. 269), a typical Moorish *patio*. "Here," says Washington Irving, " the twittering martlet, the only bird sacred and unmolested in Spain, because they are believed to have plucked off the thorns from the Crown of our Saviour as He hung on the Cross, builds his nest, breaking the silence of these sunny courts once made for oriental enjoyment, and even now just the place to read the Arabian Nights, with a charming oriental fountain, violets, Japanese medlar and orange trees, buried in the heart of the building with its roses and citrons and shrubbery of emerald green. How beauteous is this garden, says the Arab inscription, where the flowers of the Earth vie with the stars of Heaven!"

An abundant supply of water was brought by an aqueduct and

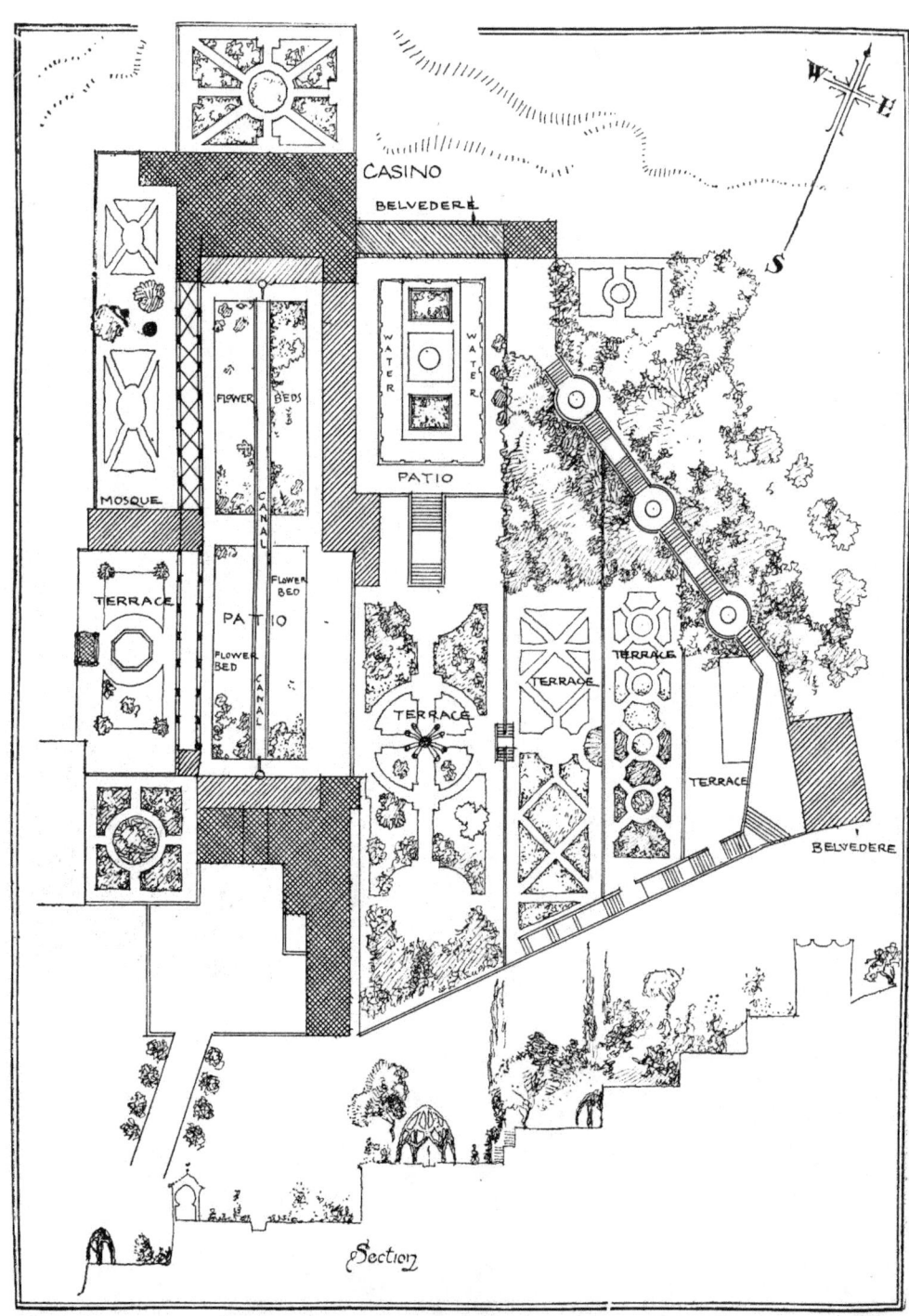

A PLAN OF THE GENERALIFE, GRANADA.

GARDEN DESIGN IN SPAIN

circulated everywhere throughout the palace, sparkling up in jets in the midst of the apartments and then tinkling through marble channels to the various courtyards and gardens, and supplying the baths and fish-pools. After it has sufficed to meet all the requirements of the palace it flows down the hillside, maintaining a perpetual verdure and coolness. The Moors carried the art of irrigation to its highest point; their hydraulic works still exist, and it is to them that Granada owes its reputation of being the Paradise of Spain and the fact of its enjoying an eternal spring in an African temperature.

THE HILL OF THE GENERALIFE.

The Generalife (illus., p. 272) (*jennatu-l'-arif*, the Garden of the Architect) is situated upon a hillside above the Alhambra, from which it is separated by a ravine. It was the *casa de campo*, or country house, of the Alhambra, where the Moorish kings came to spend the summer months. The road to this beautiful place winds through the vineyards and orchards of the farm, which extend right up to the garden walls, and for the last few hundred yards the approach is by an avenue of square cut cypress trees. The whole hillside is composed of a rich red soil, wonderfully fertile, and several streams have been diverted from their course to provide an ample supply for the fountains of the garden.

The cypress avenue leads to a small forecourt in front of the house, which like all Oriental buildings is very simple. A low Moorish portico looks out on the delicious cool greenery of an oblong enclosed garden (illus., p. 277). A canal, paved with marble, runs through the whole length of the enclosure and is bordered on both sides by numberless fountain jets which, when playing, form a sparkling arcade of water. The whole garden abounds in sweet smelling flowers, roses, carnations, lilies, jessamine and lavender. Everything blooms in luxuriant disorder and the air is heavy with the scent of orange blossom.

CYPRESS AVENUE AT THE GENERALIFE.

The flower court terminates in a porticoed gallery like the Patio of the Myrtles at the Alhambra. At the further end is an open building containing a few living rooms, the walls of which preserve traces of sixteenth century frescoes. Beyond is a balcony, affording wide spreading views of the Vega and the purple hills beyond, while the Moorish part of Granada lies at our feet. A short flight of steps leads to an open portico entirely covered with a glorious wealth of roses which forms the end of a water garden where myriads of goldfish swim in the cool green pools; along one side is a group of enormous cypresses, believed to be four centuries old.

Another broad flight of steps leads to the lower of the terraces that ascend the hillside up to the quaint two-storied whitewashed *Mirador*, or summer house crowning the garden, beyond which are some Moorish tanks and a knoll still called *La Silla del Moro*, The Moor's Chair. Each terrace

GARDEN OF ZORAYA, GENERALIFE.

has designs traced out in box and myrtle, and the topmost of all is ornamented with a row of green enamelled earthenware busts. Fountains abound everywhere; they are invariably small and often consist of merely a tiny jet of water set within a stone basin. Curious features of the garden are two cypress arbours, one in the centre of the lower terrace, made of eight cypresses bent inwards and joined at the top to form a dome (illus., p. 279). Gautier, when he visited the garden, found the arbour like an immense basket covered with flowers. The garden is bordered upon one side by a stairway, broken at intervals corresponding with the levels of the terraces by small circular resting places, which have been planned each with a tiny pool and fountain jet, shooting a crystal aigrette into the thick growth of trees overhead. Water runs down on both sides in silvery streams with a gay murmur in

THE PATIO, GENERALIFE.

channels of inverted green tiles let into the rough masonry of the balustrade walls.

After the Alhambra the most beautiful and best preserved Moorish palace is the Alcazar at Seville, constructed and decorated in the same style as the Alhambra, but on a smaller scale. The lovely *cinquecento* gardens which Charles V, with a genuine love for gardening, remodelled from the

HEAD OF THE WATER GARDEN AT THE GENERALIFE.

older Moorish gardens, are among the most curious and interesting in Spain, and although they have neither the marvellous situation nor the profusion of water that form the great delight of the Generalife they possess a charm produced by the elegance of the architecture and the wonderful richness of the vegetation.

The Alcazar lies in the south-east corner of Seville. In the time of the Moors it covered a far greater area than at present, reaching as far as the banks of the Guadalquivir and including the famous Torre del Oro within its boundary. As may be seen from the sketch plan (illus., p. 280), the gardens at present form an irregular triangle with parterres marked off into squares and divided from one another by walls of brick and tile; the compartments are arranged in quaint patterns of cut box and myrtle, and formerly contained the eagles and armorial bearings of Charles V. Walks of gaily coloured tiles or *azulejos* are here and there broken by fountains set in basins of simple design.

CYPRESS ARBOUR AT THE GENERALIFE

The gardens are entered in the angle formed by the palace façade and the gallery of Pedro el Cruel. Here is a large square pool which collects the water necessary for irrigation. In the middle is a bronze fountain and the pool is full of fish. There are several bathing pools about the gardens, the largest being the vaulted *Baños* where Maria de Padilla, mistress of Pedro el Cruel, used to bathe. The bath of Joan the Mad (illus., p. 282), with its domed pavilion and oblong tank all wrought in gaily coloured tiles, still exists surrounded by an orange grove. The pavilion has seat recesses completely covered with old purple tiles. Upon one side of the parterre is a well preserved maze, and beyond is the labyrinth of Charles V, intersected by tiled paths with seats at intervals arranged round miniature fountains; beyond again is the paved orange court which has in the centre the lovely old

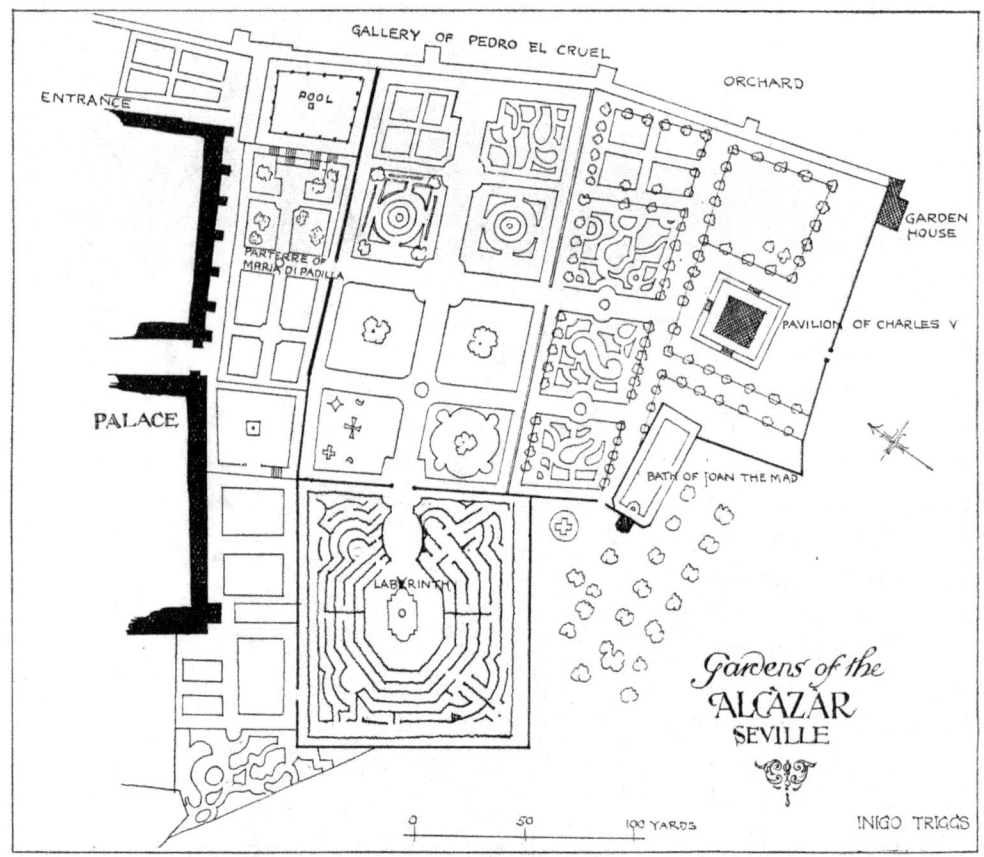

pavilion of Charles V (illus., p. 284), a square building faced inside and out with magnificent *azulejos*. The floor has a small octagonal pool and is intersected with marble channels of running water that impart a refreshing coolness in the intense heat of summer.

We must sit at the foot of the Moor if we are to learn the secret of the successful treatment of water in a garden. Living under the fierce glare

GARDEN DESIGN IN SPAIN

of a southern sky the merry tinkle of falling water was above everything a delight, the source of all that is pleasant to hear and feel and see. "It ran," says Washington Irving, "in channels along his marble pavements, it filled bath and fishpond with a sound like the murmuring of a dis-

TILED SEATS, THE ALCAZAR, SEVILLE.

tant multitude, it flowed bubbling along in underground pipes to feed basin and fountain: to-day it still offers its glassy face to image marble wall and evergreen hedge in the Court of Myrtles; it plashes in alabaster basins in the Court of Lions, it leaps from the ground in elfin jets and frolics in a hundred glistening bows in the garden of the Generalife."

FOUNTAIN IN THE PARTERRE OF MARIA DE PADILLA.

BATH OF JOAN THE MAD.

A popular Andalusian verse runs:—

Garden without water;
  House without a roof;
Wife whose talk is all
  Scolding and reproof;
Husband who forgets his home
  In the tavern revel:
Here are four things
  Ready for the Devil.

The neighbourhood of Madrid is not so conducive to good gardens; the climate in winter is cold, and icy winds sweep down from the north, whilst in summer the heat parches and burns up all vegetation, and only the public and more important private gardens can be kept green by liberal irrigation.

At the Escurial, some thirty miles from Madrid, are several lovely gardens. The monastery was originally built by Philip II as a cell in which to spend his last days, but was added to by succeeding kings and converted at last into a luxurious palace; the present gardens were mostly created by Philip IV. The Court of the Evangelists (illus., p. 285) is

INTERIOR OF THE PAVILION OF CHARLES V.

GARDEN DESIGN IN SPAIN

a most interesting courtyard garden with a central stone pavilion and four pools surrounded by a parterre laid out in regular forms with hedges of box and narrow pathways. Rising on the slope of a hill not far from the monastery is the Casita de Abajo, built for Prince Charles in 1770. The gardens are not extensive, but well worth a visit. A high cypress hedge forms an effective background to the entrance, and in front of the house is an almost square formal garden, with pools of water reflecting bright masses of colour in the box-edged beds.

Within a day's journey of Madrid are the famous summer palaces of Aranjuez and La Granja. The larger of the two palaces was one of the extravagances of Charles III. It is an oasis in the wilderness. The Tagus and the Xarama, meeting almost beneath the palace walls, keep its island garden fresh and verdant even through a burning Spanish summer. The fine old English oaks and elms

SECRET FOUNTAINS AND HEDGES OF MYRTLE.

were brought over by Philip II. They still attract as much notice in Spain as a grove of palm or prickly pears would at Hampton Court. The gardens remain as we see them portrayed in the pictures of Velasquez in the Museum at Madrid, and as they were described by Lady Fanshawe, wife of the English Ambassador, during the reign of Philip IV. Long shady avenues of planes and elms lead through closely planted woods and have been the scene of countless intrigues both in politics and love.

The Château of La Granja occupies the site of a shooting lodge built by Henry IV of Castile in 1450. The shooting lodge took its name form a *granja*, or grange, and ever since the early part of the eighteenth century, when it was much enlarged by Philip V, who came to the throne in 1701 and with true Bourbon instinct wished to surround himself with all that was best in art. Being only about 60 miles distant from Madrid, La Granja has always been a favourite summer palace of the Spanish monarchs.

ALCAZAR, SEVILLE: PAVILION OF CHARLES, V.

Both château and gardens are French in style and are an imitation on a smaller scale of those at Versailles, but the fountains, the unique and crowning joy of La Granja, are far more real than those of the celebrated French original. Great reservoirs, the largest of which is modestly called *el Mar*, the ocean, are placed high up on the mountain side, and collecting an abundance of water from streams and springs lead a vast volume to the famous cascade, *Cenador*, down to the garden level. Thence the water is led away to all manner of wonderful fountains and surprises. The great fountain, whose like is hardly to be found in Europe, represents Fame mounted on Pegasus and has a single huge jet of water rising to a height of 132 feet. In another spot, called the *Plazuela de las ocho Calles*, eight fountains unite to form a sort of Ionic temple, with columns of white marble. There are twenty-six great fountains in all; the finest are known as *los Baños de*

Diana. When Philip V was first taken to see them he is said to have stopped admiringly and remarked to his courtiers that though they had cost him three million pesetas he had been amused for three minutes.

From the scientific point of view gardening has been much neglected in Spain, and such botanic gardens as exist are hardly to be compared with those of other European countries. The study of medicine under the Moors necessitated the establishment of botanic gardens, and they are mentioned as early as the time of King Nasr, who laid out experimental gardens at Cadiz, and placed them under the direction of the botanist, Al Shafràh. In the sixteenth century Spain wished to emulate the example of Italy and Holland, who were devoting much attention to botany, and in 1555 Dr. Laguna, in his translation of Dioscorides, which he dedicated to Philip II, entreats the King to found a botanical garden which, he curiously says, would

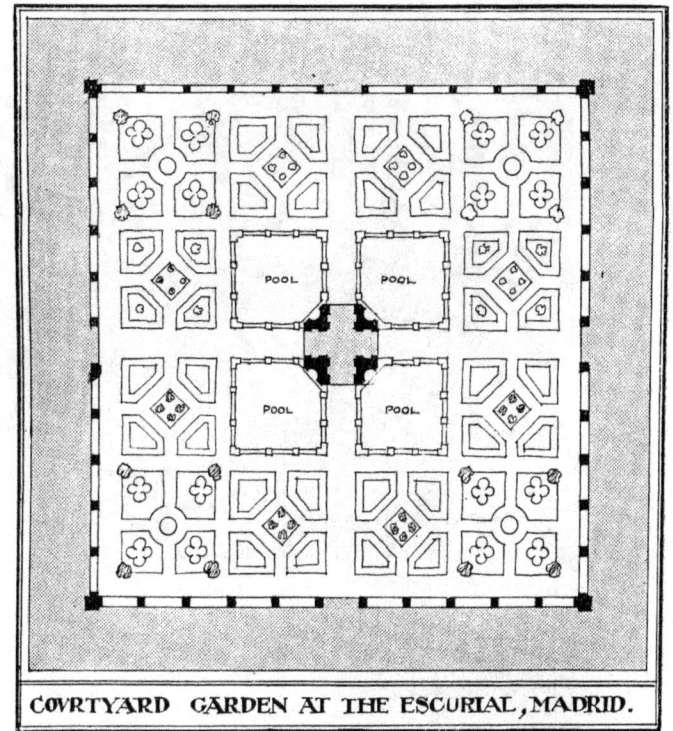

COURTYARD GARDEN AT THE ESCURIAL, MADRID.

turn to the benefit of His Majesty's health and at the same time encourage *la disciplina herbaria*. This request was granted and a portion of the royal gardens at Aranjuez allotted to that object. A few years later, in 1595, the private gardens of Simon Tovar Cortavilla were founded and at the end of the seventeenth century Jaime Salvador formed a remarkable botanic garden at San Juan d'Espe on the banks of the Llobregat, and a most interesting herbary at Barcelona. Botanic gardens were established at Seville and Madrid in the eighteenth century. At the present day the best are at Madrid, Valencia, and Barcelona.

As gardens in the country, except those attached to palaces, are rarely to be met with, greater attention has been devoted to those of towns, and thus

A MODERN PATIO, ALGECIRAS.

we find that the *patio*, or internal courtyard, is the most striking feature of all important Spanish houses. It is the direct descendant of the old Roman *atrium* with its *impluvium* and *compluvium*, as may still be seen at Pompeii, and in some ways it corresponds with the *cortile* of the Italians.

It is admirably suited to the intense heat of Spain, and forms the ordinary summer apartment where the family receive their friends. The most picturesque are to be found in Andalusia and the South, especially at Cordova and Seville. As a rule rectangular in plan, and entirely surrounded by at least two stories of arcading, they are capable of a great variety of treatment.

We frequently find them paved with marble and nearly always a small fountain bubbling up in the centre. As the entrance to the Spanish house is invariably by a broad passage leading from the street to the *patio* and divided from the latter only by an open wrought iron gate, the passerby has a delightful series of glimpses from the hot and dusty street into cool green *patios*, with myrtles, pomegranates, and jasmine trained and planted in red clay pots and forming a background to a wealth of beautiful flowers. In the words of Gautier "the *patio* is a delightful invention; it affords greater coolness and more space than a room,—you can walk about there, read, be alone, or mix with others. It is a neutral ground where people meet and when as at Granada or Seville the *patio* possesses a jet of water or a fountain, nothing can be more delightful, especially in a country where the thermometer often indicates a Senegambian heat."

PATIO AT RONDA.

CHAPTER XI

THE ENGLISH LANDSCAPE SCHOOL AND ITS INFLUENCE ON THE CONTINENT

ONDON and Wise, whose work we have already considered in Chapter VIII, were succeeded as garden designers by their pupil Stephen Switzer, the author of *Ichnographia Rustica* and other important works on gardening. The old formal gardens were ruthlessly destroyed in the extraordinary but not incomprehensible reaction against all kinds of formalism that marked the middle and latter half of the eighteenth century. The formal school had undoubtedly overstepped the mark with their monotonous statues and vases and their excesses in topiary work or " verdant sculpture " and soon fell a prey to the scathing criticism of Addison and Pope. The former, in his essays contributed to the *Spectator* on the " Pleasures of a Garden," complains that British gardeners instead of humouring nature, love to deviate from it as much as possible. He objected to " trees rising in cones, globes, and pyramids " and says that " he would rather look upon a tree in all its luxuriancy and diffusion of boughs and branches," while Pope complained that the grand manner of gardening was contrary to the simplicity of Homer. " We seem to make it our study " he says, " to recede from Nature, not only in the various tonsure of greens into the most regular and formal shapes, but even in monstrous attempts beyond the reach of the art itself. We run into sculpture, and are yet better pleased to have our trees in the most awkward figures of men and animals, than in the most regular of their own." Two years later he proceeded to lay out his fanciful garden at Twickenham which, far from being on the simple lines he professed

so much to admire, was a compendium of all sorts of rural scenery, crowded within the narrow limits of a five acre plot.

Foremost among the leaders of the new style in garden design was William Kent, who first distinguished himself as an architect and ornamental gardener at his great patron's (Lord Burlington's) villa at Chiswick; and his additions to the plans of Bridgewater and Vanbrugh at Stowe firmly established his fame. He laid out the gardens at Esher and Claremont, those at Carlton House for the Prince of Wales, and at Rousham in Oxfordshire. He

IN THE PARK AT STOWE, FROM AN ORIGINAL DRAWING BY ROWLANDSON.

appears to have been inspired with a desire to produce results that should resemble the compositions of classical landscape painters.

In the early part of his career Kent followed somewhat on the lines laid down by Bridgeman, who "disdained to make every division tally to the opposite" and though he still adhered much to straight walks with high clipped hedges, they were his only great lines; the rest he diversified by wilderness, though still within surrounding hedges. As time went on, Kent entirely left the formal garden and substituted for it the landscape style.

"Nature abhors a straight line," was one of his ruling principles, and he accordingly set himself to destroy the grand avenues left by former generations. and to make his paths wind aimlessly about in all directions, their destination always concealed by an artfully placed clump of bushes. The ornamental sheets of water were either swept away altogether or converted into artificial lakes fed by winding streams, and with miniature waterfalls. The height of absurdity was attained when he planted dead trees in Kensington Gardens "to give the greater air of truth to the scene."

LANCELOT BROWN.

The most popular of all the landscape gardeners was Lancelot Brown, Kent's collaborator and pupil, better known as "Capability Brown," from a habit he had of expatiating on the "capabilities" of any place he was asked to improve. Born in 1715, he began his career as a kitchen gardener, first at a place near Woodstock and then at Stowe. His first attempt at designing was in 1750, when he constructed an artificial lake at Wakefield Lodge for the Duke of Grafton. He was appointed Royal Gardener at Hampton Court, where he planted the celebrated vine in 1769. He soon had an enormous practice, and the old gardens disappeared with alarming rapidity before the ruthless hand of the "omnipotent magician," as Cowper calls him. The formation of artificial lakes was a strong point in his designs, and one upon which he prided himself. "Thames! Thames thou wilt never forgive me," he was overheard to exclaim when lost in admiration of one of his pet schemes. So completely did the landscape school of Kent and Brown obliterate all previous work that Repton, writing in 1806, declares that "no trace now remains" of the Italian style of gardening, which he defines as consisting of "balustraded terraces of masonry, magnificent flights of steps, arcades and architectural grottoes, lofty clipped hedges, with niches and recesses enriched by sculpture."

It would be hardly possible to enumerate all the fine old gardens remodelled by Brown, always according to the system upon which he worked with persevering uniformity. His reputation and consequent wealth gave him almost exclusive pretensions.

Brown died in 1783 and was succeeded by Humphrey Repton; fortunately the wholesale destruction of old gardens was checked, for Repton had not sufficient influence to suggest the sweeping alterations that Brown had made. At first Repton followed closely the rules laid down by his famous predecessor, but as his own reputation increased he invented for himself, trusting to his own talents. He was the first to assume the title of "Landscape Gardener" and declared himself the professor of an art to which he gave the name of "Landscape Gardening," because he says "the art can only

HUMPHREY REPTON.

be advanced and perfected by the united powers of the landscape painter and the practical gardener." In 1795 he published *Sketches and Hints on Landscape Gardening*, wherein he lays down the four following rules for the design of a garden. "First it must display the natural beauties and hide the natural defects of every situation. Secondly, it should give the appearance of extent and freedom, by carefully disguising or hiding the boundary. Thirdly, it must studiously conceal every interference of art, however expensive, by which the scenery is improved; making the whole appear the production of nature only; and fourthly, all objects of mere convenience or comfort, if incapable of being made ornamental, or of becoming proper parts of the general scenery, must be removed or concealed." He was the author of several other works on the same subject and continued to practise his profession of "producing beautiful effects" until his death in 1818.

A further impetus to the landscape school was given by Sir William Chambers, who published *A Dissertation on Oriental Gardening* in 1772. This work created a commotion quite out of keeping with its value, and it is said that with the exception of the preface, which is in earnest enough, the book is really a solemn joke intended to mystify the public, and prompted to a certain extent by a personal feeling against Capability Brown, who had obtained a commission for laying out an important estate which Chambers coveted. It is this which gives point to the following sarcastic description of the English garden of his day, a description little exaggerated, as we know from other records of Brown's methods of dealing with the surroundings of a house. "Our gardens," he says, "differ very little from common fields, so closely is common nature copied in most of them. There is generally so little variety in the objects, such a poverty of imagination in the contrivance, and of art in the arrangement, that these compositions rather appear the offspring of chance than design, and a stranger is often at a loss to know whether he is walking in a meadow or in a pleasure-ground, made and kept at a considerable expense. He sees nothing to amuse him, nothing to excite his curiosity, nor anything to keep up his attention. At his first entrance, he is treated with the sight of a large green field, scattered over with a few straggling trees, and verged with a confused border of little shrubs and flowers; after further inspection, he finds a little serpentine path, twining in regular esses (*sic*) among the shrubs of the border, upon which he is to go round, to look on one side at what he has already seen—the large green field,

A View of the Wilderness, with the Alhambra, the Pagoda and the Mosque.

THE PAGODA AT KEW.

THE ENGLISH LANDSCAPE SCHOOL

and on the other side at the boundary, which is never more than a few yards from him and always obtruding upon his sight; from time to time he perceives a little seat or temple stuck up against the wall; he rejoices at the discovery, sits down, rests his wearied limbs, and then reels on again, cursing the line of beauty; till, spent with fatigue, nearly roasted by the sun, for there is never any shade, and tired for want of entertainment, he resolves to see no more; vain resolution! There is but one path; he must either drag on to the end, or return back by the same tedious way he came. Such is the favourite plan of all our smaller gardens, and our larger works are only a repetition of the smaller ones; more green fields, more shrubberies, more serpentine walks, and more seats."

In his own work Chambers brought to bear a highly cultivated mind upon the subject of garden design and did what he could to check the absurdities that were being perpetrated everywhere. In this, however, he was not altogether successful, and the Chinese style, in the hands of less skilful designers, led to the erection of the most amazing of garden freaks.

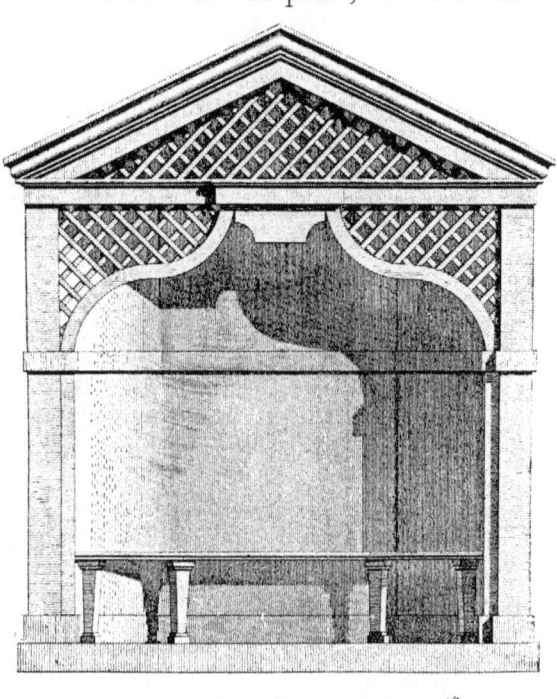

AN ARBOUR AT KEW, DESIGNED BY SIR WILLIAM CHAMBERS.

The interest in China was further stimulated when Lord Macartney conducted the first diplomatic mission to that country. Chambers was afterwards appointed superintendent of the royal gardens and designed the gardens at Kew in 1730; he constructed several Chinese buildings, including the Pagoda (illus., p. 293) which still remains a monument to this extraordinary passing craze for things Chinese. He is more happy when designing the graceful little garden buildings; the little circular Temple of Æolus is one of the most pleasing buildings of its kind that has been seen.

Although during the greater part of the eighteenth century the landscape style reigned supreme, in the remoter parts of the country the less pretentious gardens of the middle classes still adhered to the best principles of the formal school. During the nineteenth century, the introduction of many new plants and improved methods of cultivation and the more extended use of hothouse and conservatory have brought about many changes. In the early part of the century landscape gardening was all the fashion, but towards the middle of the century, with a revival of Italian architecture, an attempt was made to introduce the Italian garden. Several large schemes were designed by Sir Charles Barry, amongst which are the gardens of Trentham and Shrublands. The practice of bedding-out plants came into vogue, and instead of the glorious borders of old-fashioned perennials which for years had been the pride of English gardens, we were asked to admire rows of blue lobelia planted in front of scarlet geraniums against a gorgeous background of yellow calceolaria.

A CHINESE PAVILION AT KEW.

The taste for landscape gardening quickly spread all over the Continent, and after the peace of 1762 the *Jardin à l'anglaise* became all the fashion in France. It seems strange indeed that, with the great examples of garden design that then existed, the French should have been content to follow the

THE ENGLISH LANDSCAPE SCHOOL

lead of England and to replace the magnificent tradition of Le Nôtre with the ridiculous fancies of the landscape gardener.

Although the landscape garden was generally called *le jardin anglais* in France, and might be supposed to have mainly originated in England, there had already been several attempts to break away from the stiff formality of the seventeenth century. A designer named Dufrény, born in Paris in 1648, has been regarded as one of the pioneers of the natural style, and according to D'Alençon, when Louis XIV first resolved upon laying out Versailles on an extensive scale, Dufrény submitted two different schemes which were refused by the King, on account of the expense; some of these designs were published in 1731. Dufrény said that he preferred to lay out his gardens upon an irregular site, and when Nature offered no obstacles to overcome he created them himself, that is to say, when he had to deal with a flat site he promptly raised a hill and utilized it for a belvedere. He designed the gardens of Mignaux near Poissy, and also laid out a piece of ground which belonged to him in the Faubourg St. Antoine, in the natural style.

THE TEMPLE OE ÆOLUS, KEW.

Paramount above all was the influence of Jean-Jacques Rousseau, who as Taine said " made the dawn visible to people who had never risen till noon, the landscape to eyes that had only rested hitherto upon drawing-rooms and palaces, the natural garden to men who had only walked between tonsured yews and rectilinear flower borders." Rousseau in *La nouvelle Hélöise* explains the radical change of taste that was taking place in garden design. Describing an imaginary garden on the banks of the Lake of Geneva he says, " you see nothing regular and nothing levelled; the gardener's line is unknown here. Nature never plants anything in line, the windings of paths and streams in their intentional irregularity are designed with art, the better to prolong the promenades, hide the extent of the island, and increase its apparent size."

Horace Walpole never made a greater mistake than when he predicted the failure of the introduction of the English garden in France. "The people of the eighteenth century," says Riat, " with their refined cultivation, their exquisite delicacy and remarkable adaptability, perceived at once all the advantages of Kent's theories and did not trouble themselves that the innovation proceeded from England." French society had passed through such changes that the architectural garden of Le Nôtre was no longer suitable. In France, as in England, it was left to literature to lead Fashion away from the best ideals of the Formal garden. Langier was the first French author to popularize the English style of gardening in his *Essai sur l'Architecture*, published in 1753. In 1760 Thompson's *Seasons* was translated into French, and the following year Rousseau wrote *La nouvelle Héloïse* with the description of the landscape garden of Clarens. In 1770 appeared *Les Ruines des plus beaux Monuments de la Grèce*; in 1764, *Les Saisons*, by Saint-Lambert; in 1777, *La Composition des Paysages*, by the Marquis de Girardin; then, in 1779, *Le Jardin de Monceau*, by Carmontelle, and in 1784, *Etudes de la Nature*, by Bernardin de Saint-Pierre; in 1787, *Paul*

ENGLISH GARDEN AT THE PETIT TRIANON.

et Virginie, in which the descriptions of nature created a great impression; in 1782, *Le Voyage en Grèce*, by Gouffier; in the same year *Les Jardins* of Delille, and also the Idylls of Gessner, and *La Nature Champêtre*, by Marnézia.

This revulsion of feeling was quite in accordance with the taste of the time, which tended towards the life of the fields and opposed the simplicity of rustic manners to the luxury and artificiality of town life. It soon became the fashion for landscape gardens to have an entire rustic village or *hameau*;

THE HAMLET AT THE PETIT TRIANON.

one of the first was laid out at Chantilly about 1780. A water mill was set on the bank of a meandering stream with several groups of thatched cottages. One farmhouse of modest exterior contained a richly decorated salon and boudoir, and a dining hall with ceiling painted to represent foliage, that one might fancy oneself in a dense forest; other thatched cottages were devoted to the billiard-room, library, etc.

According to Delille, the two first landscape gardens were those of Tivoli, laid out by Boutin near Paris, and those of the Duchesse de Boufflers; but the perfect type of the new style was the Petit Trianon at Versailles.

Marie Antoinette had always been fond of gardening, and whilst still Dauphine had much wished to own a country house. Fired with envy at the gardens which the Duc de Chartres had laid out at Monceau, she determined to imitate him. The King therefore gave her Trianon, and an English gardener, Richard, was employed to lay out the grounds. He accumulated a variety of garden buildings, a pagoda, Chinese aviary, theatre, Temple of Diana, Turkish fountains, dairy, farm. His work, however, did not give satisfaction, and the Count de Caraman put before the Queen

THE MILL AT THE HAMLET, PETIT TRIANON.

another project, which was accepted. The works were at once begun, but were stopped soon after for lack of funds. In 1776 the *jeu de bague* was set up, then once again the plans were discarded and the architect Mique elaborated an entirely new plan. Amongst his innovations were a hermitage, a *salon hydraulique*, Chinese decorations, an ancient temple on a large rock, and a belvedere. Between 1778 and 1782 further works were carried out—a thatched cottage, a stone bridge and on a grassy island *Le Temple d'Amour* was erected from the designs of the sculptor Deschamps. The next year Mique also planned for the Queen a little hamlet like that at Chantilly.

The head gardener by this time was Claude Richard, who had succeeded his father and greatly delighted the Queen by his abundant cultivation of flowers.

The building of the hamlet was the last flight of Marie Antoinette's imagination. It is still kept up as one of the most curious of the attractions of Versailles. The two groups of cottages were formerly occupied by several rustic households, who carried out real farming operations on the spot. The farm stands a little aloof from the other buildings. It was famous for its herd of Swiss sheep, and there was also an excellent dairy, where the Queen amused herself and her friends by making butter and cheese under the direction of the farmer's wife. A mill, manor house, grange and boudoir completed the bijou village, which was finished and in full swing by 1784. Mique wanted to enlarge the scheme, and proposed the addition of a "Temple of the Muses," but the Queen would not give her consent, and built the *Tour de Marlborough* instead.

Though not the first in France, the Trianon garden soon became the model of the Anglo-Chinese style, and no money was spared to adorn it with everything that was charming and novel. For several years the Queen led a simple life here with a few companions, amusing herself by occasionally giving small receptions to the King and his courtiers.

In 1763 the estate of Ermenonville was acquired by the Marquis de Girardin, large sums were spent on laying it out, and after Trianon it became the most famous landscape garden in France. In 1778 Rousseau, being obliged to quit Paris, was invited to take up his residence here, but only enjoyed two months of the quiet rest before he died. His body was embalmed and buried by moonlight on the *Ile des Peupliers,* and the spot soon became a popular shrine. An account of this place was written by Girardin himself in 1775 and translated into English. Among other objects of interest in the grounds were Rousseau's cottage, a garden in ruins, and a cascade. Girardin had travelled much in England and drew his ideas from the English garden designers. He professes, however, that his object is "neither to create English gardens, nor Chinese gardens, and less to divide his grounds into pleasure grounds and parks than to produce interesting landscapes." He was assisted by J. B. Morel, the "Kent" of France, who afterwards published the *Théorie des Jardins,* and probably also by his guest, Rousseau. Girardin kept a band of musicians, who constantly perambulated the grounds, playing sometimes in the woods and at other times on the waters, and in scenes devised for particular seasons, so as to draw the attention of visitors to them at the proper time. The Marquise and her daughter wore dresses of common brown stuff "*en amazone*" with black hats, while the boys wore "*habillements les plus simples et les plus propres à les faire confondre avec les enfants des campagnards.*"

In 1774 C. H. Watelet published an *Essai sur les Jardins*, wherein he professed to take utility for the basis of his art. With this end he laid out

ENGLISH GARDEN AT "LE MOULIN-JOLI," NEAR PARIS.

the *Moulin-joli* on the Seine near Paris, of which the Prince de Ligne wrote:—

"Here is a place more after my own heart than Ermenonville, and nearer to Paris. Having turned my back on the gaieties of Paris, I was wandering aimlessly along the banks of the Seine and at last, losing sight of the City at Moulin-Joli found myself, for it is only alone with Nature that one finds oneself. Whoever you may be, if your heart be not hardened, perch yourself in the branches of a willow at Moulin-Joli on the banks of the river.

Read, gaze and weep. It will not be from sadness, but from delighted emotion. You may see your innermost soul, meditate with the sage, sigh with the lover, and bless Watelet."

Morfontaine, near Chantilly, famous as the place where the Treaty between France and America was signed, was laid out about 1770 upon a waste piece of land presenting enough obstacles to please any landscape designer. In the early nineteenth century it became the favourite

THE AVIARY AT MORFONTAINE.

residence of Joseph Bonaparte, who only quitted it in 1806 to accept the Crown of Naples. There was a small garden theatre here with a screen, which being removed, disclosed a natural sylvan background.

In the *Bibliothèque Nationale* is a curious volume of Chinese drawings of the eleven principal pleasure houses of the Emperor of China, taken from a collection of pictures on silk that was presented to Louis XVI. These, together with the Chinese text, were published by Le Rouge, who in 1784 also published an extraordinary project by an Italian, Francesco Beltini, for a combined English, French and Chinese garden. The garden was designed for the Venetian Ambassador, and its description is worth transcribing to show the wild excesses to which a French gardener could run. Like the Chinese gardens, its perfection was to consist in the number and diversity of its scenes, and in the artful combination of their parts, planned to suit every mood of the owner. Arriving by the grand avenue we find the château placed in the midst of the gardens, which are laid out regularly upon the side of approach, with a path leading to the *Hameau,* and a tiny Gothic ruined chapel and group of cottages, each with its separate garden, a pyramid overlooking a pond, a fishing lodge, dairy and sheep-fold. Hard by is an Italian vineyard, overlooked by a Temple appropriately dedicated to Bacchus; as a great contrast the visitor passed from this joyous spot to one more serious, "The Isle of Tombs," with monuments dedicated to the great dead of all time, virtuous citizens, dead or even living friends; this scene we are told would always evoke emotion. The next is of quite a different kind; a triumphal bridge decorated with military trophies and two rostral columns, leads from the Island of Sadness to the Temple of Momus, placed within gay surroundings, well cut lawns, flowery parterres; here were established all sorts of *Jeux Champêtres,* a *Balançoire,* and *Jeu de Bague.* It was even suggested that failing a better use the temple might be a fitting place for a billiard table. Now we pass to the English garden, whose principal feature was to be the collection of evergreen trees, and then on to the Dutch garden, formally laid out with tiny canals and a Temple of Venus decorated with shells and

MONUMENT TO THE MEMORY OF CAPTAIN COOK AT MEREVILLE.

coloured spar, in the usual Dutch manner. This garden was to be surrounded by roses, and to be as gay as possible in order to form the greater contrast to the next scene, which was to represent a fearsome desert, a scene which the writer says is very difficult to treat, and ought not only to offer a spectacle of sterility, but one which by means of ruined habitations, the débris of burnt houses, trees overturned by the tempest, and caverns inhabited by monsters, is calculated to inspire sadness. It is suggested that

BRIDGE AND CLASSIC RUIN AT MEREVILLE.

the effect might be still further heightened by a volcano artfully constructed in imitation of Vesuvius, emitting smoke by means of a coal fire. An underground passage leads from this dreadful spot to the *Champs Elysées* where abundance reigns supreme. Then came the Chinese garden, where plenty of water was necessary for the meandering streams. Marble pavilions, bridges, and pagodas were interspersed with rare trees and plants from China and Japan. The side of the château which faced this garden was to be decorated in the Chinese manner; in fact, each elevation of the house was to be treated in a different style to suit the garden it overlooked.

Le Rouge published a number of landscape garden schemes, including that of the Duc de Chartres at Monceau, Bagatelle in the Bois de Boulogne, the retreat of the Comte d'Artois, Bagnolet, laid out by La Chapelle for the Duchesse d'Orléans, Gennevilliers, near Paris, laid out in 1785 by Labrière, Romainville, the seat of the Marquis de Ségur, and the Château de Brunoy or the King's brother. He also published detailed descriptions of the Royal

Vue de la Cascade ou rocher, près la Cabane des Druides, dans le Jardin de Bagatelle,
¹ Situé dans le Bois de Boulogne

THE CASCADE AT BAGATELLE.

Gardens at Richmond, Lord Burlington's garden at Chiswick House, and that of the Princess of Wales at Kew Palace.

The Duc de Chartres' garden at Monceau is also described by Carmontelle. It was designed by a Scotchman named Blaikie, who had worked under Richard at the Trianon, and later on at Malmaison. He first went to France in 1776, and remained there during the Revolution, when he was engaged by the National Assembly to plant the Tuileries with potatoes. He was next

THE ROCHER AT BAGATELLE.

offered the appointment of Commissioner for the establishment of a botanic garden at Versailles, but as he had never been paid for his work at the Tuileries he respectfully declined the appointment and preferred to return to his old profession of garden-designer. He was one of the most famous designers in the *style anglais* on the Continent, and his work extended to Holland, Germany and Austria. At Monceau there was a grove of tombs, an Italian vineyard, and a very curious hexagonal plot with central space laid out for roses, to which were added three other gardens, each containing flowers of one colour only; there was a group of rustic cottages, a Dutch windmill upon a foundation of rock, a Tartar tent, and lastly the *Jeu de Bague*, with real Chinese attendants.

In 1778 the Comte d'Artois, who had just completed the little château of Bagatelle, secured the services of Blaikie to lay out the gardens. The pavilion had been planned upon an oblong piece of land bordering the kitchen gardens of the "Château de Madrid" in the Bois de Boulogne, and remained until in 1777 the Count made a wager with the Queen that he would erect another pavilion in two months, a feat which he accomplished at enormous expense. In later times Bagatelle came into the hands of Sir Richard Wallace, who made the place famous for its wonderful flower display, and recently the whole property has been bought by the City of Paris.

BAGATELLE.

In 1808 Alexandre Laborde published his *Description des nouveaux Jardins de la France et de ses Châteaux*. Laborde's work gives the best account we have of the "English garden" in France, and having been written at the beginning of the nineteenth century gives an accurate picture of the absurd excesses into which the new system had fallen. In 1830 Boitard published a more practical volume, *L'Art de composer et décorer les Jardins*.

In Germany, quite as much as in France, the English School became the fashion. The first "English garden" to start the fashion was that at Munich, laid out in 1789 under the direction of Count Rumford by Louis Sckell, who afterwards had a great reputation as a landscape gardener. At Sans Souci Frederick William IV soon began to alter the designs of his ancestors and to set up sham ruins, a mausoleum, Roman baths and even a Japanese house. His example was followed at all the Royal Palaces in Germany, at Nymphenburg in Bavaria, Wilhelmshöhe near Cassel, Laxenbourg and Ludenbourg in

THE FORECOURT AT MALMAISON.

Austria. All through the nineteenth century the landscape style has been followed in Germany, resulting everywhere in gardens so uninteresting and appalling as to make us long for the old court gardens of the seventeenth and eighteenth centuries. Loudon, writing in the early nineteenth century, says that " there are specimens of English gardening more or less extensive in or near the capital towns of every state in Germany, but by far the greater number are of very inferior description; they have a distracting confusion arising from too many buildings and walks, and are crowded with winding sanded paths continually intersecting each other, little clumps, and useless seats or temples; the defects of the English style are copied more than the beauties."

No important gardens were laid out in Russia before the time of Peter the Great, whose first effort was made in 1714, when the garden of the summer Palace on the banks of the Neva was laid out in the Dutch style, but, dissatisfied with this first palace, he soon after laid out Peterhof, which was designed by Le Nôtre's pupil Le Blond. The garden of Tsarkoie Selo (Imperial spot) was laid out by Catherine II about 1768. Loudon says that her own architect and gardener, being unable to satisfy her orders " to follow Nature," she sent to England for a landscape gardener in the person of John Bush of Hackney. In 1772 he begun his work at Pulkora with winding shady walks and fine lawns. He was then transferred to Tsarkoie Selo, where he gave rein to all the absurd fancies of the period. One part of the garden, writes a contemporary, has been laid out in the regular lines of the best traditions of Le Nôtre, the other in the style of the English school, where every means has been employed to impart a picturesque air.

A GARDEN HOUSE FROM LABORDE.

Although the soil is unfavourable, woods have been planted, traversed by winding walks and rivulets, and the visitor will find all the usual concomitants of the English garden. The writer concludes his catalogue of the tombs and monuments by saying that the Olympians must indeed be hard to please if they are dissatisfied with the attention accorded them here.

Near St. Petersburg were also the park of Oranienbaum and the palace of Paulowsky. This was begun in 1780 from a design said to have been furnished by " Capability " Brown. Prince Potemkin's extravagant excesses in gardening were situated in different parts of Russia; the largest were in the Ukraine, but the most celebrated were those of the Palace of Taurida. He employed an Englishman, Gould, who was one of Brown's most able pupils.

Loudon relates a story that in one of the Prince's journeys to the Ukraine, Gould travelled with him with several hundred assistants to lay out the Prince's grounds at his Crimean residence, and that wherever the Prince halted, if only for a day, a little garden was laid out round his travelling pavilion in the English style, with trees and shrubs, and divided by winding gravel walks; the seats and statues were carried forward with the cavalcade.

CHINESE BRIDGE AT BAGATELLE NEAR PARIS.

The English landscape garden was introduced into Poland by the Princess Czartoryska at Pultawa. This lady, highly accomplished, of great taste, and much good sense, had been a considerable time in England. She carried to Poland a gardener, Savage, and with his assistance and that of Vogel and Frey, artists of Warsaw, she laid out Pultawa between 1780 and 1784, and published a work in Polish on English gardening in 1801. In Sweden, Gustavus III laid out the garden at Haga in the English landscape style towards the latter part of the eighteenth century from the plans of a certain Masretier. At Drottingholm the garden was planned in the Anglo-Chinese manner, and the prevailing fashion was fostered in the gardens of the British merchants of Gothenburg in Sweden, and Christiania and Trondhjem in Norway.

In Switzerland, where Nature has been prodigal in her gifts of landscape beauty, the English style was in more appropriate surroundings. "Almost all the gardens," writes Hirschfeld, "are theatres of true beauty without vain ornaments or artificial decorations." He mentions several gardens near Geneva and Lausanne. Les Délices is chiefly remarkable because it was inhabited by Voltaire, and La Grange and La Boissier were other well-known gardens of the late eighteenth century.

Happily during the last quarter of a century a revival of the best traditions of the formal garden has taken place, and as throughout the Renaissance period architects were invariably employed to plan the garden settings of the houses they built, so it is gratifying to note that this practice is once more becoming usual in England and America. There can be no doubt that the work is quite within their province, and that a much more pleasing and harmonious result is likely to be attained when the main lines of a garden are set out by those who have designed the building and who, owing to their training, should have a keen sense of proportion and beauty.

BIBLIOGRAPHY

OF THE PRINCIPAL WORKS TREATING OF EUROPEAN GARDEN DESIGN AND ITS HISTORY, TOGETHER WITH THE NAMES OF THE CHIEF ENGRAVERS OF VIEWS OF GARDENS

GENERAL.

ANDRÉ, E.   L'Art des Jardins.   Paris, 1879.
HAZLITT, W. C.   Gleanings in Old Garden Literature.   London, 1887.
HIRSCHFELD, C. C. L. von.   Theorie der Gartenkunst.   5 vols.   Leipzig, 1779–85.
—— Théorie de l'art des Jardins.   (French translation of above.)   5 vols.   Leipzig, 1779–85.
JÄGER, H.   Gartenkunst und Gärten sonst und jetzt.   Berlin, 1888.
MANGIN, A.   Histoire des Jardins anciens et modernes.   Tours, 1889.
RIAT, Georges.   L'Art des Jardins.   Paris, 1900.
SIEVEKING, A. Forbes.   In Praise of Gardens.   London, 1899.

CLASSIC GARDENS.

ARNOLD, B.   De Graecis florum et arborum amantissimis.   Göttingen, 1885.
BÖTTIGER, C. A.   Racemazionen zur Gartenkunst der Alten.
BRADLEY, R. A.   Survey of the ancient husbandry and gardening collected from Cato, Varro, etc.   1725.
BROWNE, Sir Thomas.   The Garden of Cyrus.   1658.
CASTELL, ROBERT.   The Villas of the Ancients, Illustrated.   London, 1728.
CATO, M. P.   De Re Rustica.   B.C. 234–149.
COHN.   Die Gärten in alter und neuerer Zeit, Deutsche Rundschau, 1879.
COLUMELLA.   De Re Rustica.   1st Century A.D.
COMES, Dr. Orazio.   Illustrazione delle piante rappresentate nei dipinti Pompeiani.   Naples, 1879.
FALCONER.   Historical view of the Gardens of Antiquity.   1785.
FÉLIBIEN, J. F.   Les Plans et les Descriptions de deux des plus belles maisons de Campagne de Pline le Consul.   1699.

JORET. Les Jardins de l'ancienne Égypte. 1894.
—— Les plantes dans l'antiquité et au moyen âge. 1897.
—— La rose dans l'antiquité et au moyen âge. Paris, 1892.
NICCOLINI. Le Case ed i monumenti di Pompei disegnati e descritti, Naples. 1854, etc.
PALLADIUS, RUTILIUS. De Re Rustica. Fourth or fifth century A.D.
PLINY THE ELDER. Natural History. Translated by Philemon Holland, 1551–1636.
PLINY THE YOUNGER. Letter to Apollinaris translated by William Melmoth.
SIMONIS. Ueber die Gartenkunst der Römer. Blankenberg, 1865.
STEPHANUS, C. De re Hortensi Libellus. 1536.
STENGEL. Hortorum Florum et Arborum Historia. 1650.
TEMPLE, Sir William. Miscellanea : Upon the Garden of Epicurus.
TRINKHUSII. Dissertatio de Hortis et Villis Ciceronis.
VARRO, M. T. De Re Rustica. Last Century B.C.
WÜSTEMANN, C. F. Über die Kunstgärtnerei bei den alten Römern, Gotha, 1846.

MEDIAEVAL GARDENS.

Art et Décoration, vol. xvi, p. 95.
BERNARD, A. Orchards and Gardens, Ancient and Modern.
British Museum. Harleian MSS., Nos. 18852, 26667, 4425, 5763, 35314.
DE GARLANDE, Jean. Le Ménagier de Paris, composé vers 1393 par un bourgeois parisien.
DELISLE, Leopold. Études sur la condition de l'agricole et l'état de l'agriculture en Normandie au moyen âge. Evreux, 1851.
GAUTIER, Léon. La Chevalerie. Paris, 1895.
JORET, Charles. La Rose dans l'antiquité et au moyen âge. Paris, 1892.
KEMP-WELCH. Article on Mediaeval Gardens, *Nineteenth Century*. June, 1905.
Romance of the Rose. Harleian MSS. 4425, British Museum.
SAUVAL, Henri. Histoire et recherches des antiquités de la Ville de Paris. Paris, 1724.
Scribner's Magazine, vol. xxxv, p. 131.
TURNER, T. H. State of Horticulture in England. *Archæol. Journal*, vol. v.
VIOLLET LE DUC. Dictionnaire raisonné de l'Architecture française du XIe au XVIe siècle. Paris, 1868.
WALCOTT. Church and Conventual Arrangement. London, 1861.

BIBLIOGRAPHY

ITALIAN GARDENS.

BURCKHARDT, Jacob. Der Cicerone. Basel, 1855 and Leipzig, 1898.
——— Geschichte der Renaissance in Italien. Stuttgart, 1868 and 1904.
BUSSATO, M. Giardino di Agricoltura. Venice, 1592.
COLONNA, Fra Francesco. Hypnerotomachia Poliphili. Venice, 1499. Reprinted London, about 1906.
COSTA, Gianfrancesco. Le Delizie del Fiume Brenta. 1750.
CRESCENZI, Pietro. Opus Ruralium Commodorum. Bk. VIII, 1471.
ELGOOD, G. S. Italian Gardens after Drawings by, with Notes by the Artist. London, 1907.
FALDA, G. B. Li Giardini di Roma con le loro piante alzate e Vedute in prospectiva. Rome, 1670.
——— Le Fontane di Roma. Rome, 1675.
FERRARI, J. B. De Florum Cultura, Rome. 1633.
GAUTHIER, M. P. Les plus beaux Edifices de la Ville de Gênes et de ses Environs. Paris, 1832.
KYSELL MELCHIOR, Recueil des Jardins Italiens, Augsburg, 1682.
LATHAM, Charles. The Gardens of Italy. London, 1906.
LEBLOND, Mrs. Aubrey. The Old Gardens of Italy. How to visit them. London, 1912.
MONTAIGNE, Michel de. Journal du voyage en Italie etc. en 1580 et 1581. Rome et Paris, 1774.
PERCIER ET FONTAINE. Choix des plus célèbres Maisons de Plaisance de Rome et de ses environs. Paris, 1809.
PIRANESI, G. B. Vedute di Roma. 1765.
PLATT, C. A. Italian Gardens. 1894.
POLITIANUS, Angelus. Rusticus. 1486.
RE, A. dal. Maisons de Plaisance de l'Etat de Milan. Milan, 1743.
ROSS, Janet. Florentine Villas. London, 1901.
RUBENS, P. P. Palazzi di Genova. Antwerp, 1622.
SILVESTRE, Israel de. Alcune vedute di Giardini e Fontane di Roma e di Tivoli. Paris, 1646.
SITWELL. An Essay on the making of Gardens. A Study of Old Italian Gardens, etc. London, 1909.
TAINE, H. Voyage en Italie. Paris, 1884.
TRIGGS, H. Inigo. The Art of Garden Design in Italy. London, 1906.

TUCKERMANN, W. C.   Die Gartenkunst der italienischen Renaissance-Zeit. 1884.
VANVITELLI, L. Disegni del Reale Palazzo di Caserta. 1756.
VITRUVIUS, M. Pollio. Architectura.
WHARTON, Edith. Italian Villas and their Gardens. London, 1904.
ZOCCHI, Giuseppe. Vedute delle Ville ed'altri luoghi della Toscana. Florence, 1744.

FRENCH GARDENS.

BETIN, Pierre.   Le fidèle Jardinier, ou différentes sortes de parterres tant de plaine broderie que meslée de pièces à mettre fleurs pour servir d'instruction à ceux qui se délectent en cest art. Paris, 1636.
BLONDEL, J. F.   De la Distribution des Maisons de Plaisance. Paris, 1737-8.
BOYCEAU, Jacques. Traité du Jardinage selon les raisons de la nature et de l'art. Paris, 1638.
CHATILLON, Claude. Topographie Française, etc. Paris, 1648.
D'ARGENVILLE, A. J. D.   La Théorie et la pratique du Jardinage. Paris, 1713.
DE SERRES, Olivier. Le Théâtre d'Agriculture et mesnage des Champs. Paris, 1603.
DU CERCEAU, Androuet. Les plus excellents bastiments de France. 1576. The original drawings are in the Print Room at the British Museum. A re-engraved issue, edited by H. Destailleur. Paris, 1865. A selection of the original drawings was published by W. H. WARD, entitled,—French Châteaux and Gardens. London, 1908.
ESTIENNE, Charles. La Maison Rustique. Paris, 1570. English editions, 1600 and 1616.
FOUQUIER, Marcel. De l'art des jardins. Paris, 1911.
FRANÇOIS, Jean. L'Art des Fontaines. Rennes. 1665.
GALIMARD, fils. Architecture des Jardins. 1765.
LANGLOIS, N.   Parterres, 23 plans after Le Nôtre, Le Bouteux, etc.
LE BLOND, A. J. B. Engravings of plans for Gardens. 1685.
—— Parterres de Broderie. 1688.
—— La Théorie et la Pratique du Jardinage.
LE CLERC, Sébastien. Le Labyrinthe de Versailles. 1679.

LE PAUTRE, J. Nouveaux desseins de jardins, parterres et fassades, Jets d'eau nouvellement gravés par Le Pautre. *Several series of Plates*, n.d.
LIGER, Louis. Le Jardinier, Fleuriste, et Historiographe. Amsterdam, 1703.
MARIETTE, J. Parterres de Broderie. c. 1730.
MAROT, Jean. Architecture. Paris, n.d.
MIZAULD. Le Jardinage de Mizauld. Paris, 1578.
MOLLET, André. Le Jardin de Plaisir. Stockholm, 1651.
NOLHAC, Pierre de, Histoire du château de Versailles. Paris, 1911.
PALISSY, Bernard. Recepte véritable, etc. . . . Rochelle, 1563.
PERELLE, Adam. Divers Veuës et Perspectives des Fontaines et Jardins de Fontainebel-eau et autres lieux.
QUINTINYE, Jean de La. Instructions sur les Jardins fruitiers et potagers avec un traité des orangers. Paris, 1690.
RIGAUD, Jean. Recueil choisi des plus belles Vues de palais, châteaux, maisons de plaisance, etc., de Paris, et de ses environs. Paris, 1752.
ROUBO. L'Art du Treillageur. Paris, 1775.
SCHABOL, R. Dictionnaire du Jardinage, 1767.
—— La Théorie du Jardinage, 1785.
SILVESTRE, Israel de. Jardins et Fontaines. Paris, 1661.
VALLET, Pierre. Le Jardin du Roy tres chrestien Henri IV. Paris, 1608.

DUTCH GARDENS.

BEUDEKER, Christoffel. Germania Inferior. *A collection founded on Blaeu's Views.*
CAUSE, D. H. De Koninglycke hovenier. Amsterdam, 1676.
COMMELYN, Jan. The Belgick or Netherlandish Hesperides. 1683. English translation by G. V. N.
COMMELYN, Gaspard. Horti Medici Amstelodamensis. Amsterdam, 1678.
DANCKERTS, J. Engraved views of Het Loo.
DE CANTILLON, Philippe. Délices de Brabant et de ses Campagnes. Amsterdam, 1757.
DE CLOET, J. J. Châteaux et monuments des Pays-Bas. Brussels, 1826.
DE GROOT. Les Agréments de la Campagne. 1750.
DE HOGUE, Romeyn. Villa Angiana and engraved views of Het Loo.

DE LETH, Hendrik. Het zegepralent Kennemerlant. Amsterdam, 1730.
    (Engraved views of Dutch Country Seats.)
DE PASSE, Crispin. Hortus Floridus. Arnhem, 1614. English edition, 1616.
DU VIVIER. Le Jardin de Hollande. Amsterdam, 1710.
GORIS, Gerard. Les délices de la Campagne à l'entour de la Ville de Leide.
    Leyden, 1712.
HARTLIB, Samuel. Discourse of Husbandrie used in Brabant and Flanders.
    London, 1645.
HOLLANDSCHE ARKADIA. A series of views engraved by A. Rademaker,
    C. Pronk, H. de Winter, D. Stoopendaal.
MOUCHERON, I. de. Engraved views of Honslaardijk.
NUMAN, H. 24 Vues des Maisons de Campagne situées en Hollande. 1797.
POST, Pierre. Les Ouvrages d'Architecture. Leyden, 1715. *Gives plans
    of the Huis 'ten Bosch, Swanenburg, Ryxdorp, Vredenburg, etc.*
RADEMAKER, A. Rhynland's Fraaiste Gezichsten. Amsterdam, 1732.
—— French Translation (Les plus agréables Vues de Rhynland). Amsterdam, 1732.
—— Holland's Tempe vereherelijkt, etc. *c.* 1730.
—— L'Arcadie Hollandoise. Amsterdam, 1730.
RAY, John. Observations on a Journey through the Low Countries. 1673.
SANDREMIUS, Dr. A. Flandria Illustrata. 1641.
SCHENCK, Peter. Many engraved views of Dutch country houses, including
    the Loo, Dieren, Zutphen, Duinrel, Roosendaal.
SMALLEGANGE, M. Cronyk van Zeeland. 1696.
SPRINGER, L. A. De Oud-Hollandsche Tuinkunst. Haarlem, 1889.
STOOPENDAAL, D. De Vechtstroom, 1790, and engraved views of Rijswijck.
VALCK, G. Engraved views of the Huis-ten-Bosch, and many designs for
    garden detail, as treillage, vases, etc.
VAN DER GROEN, J. Le Jardinier des Pays-Bas. Brussels, 1672.
—— De Nederlandischen Hovenier.
VAN OOSTEN, H. The Dutch Gardener. London, 1710.
VISSCHER, N. La triomphante Rivière de Vecht. Amsterdam, 1719.
—— Engraved views of Clingendaal.
VREDEMAN DE VRIESE, J. Hortorum viridariorumque elegantes et multiplicis formae architectonicæ, etc. Antwerp, 1583.
WIERIX, Jean, Jerome, and Antoine. Theatrum vitae humanæ; engravings of gardens in perspective. 1577.

ENGLISH GARDENS BEFORE THE LANDSCAPE SCHOOL.

AMHERST, Hon. Alicia. A History of Gardening in England. London, 1896.
BACON, Francis. Of Gardens (Essays).
BADESLADE, T. Thirty-six different views of Noblemen and Gentlemen's Seats in the County of Kent. London, n.d.
BEEVERELL, James. Les Délices de la Grand' Bretagne et de l'Irlande Leyden, 1727.
BLOMFIELD, R., and F. Inigo THOMAS. The Formal Garden in England. London, 1892.
BOORDE, Dr. Andrew. The boke for to Lerne a man to be wyse in buyldyng of his howse. About 1540.
CAMPBELL, WOOLFE and GANDON. Vitruvius Britannicus. 1715-71.
DE CAUX, Isaac. "Le Jardin de Wilton." c. 1615; reprinted by Bernard Quaritch, 1895.
—— New and Rare Invention of Water-Works shewing the easiest waies to raise Water higher than the Spring. London, 1659.
DE PASSE, Crispin. A Garden of Flowers, etc. Utrecht, 1615.
ELGOOD, G. S. and Gertrude JEKYLL. Some English Gardens. London, 1904.
ESTIENNE and LIEBAULT-SURFLET. Maison Rustique, or the Covntrie Farme. 1600.
GERARDE, John. The Herball, or generall Historie of Plantes. London, 1597.
HILL, Thomas. The proffitable Arte of Gardening. London, 1568. See also Mountain.
—— A most briefe and pleasaunt treatyse teachynge howe to dress, sowe, and set a garden. London, 1563.
KIP and KNYFF. Britannia Illustrata. London, 1707, etc.
LANGLEY, Batty. New Principles of Gardening, or the laying-out and planting Parterres. London, 1728.
LAWSON, William. A new Orchard and Garden. 1618.
LE BLOND. The Theory and Practice of Gardening. Translated from the French of A. le Blond by John James. London, 1703.
LOGGAN, David. Oxonia Illustrata. Oxford, 1675.
—— Cantabrigia Illustrata. Cambridge, 1690.
LONDON and WISE. The Compleat Gard'ner (of J. de la Quintinye). London, 1699.
—— The Retir'd Gardener. From the French of le Sieur Louis Liger of Auxerre. London, 1706.

MARKHAM, Gervase. The Country Housewife's Garden. 1617.
—— Maison Rustique; or the Countrey Farme. London, 1616.
MAWSON, T. H. The Art and Craft of Garden-making. London, 1912.
MEAGER, L. The English Gardener. London, 1670.
—— The new arte of Gardening. London, 1697.
MOUNTAIN, DIDYMUS (Thomas Hill). The Gardener's Labyrinth. London, 1577.
PARKINSON, John. Paradisi in Sole Paradisus Terrestris, or a choice Garden of all sortes of rarest Flowers. London, 1629. Reprinted London, 1904.
SEDDING, John D. Garden Craft, Old and New. London, 1895.
SWITZER, Stephen. The Nobleman, Gentleman, and Gardener's Recreation, etc. London, 1715.
SHORT INSTRUCTIONS very profitable and necessary for all those that delight in Gardening . . . From the French. London, 1592.
TRIGGS, H. Inigo. Formal Gardens in England and Scotland. London, 1902.
TUSSER, Thomas. A hundreth good pointes of husbanderie. London, 1557.
WILLIAMS, W. Oxonia Depicta, etc. London, 1733.
WORLIDGE, John. Systema Horticulturae, or the Art of Gardening. London, 1677.

GERMAN AND AUSTRIAN GARDENS.

BÖCKLERN, G. A. Architectura curiosa nova. Nuremberg, 1673.
BOETTICHER, C. G. W. Die Königlichen Schlösser und Gärten zu Potsdam, 1854.
BESLER, Basil. Hortus Eystettensis. 1613.
CAUS, Salomon de. Les Raisons des Forces mouvantes. Frankfort, 1615.
—— Hortus Palatinus a Frederico . . . Electore . . . Heidelbergae exstructus. Frankfort, 1620.
DANREITER, F. A. Die Garten Prospect von Hellbrünn bei Salzburg. 1740.
DECKER, Paulus. Fürstlicher Baumeister; oder, Architectura Civilis. Augsburg, 1711-1716.
DIESEL, Matthias. Erlustierende Augenweide in Vorstellung Herrlicher Garten und Lustgebäude. 3 vols. Ausburg, 1725.
ELSZHOLZ, J. S. Vom Garten-baw. Cologne, 1666.
GRISEBACH, August. Der Garten: eine Geschichte seiner künstlerischen Gestaltung. Leipzig, 1910.
HESSE, H. Neue Garten-Lust. Leipzig, 1713.

Hoghenberg. Hortorum ... formae. Cologne, 1665.
Jung and Schröder. Das Heidelberger Schloss und seine gärten .. und der schlossgarten zu Schwetzingen. Berlin, 1898.
Kleiner, Salomon. Vera et accurata delineatio omnium Templorum ... in urbe Viennæ. Amsterdam, 1724-37.
—— Maisons de Plaisance Impériales. Augsburg, 1724?
Laurenberg, Peter. Horticultura, Lib. II. Plans of gardens by Merian. Frankfort, 1631.
Royer, Johann. Beschreibung des gantzen Fürstlichen Braunschweigischen Gartens zu Hessen. Halberstadt, 1648.
Volckamer, J. C. Nürnbergische Hesperides. Nuremberg, 1708-14.
Wolff, J. Fortsetzung erlustierenden Augenweide in Vorstellung herrlicher Garten und Lust-gebäude. n.d.

SPANISH GARDENS.

Banqueri, Josef Antonio. Libro de agricoltura. 1802.
Fanshawe, Lady Anne. Memoirs. 1766.
Gautier, T. Voyage en Espagne.
Gayangos, Pascuel de. Translations of works of Ahmed Ibn Mahommed Al-Makkari.
Girault de Prangey. Souvenirs de Grenade et de l'Alhambra. Paris, 1837.
Herrera, Gabriel Alonso de. Libro di Agricultura. Folio. Toledo, 1546.
Jones, Owen. The Alhambra. London, 1842-5.
Junghändel. Die Baukunst Spaniens. Dresden, N.D. (c. 1894.)
Meusnier, Louis. Veuë du Palais Jardins et Fontaine; d'Arangouesse; Maison de Plaisance du Roy d'Espagne. Paris, 1665.
Rusinol, S. Jardins d'Espagne. Barcelona, 1903.
Theatrum Hispani. Amsterdam, 1660.

THE LANDSCAPE SCHOOL IN EUROPE.

Alphand, A. Les promenades de Paris. Paris, 1867-73.
Attiret, J. D. A particular account of the Emperor of China's Gardens near Pekin. Translated from the French by Sir. H. Beaumont. London, 1752.
Carmontelle, L. C. de. Jardin de Monceau. Paris, 1779.
Chambers, Sir William. A dissertation on Oriental gardening. London, 1772.

De Lille. On Gardening. Translated from the French of l'Abbé de Lille. 1783.
Ermenonville–Malthus. An Essay on Landscape. From the French of Ermenonville. 1783.
Girardin, R. L. De la composition des paysages sur le terrain, et des moyens d'embéllir les campagnes autour des habitations, etc. Genève, 1777.
Knight, R. P. The Landscape : a Didactic Poem. 1794.
Krafft, J. C. Plans des plus beaux Jardins pittoresques de France, d'Angleterre, et d'Allemagne. 2 vols. 1809–10.
Laborde, Alexandre de. Descriptions des nouveaux Jardins de la France. 1808–21.
Le Rouge, G. L. Recueil des plus beaux Jardins de l'Europe. 1776–87.
Loudon, J. C. Observations on the formation of useful and ornamental plantations. Edinburgh, 1804.
—— Hints on the formation of Gardens and Pleasure Grounds. 1812.
—— The Encyclopedia of Gardening. London, 1822.
Mason, G. An Essay on Gardening design. 1768.
Mérigot. Promenade ou Itinéraire des Jardins d'Ermenonville. Paris, 1788.
Morel, N. Théorie des Jardins. 1776.
Milner, H. E. The Art and Practice of Landscape Gardening. London, 1890.
Repton, Humphrey. Sketches and Hints on Landscape Gardening. London, 1795.
—— Observations on the Theory and Practice of Landscape Gardening, etc. London, 1803.
—— The two above Reprinted. Edited by John Nolen. Boston, U.S.A., 1907.
—— Fragments on the Theory and Practice of Landscape Gardening. London, 1817.
Rudder, Samuel. History of Gloucestershire. Cirencester, 1779.
Scott, Sir Walter. On Ornamental Plantations and Landscape Gardening. (*Quarterly Review*.) 1828.
Walpole, Horace. Essay on Modern Gardening. 1785.
Watelet, Claude. Essai sur les Jardins. Paris, 1774.
Wheatley, Thomas. Observations on Modern Gardening. 1770.

INDEX TO TEXT AND ILLUSTRATIONS.

References in heavy type denote illustrations, and indicate the pages on which they occur. References thus, f. 202, are to the collotype plates.

Abd-er-Rahman I, Sultan of Morocco, 265
Abd-er-Rahman III, Sultan of Morocco, 266, 267
Abu Concind, Moorish architect, 270
Abu-el-Thair, Moorish gardener, 266
Abu Xacer, Moorish gardener, 266
Abu Zacharias, Moorish gardener, 266
Acilius Glabius, his gardens on the Pincian Hill, 10
Addison, on the pleasures of a garden, 288
Aix-la-Chapelle, Charlemagne's Palace and Menagerie at, 13, 14
Al Shafrah, Moorish botanist, 285
Albani, Villa, Rome, **44**
Alcazar, the, Cordova, 268
Alcazar, the, Seville, **280, 281, 282, 284**
Alcinous, the garden of, 2, 3
Aldobrandini, Villa, Frascati **54, 55,** 57, 149
Alençon, D', on Versailles, 297
Alexandria, gardens at, 1
Algeciras, a modern patio at, **286**
Alhambra, the, at Granada, **268, 269, 270,** 274, 281
Alkmaar, bulb-growers of, 182, 183; gardens at, 187
Allées d'eau at Fontainebleau, **113**; at St. Cloud, f. **150**; and *see* Canals
Alleys or Walks, 85, 172, 173, 210, 222, 223
Ambargalia, the, 13
Amboise, Château d', 70
Amboise, Cardinal Georges d', 71
Amelia of Solms, and the "House in the Wood," 195, 196
Amicis, De, his *Holland*, 200
Amphitheatres, *see* Theatres
Amsterdam, gardens at, 159, 177, 184, 187; botanic garden at, **201,** 202
Ancy-le-Franc, Château d', 70
Anet, Château d', 70, 74, 77, 121
Angle towers, 238, 241
Anglo-Saxon gardens, 25
Anne, Queen, and Hampton Court, 218
Antium, villas at, 7
Aqueducts, 8
Apuleius, the *Herbal* of, 12
Aranjuez, Palace of, 283

Arbours, *see* Summer-houses
Archery Greens, 215
Argenville, D', garden designer, 190
Aristotle, 2
Artois, Comte d', at Maisons, 150; at Bagatelle, 306, 307
Athens, Lyceum at, 2
Atkyns, engraver, 231
Atrium, the, 11, 286
Augustus, his gardens, 10
Aumale, Duc d', and the Chateau d'Anet, 77
Austrian Gardens, 238 *et seq*
Avenues, 77-79, f. 150, 152, 174, 188, 218, 248, **274**
Aviaries, 5, 11, 25, 81, 160, 245; at Villa Borghese, **42**; at Westerhof, **181**; an eighteenth century, **182**
Babylon, gardens of, 3
Bacon, *Essay upon Gardening* quoted, 76, 211, 213
Baden, Margrave of, Schloss at Carlsruhe, 258
Badeslade, engraver, 231 **223, 224**
Bagatelle, Château de, **306,** f. **306, 307,** 310
Bagnolet, Château de, 90 *n*., 121, 306
Baiae, Villas at, 7
Ballin, vase by, **115**
Balustrades, 70, 76
Banqueting-houses, *see* Summer-houses.
Barcelona, botanic gardens at, 285, 386
Barry, Sir Charles, garden designs by, 296
Bathing pools, 8, 15, **16,** 163, 213, 279, **282**
Beaumont, M., garden designer, 221.
Beauregard, Château de, 72, **73**
Beckford, Alderman, his *Diary* quoted, 167, 168, 192
Beckington, The Cedars, 226
Bedding out, 296
Bedford, Duke of, and the Hôtel St. Paul, Paris, 22
Belling, Johann, gardener, 247
Beltini, Francesco, his combined English, French and Chinese Garden, 303-305
Belton House, two ironwork gates, f. **288,** sundial at, **230**
Bentinck, Count, *see* Portland
Berlin, Palace of the Kurfurst, 241

INDEX

Besler, Basil, apothecary and botanist, 232; his *Hortus Eystettensis*, 233
Beyer, sculptor, at Schönbrunn, 261
Blaikie, Richard, garden designer, 306, 307
Bleaching grounds, 162
Bois, Château de, 70, 72; plan, **71**
Blondel, François, his *Architecture à la Mode*, 152
Boboli Gardens, Florence, 30, 31, **32, 33,** 79
Boccacio, his *Decameron*, 28
Bocchi, quoted, 32
Boendermaker on the Vecht, **186**
Bois-le-Vicomte, Château de, 134
Boitard, his *L'Art de composer et de décorer les Jardins*, 308
Bologna, John of, sculptor, 32, 33
Boorde, Andrew, his *The Boke*, etc., 210
Borghese, Scipione, 42
Borghese, Villa, Rome, **42, 46**
Borromeo, Count Carlo, at Isola Bella, 61
Bosch-en-Hoven, **183,** 184
Boscobel, mount at, 205
Bosquets, Boschetti, or Boschi, 3, 41, 58, 62, 88, 136, 145, 146, 152, 171, 172, 188.
Bosse, Abraham, engraver, 83
Botanic gardens, in Italy, 15, 38; in France, 79, 151; in Holland, 201, 202; in England, 212, 213; in Germany, 232; in Austria, 261; in Spain, 285, 286
Bouteaux, Michel, or Le Bouteux, garden designer, 121, 219
Bowers, see Summer-houses
Bowling greens, 135, 142, 191, 215, 223, 225–228
Box edging and scroll work, 8, **51,** 69, 99, 126, 165, 184, 218, **277, 279,** 283
Boyceau, Jacques, his *Traité du Jardinage*, 83, 84, 94; remarks on water, 150
Bramante, architect, 39, 40
Bredby, Derbyshire, 227
Brickwall, Sussex, stewponds at, **213,** 214
Bridgeman, garden designer, 224, 228, 289
Brock, gardens at, 200, 201
Brosses, Charles de, on Marly, 139
Brown, Lancelot, "Capability," landscape gardener, 290, 291, 309; portrait, **290**
Brunswick, gardens of, 241
Bulbs, 3, 4, 182, 183
Buontalenti, architect, 30, 33
Burleigh, Lord, and Gerarde, 211
Burlington, Lord, his villa at Chiswick, 289, 306
Bush, John, landscape gardener, 309

Cabinets de Verdure, 77, 191, and *see* Summer-houses
Cadiz, gardens at, 285
Caffaggiuolo, fortress villa at, 30

Caligula, his gardens, 10
Call, Jan van, Dutch garden designer, 175
Calypso, the garden of, 2
Canals, Egyptian, 1; at Chantilly, **91**; at Versailles, 104, 139, 140; at Sceaux, 141; at St. Cloud, **150**; at Rambouillet, **150**; at Maisons, 151; at Commercy, 156; Dutch, 166, 167, 177, 199, 200; at Hampton Court, 218; at Westbury, **222,** 223; at Nymphenburg, **255**; German, 257; Moorish, 274
Candid, Peter, garden designer, 242
Canons Ashby, f. **203**
Cantillon, De, his *Vermakelykheden van Brabant*, 170
Caprarola, Villa, 46, **46, 47, 49**
Careggio, villa at, 29, 38
Carlotta, Villa, Cadenabbia, **61**
Carlsruhe, gardens of, 258
Carlton House, gardens of, 289
Carmontelle, his *Le Jardin de Monceau*, 298, 306, 307
Cascades, at Villa Aldobrandini, **54, 55**; at Villa Torlonia, **59**; at Chantilly, **91**; at St. Cloud, **122, 146**; at Marly, **137**; Dutch, 192; at Nymphenburg, **255**; at La Granja, **284**; at Ermenonville, 301; at Bagatelle, **306**
Caserta, Palace of, 61
Casinum, Verro's Villa at, 5
Casita, de Abaja, Madrid, 283
Cassel, gardens at, 259
Cassiobury House, 228
Castellazzo, Villa, 61
Castello, Villa, Florence, 33, 79, f. **34**
Castle gardens, 17, 23, **25,** 163, 164, 165, **171,** 172, 204, **233, 234, 233,** 239, 241, 245–247
Catherine de Medici, 79–81
Catherine II of Russia, 309
Cato on gardens, 4, 23
Caus, Salomon de, 233, 234, 237–239; design by, 235
Cecil, Lord Salisbury, and Hatfield, 207, 217
Chambers, Sir William, his *Dissertation on Oriental Gardening*, 292, 295; his buildings at Kew, etc., 295, 296.
Chambord, Château de, 65, 70.
Chantilly, Château de, 66, 70, 88, 89, **90, 91, 93,** 121, **126,** 299, 300; the Temple d'Amour at, **129**
Charbonnier, father and son, garden designers, 248
Charites, the, 2
Charlemagne, his palaces, 14
Charles II of England, 121, 218, 221
Charles V of France, 21, 22, 73, 82
Charles III of Spain, 283
Charles V of Spain, 269, 278–280
Charles XII of Sweden, 156
Charlottenberg, gardens of, 259

INDEX

Chartres, Duc de, his gardens at Monceau, 300, 306
Chatelet, Marquise de, on Enghien, 172
Chatsworth, gardens of, 227, 228
Chaulnes, Château de, 75
Cheere, lead modeller, 229
Chelsea botanic gardens at, 202
Chenonceaux, Château de, 66, 70, 75
Chilson Manor House, **224**
Chinese influence on landscape gardening, **292**, 295, **296**, 301, 303-305, 310
Chiswick House, 227, **230**, 289, 306
Choisy, Château de, 134
Cicero, his Villa at Tusculum, 4
Cistern, Lead, v. Leadwork
Civita Vecchia, villas at, 7
Clagny, Château de, 121, 123, 135-**137**
Clairvoyé, The, 177, 205, 223
Claremont, gardens of, 289
Cleeve Prior Manor House, yew hedge, f. **205**
Clifton Maubank, garden house at, 225
Clingendaal, gardens at, 175, 199
Clusius, translates Dodoens' *History of Plants*, 211
Cluyt, botanist, 201, 202
Cobham, Lord, 224, 288
Coke, Thomas, Vice-Chancellor, 222
Colbert, controller of the Royal Palaces, 129, at Sceaux, 141
Colonnade hydraulique, **156**
Colour in gardens, 70
Columella, on gardens 4, 23
Commelyn, Jan, botanist, 178, 202; Gaspard, 202
Commercy, *Colonnade hydraulique* at, **156**
Commines, Château of, 23
Como, Lake, gardens on, 61
Condé, Prince de, and Chantilly, 89
Conservatories, 9, 189, 213, 296
Constantinople, Sultan's gardens at, 121
Cordova, gardens of, 265-268, 287; and *see* Alcazar
Cortavilla, Simon Tovar, botanist, 285
Cosimo I, of Tuscany, and Petraja, 34
Conrart, garden of, Paris, 79
Coustou, sculptor, 140
Cowper, quoted, 290
Coysevox, Antoine, sculptor, 93, 100, 140, 149
Creil, Château de, 70, 73
Crescenzi, Pietro, his *Opus Ruralium Commodorum*, 23-25, 28
Crusades, influence of the, 15, 16
Czartoryska, Princess, introduces the English garden into Poland, 310

Dachau, gardens of, 257
Dal Ré, Alberto, his *Ville di Delizia di Milan*, 61-**63**
Damascus, Plants from, 16, 226; gardens of, 266; the *ghauttah* of, 268

Dampierre, Château of, 70
Danby, Henry, Earl of, 212, 213
Dangeau, on the Trianon 130
Debucourt, engraving by, **124**
Deleuze, quoted, 202
Délices, Voltaire's garden at, 311
Delille, his *Des Jardins*, 299
Della Bella, engraving by, **32**
Della Porta, Giacomo, atrchitect, 53, 54, 62
De l'Orme, Philibert, architect, 65, 66, 74, 134
Des Hours, Yves, designs the gardens of Luneville, 155
Deschamps, sculptor, 300
Desgots, Claude, garden designer, 90, 122
Demetrius, his museum at Athens, 2
Democritus, on Greek gardening, 3
Diane de Poitiers, at Chenonceaux, 66; at Anet, 74
Dieren, Huis-te-, William III's house at the Hague, 175
Diesel, M., designs the gardens of Schloss Hellbrun, 252
Dionysus, temple dedicated to, 2
Dioscorides, Laguna's translation of, 285
Dodoens, Rembert, botanist, 211
Domitian, his garden on the Palatine, 10
Dovecotes, 164, 245
Dreihock, de la Court's gardens at, 202
Dresden, Elector's Palace at, 258, 259
Du Cerceau, Jacques Androuet, his *Les plus excellents bastiments de France*, 65-75, 165; illustrations from, 66, **70**, **72**, **73**; gardens designed by, 81, 90, 145
Duchesne, André, his description of Saint-Germain, 83
Dufreny, landscape gardener, 297
Dugdale, Sir William, his engravings, 231
Duperac, designs the gardens of Saint-Germain, 83
Durusé, architect at Clagny, 136
Düsseldorf, the orangery of, 247
Dutch gardening, 159-161, **162**, 163-202; in England, 221

Ecouen, Château d', 70, 75
Edward I, 26
Egyptian gardens, 1
El-Avram, Ebu, his works on gardening, 266
El-Hadj of Granada, gardener, 266
Elizabeth, Queen, her love of flowers 204,
English gardens, 25-27, 203 *et seq.*; and *see* Landscape
Enjhien, Castle of the Duc d', 172, **173**, **174**
Erasmus, his *Colloquies* quoted, 159
Erlach, Fischer von, architect, 260
Ermenonville, Chateau d', 301, 302
Escurial, The, 61, 282, 283; courtyard garden, **285**
Esher Place, 228, 289

INDEX

Este, Cardinal, Ippolito d', 40, 49, 50
Este, Villa d', at Tivoli, 49, **50**, 53
Estienne, Charles, physician, 66, 160, 162; his *La Maison Rustique*, 69, 215, 216
Evelyn, John, quoted, 53, 54, 57, 82; gardening works, 221, 222

Faglietta, Uberto, quoted, on the Villa Pia, 50
Falconiere, Villa, Frascati, 58
Falda, his *I Giardini di Roma*, 41, **44, 45**
Fanshawe, Lady, at Aranjuez, 283
Farnese, Cardinal Alessandro, 46
Farnese, Cardinal Odoardo, 49
Farnese, Villa, 40, 49
Ferdinand of Spain, 268
Ferrari, his *De Florum Cultura* quoted, 37, 38
Fish-ponds, and stewponds, 18, 24–26, 167, 177, 199, 205, **213**, 214, 222
Fitzherbert, Sir Antony, his *Boke of Husbandrie*, 210
Florence, gardens of, 28–39
Flower beds, 3, 8, 21, 204, 205
Flower garden, the, 16
Flowers, in Greek and Roman gardens, 3–7; in Medieval gardens, 16, 24; grown for ornament, 74, 130; for perfume, 130, 209; in France, 136; in Holland, 159, 182, 202, in English gardens, 204, 207, 208; in Spain 266
Fontainebleau, 65, 70, 134, 148, 145; plans of, **66, 67, 112-113, 144-5**; canal at, **145**; orangery, **144**; parterres, **141**
Fontana, Carlo, architect, 61
Fontana, Giovanni, architect, 54, **55**
Fortifications, gardens on, 242
Fountains, Roman, 8, 11; Medieval, 17, 18, **19**; at Florence, **30, 31**; by Il Tribolo, **35**; at Villa Borghese, **42, 45**; at Caprarola, **47**, 49; at Villa d'Este, 53; at Villa Torlonia, **59**; at Villa Carlotta, **61**; at Verneuil, **69**; at Gaillon **70**, 72; at the Luxembourg, **81, 82**; at Versailles, 94, **97, 100, 103, 104, 105, 107**, 109, **110, 116**, 117; at Trianon, **130, 133**, 300; at Meudon, 134, **135, 136**; at Fontainebleau, **144, 141, 142**; at St Cloud, **145, 149**; at Liancourt, 152; Dutch, 159, **164**, 166, 172, 191, 192; English, 206, 209; German, **245, 251, 258**, 261; Moorish, **265, 267, 269, 270, 275, 277, 279, 280, 281**; Spanish, **282, 283, 284**
Fouquet, his château of Vaux-le-Vicomte, 87–89, 94, 143
Fragonard, his *Fête de St Cloud*, 146
Francini brothers, fontaniers, 65, 83, 94
Francis I, Emperor, and Schönbrunn, 261
François I of France, his encouragement of garden design, 65, 66, 83, 145, 204
Frankfort, the Swindscher garden at, **243**

Frascati, gardens near, 51–58
Frederick the Great, 259, 260
Frederick William IV, 308
French gardens, **20, 21**, 65–156
Frey, artist, 310
Fruit gardens, *see* Orchards
Furniture, Garden, 18, **188**
Furttenbach, Joseph, his *Architectura Recreationis et Privata*, **234, 237**, 238, **239**

Gaillon, Château de, 70, 72, 81; plan, **71**
Galleries, 21, 72, **74**, 161, 163, 166, 167, **173**, 205
Gambara, Cardinal, his gardens at Villa Lanti, 49
Gamberaia, Villa, **34**
Garda, Lago di, 61
Garden houses, *see* Summer-houses.
Garlande, John de, his garden in Paris, 26
Garlands, 3, 4, 13
Gates, 1
Gauthier, M. P., his *Les plus beaux edifices de la ville de Gênes*, 62
Gautier, 277; quoted, 287
Gazebo, *see* Summer-houses
Gemmingen, John de, Bishop of Eichstatt, his collection of plants, 233
Genbach, gardens at, 262
Generaliffe, the, Granada, **273**, 274–281; plan, **266**, 272; Fountain in the garden, **267**; Cypress Avenue, **274**; Garden of Zoraya, **275**; Patio, **277**; Head of the Water Garden, **278**; Cypress Arbour, **279**
Geneva, gardens at, 311
Gennevilliers, landscape garden at, 306
Genoa, villas near, 62
Geoponica, The, 3
George, Prince of Wales, 289
Gerarde, John, portrait, **210**; his *Herbal*, 211
Gerarden, or Gerardin, Marquis de, his *La Composition des Paysages*, 298, 301, 302
German gardens, 232 et seq.; **233, 238, 262**
Gervais, Louis, garden designer, 155
Gessner, Salomon, his *Idylls*, 299
Giessen, botanic garden at, 232
Girardon, François, his fountains at Versailles, 104, 109
Giraud, Sieur, garden designer, 254, 257, 261
Gitard, Daniel, architect, 90
Gomboust, his *Plan of Paris*, 78, **79, 80**
Goncourt, de, quoted, 45
Gori, Villa, Siena, **57**, 58
Gothen, Castle of, tilt yard at, 245
Goujon, Jean, arachitect, 65
Gould, English gardener, 309, 310
Graces, The, 2
Grahme, Colonel James, of Levens Hall, 221
Granada, 268–278; and *see* Alhambra, Generaliffe

Greek gardens, 2, 3
Greenhouses, see Conservatories
Greenwich Park, 121, 233
Grimani breviary, the, 18, **24, 25, 27**
Grimsthorpe, bowling green at, 228
Groen, Jan van de, his *Nederlandsche Hovenier*, 175, 176
Groningen, botanic garden at, 202
Groombridge, Manor House at, 222
Grosbois, Château de, 134
Grosseteste, Bishop of Lincoln, 26
Grottoes, 34, 42, 46, 49, 54, 81, 83, 94, 146, 156, 192, 234
Guisborough, bowling green at, 228
Gunterstein, gardens at, **176**, 199
Gustavus III, his English garden at Haga, 311

Haarlem, 182, 184, 187, 189, 248 ; Gazebo near, **177** ; Country-house near, **179**
Hadrian's Villa, 8, 9
Haga, English garden at, 311
Hague, The, gardens at or near, 175, 176, 184, 192, 196, 221
"Ha-ha," the, 205
Hameau, 299
Hampton Court, 121, 175, 183, 205, 206, 215, 217 ; its orange trees, 178, 191 ; terrace, 209 ; avenues and canals, 218 ; parterre, **219** ; vine, 290
Hanging gardens, 21
Harrewyn, artist, 163
Harris, Dr. W., his discription of the Loo, 191
Hatfield House, 207, 217
Haudebourt, his restorations of Pliny's Villa, **5, 6**
Hedges, 8, 24, 28, **234**
Heidelberg, Castle of, **233**, 234, 237, 246, 247
Hellbrünn, Schloss **252**, 253
Henri II of France, 66, 134
Henri IV of France, 65, 66, 77, 83
Henriette d'Orleans, and St. Germain, 142
Henry III of England, and Woodstock, 26
Henry VIII of England, influence on garden design, 204–206
Henry, Prince of Wales, 233
Hentzner, quoted, 206
Herb, gardens, 23, 159, 160, 204, 245
Herbals, 12, 211
Herbularis, see Physic garden
Herculaneum, 11
Héré, Emmanuel, architect, 156
Herrenhausen, 196, 248–252 ; orangery, **247** ; Castle and gardens, **249**
Hesse, Prince of, 259
Hessen, Castle of, **242**, 245
Hill, Thomas, his *Profitable Arte of Gardening*, and *Gardener's Labyrinth*, 210, 211
Hippodrome, The, 7

Hirschfeld, quoted, 232, 311
Hoghton Tower, leaden statue at, 229
Hollar, Wenceslaus, engraver, 163
Holyrood Palace, 230, **231**
Homer, quoted, 2, 3
Honsholredyk, gardens at, 176
Honslaerdyk, gardens at, 192, **193**, 221
Hooghe, Romain de, engraver, 172
Horace, 4
Hothouses, see Conservatories
Houel, Nicholas, botanist, 79
House-in-the-Wood, see Huis-'ten-Bosch
Huis-te-Dieren, 175
Huis-'ten-Bosch, the Hague, 176, 192, **194**, 195, **196**
Hydraulic organs, devices and surprises, see Waterworks

Il Tribolo, see Tribolo
Impluvium, the, 11
Ingelheim, Charlemagne's Palace at, 13
Ironwork, 89
Irving, Washington, quoted, **270**, 281
Island gardens, 165, 172, 173
Isola Bella, gardens of, 61, **63**
Italian gardens, 28–63 ; in England, 296

James, I, 207, 212, 217
James II, 142
Japanese gardens, 199
Jeu de bague, The, 300
Joan the Mad of Spain, 279 ; Bath of, **282**
John Frederick, Duke of Hanover, 248
John of Bologna, sculptor, 32, 34
Jones, Inigo, architect, 212
Joseph II, Emperor, 261
Julius IV, Pope, 40
Julius Caesar, 7, 10

Kaempfer, quoted, 199
Karl Ludwig, Prince of Pfalz, 247
Karl Theodore, Elector, 247
Kasteel van Tervueren, garden at, **170**
Keller, Brothers, bronze casters, 100
Kennemerlant (district near Haarlem), The, 187
Kensington Gardens, 290
Kensington Palace, Parterre at, **220**
Kent, William, architect and gardener, 218, 289–291, 298
Keulen, Albrecht van, writer, 17
Kew, **293, 295, 296**, 306 ; Temple of Æolus at, **297**
Kielmännischer Garten, near Vienna, 238, **241**
Kinross House, **227**
Kip, views by, 218, **219, 223**, 227, 231
Kitchen gardens, see Herb gardens
Kleef, Lime Tree Arbour at, **200**
Kleiner, Salomon, engravings by, 262

INDEX

Knole Park, 228
Knots, 205, and *see* Parterres.
Koniglyck Hovenier. De, 176, 183

La Bossier, garden near Geneva, 311
La Caille, André de, physician, 78
La Court, Pierre de, his gardens at Dreihock, 202
La Grange, near Geneva, 311
La Granja, palace of, 283-285
La Meutte, Château de, 152, 153
La Pointe, his plan of the parterre at Versailles, 99
La Quintinie, gardener, 90
Laborde, Alexander, his *Description des nouveaux jardins de la France et de ses Châteaux*, 307, 308, **309**
Labyrinths or Mazes, 8, 21, 141, 173, 191, 192, 199; at the Tuileries, 81; at Versailles, 113, 114; at Fontainebleau, 184; at Seville, **280**
Laguna, Dr., quoted, 285
Lancelotti, Villa, Frascati, **51**
Landscape or English Gardening, 225, 246, 288; in France, 297 *et seq.*; in Germany, 308
Langier, his *Essai sur l'Architecture*, 298
Langley, Batty, on formal gardens, 225
Lante, Villa, Viterbo, 49, f. **47**; plan of, **47**
Laurentine Villa, Pliny's, **5, 6**
Lausanne, gardens near, 311
Lawson, William, his *A New Orchard and Garden* quoted, 205, 209, 216
Laxenbourg, English garden at, 308
Lazienski, palace of, 262, 263
Le Barbier, picture by, **120**
Le Blond, remarks on water, 150; designs Peterhof, 309
Le Bouteux, *see* Bouteaux
Le Brun, Charles, sculptor, 86; his work at Versailles, 104, 109; at Marly, 140; at Sceaux, 141; at St Cloud, 149
L'Ecluse, botanist, 201
Le Comte, sculptor, 113
Le Gros, sculptor, 113
Le Hongre, sculptor, 100 **107**
Le Manse, water engineer, 90
Le Nôtre, André, garden designer, 61, 75, 83, 124, 125, 140, 152, 155, 284; account of, 86-117; portrait, *frontispiece*; at Vaux-le-Vicomte, 87-89; at Chantilly, 89; at Versailles, 89-104, 110-113, 117; his style and influence, 121, 156, 170, 171, 174, 177, 187, 193, 218, 221, 232, 262; his parterres, 125; at Meudon, 134-136; at Sceaux, 141; at St. Germains, 142; at Fontainebleau, 145; at the Tuileries, 145, 146; at St. Cloud, 146; at Rambouillet, 151
Le Pautre, garden designer, **123**, 149
Le Rouge, publisher, 303, 306
Le Sueur, artist, 86

Leadwork, 110, 115, **228, 229, 230**, 246
Lechmere, Judge, his garden house at Severn End, 227
Lees Court, Kent, **223**
Leipzig, botanic garden at, 232
Leland, quoted, 205
Leminius, Levimus, quoted, 209
Lescot, Pierre, architect, 65
Lespignola, sculptor, **100**, 113
Leth, Hendrik de, his *Het zegepralent Kennemerlant*, 187
Levens Hall, gardens at, 221
Leyden, flower culture at, 183; gardens at, 184; botanic garden of, 201, 202
Liancourt, Château de, 152
Liebault, Jean, his *La Maison Rustique*, 69, 216
Liechenstein, Prince, his garden at Vienna, 261
Liger, Sieur Louis, his *Le Jardiner Solitaire*, 222
Ligue, Prince, de, quoted, 302, 303
Ligorio, Pirro, architect and garden designer, 40, 41, 50, 53, 62
Lilliputian gardens in Holland, 200
Linderhof, Castle of, **257**
Lippe, Annibale, architect, 41, 62
Lisle, de, French garden designer, 259
Lobel, Matthias de, botanist, 217
Loggie, 7, 11, **44**, 46
London, George, landscape gardener, 218, 223, 288
London, medieval gardens of, 26-7
Long Acre, Parkinson's garden in, 212
Long Melford Hall, Garden-house in Moat, **226**
Loo, Het, gardens of, 171, 173, **176, 177**, 178, 191, 221
Loppin, fontanier, 134
Lorraine, Cardinal Charles de, 134
Lotel, his *Histoire des Plantes*, 182
Lothen, Schloss, 245, **253**
Lotto, Lorenzo, picture by, 28, **29**
Loudon, John, botanist, 173, 182, 202; quoted, 262, 308-310
Louis XIII, of France, 77, 84
Louis XIV, 65, 84, 297; and Le Nôtre, 88, 89 93, 94; and the Trianon, 126, 130, 133; and Meudon, 134; and Clagny, 135; and Marly, 139; and St. Germain, 142; and St. Cloud, 146; at the Tuileries, 146
Louis XV, 133, 140
Louis XVI, 140, 150, 151
Louis Elizabeth, Madame, 155
Louvois, Marquis de, and Meudon, 134
Louvre, The, 70, 85, 93
Lucullus, his gardens, 4
Ludenbourg, palace of, 308
Lunéville, Château de, **155**, 156
Lustheim, palace of, 257, 258

INDEX

Luststuck at Herrenhausen, 248
Luxembourg, The, 79, **80, 81, 82**, 196
Lyceum, Athens, 2
Lycurgus, his plantations at Athens, 2

Machiavelli, Niccolo, 39
Madama, Villa, Rome, 40
Madrid, gardens at or near, 282, 283, 286
Madrid, Château de, 70, 75, 307
Maecenas, his Villa at Rome, 9
Maerland, Jacob van, his *De Naturen Bloeme*, 17
Maggiore, Lago di, 61
Maintenon, Madame de, at Sceaux, 141
Maison de Dédale, a labyrinth, 21
Maisons, Château de, 150, 151
Mall, The, at Enjhien, **174**, at Nymphenberg, 255
Malmaison, Château de, 306, **308**
Mannepall, country-house at, 187
Mannheim, gardens at, 247, 248
Mansart, J. H., architect, at Versailles, 110, **114**, 124, 125, **129**, 133; at Marly, 136, 140; at St Cloud, 145, 146, 149, 150; at Maisons, 150
Marcus Lucretius, his house at Pompeii, **10**
Marie Antoinette, and Marly, 140; at Maisons, 150; and the Trianon, 300, 301
Marie de Medici, and the Luxembourg, 79, 82, 196; at the Tuileries, 86
Markham, Gervase, his *The Country Housewife's Garden*, 69, 216
Marlia, Villa, Water Garden, f. **34**
Marly, Château de, 121, 134, 136, **137**, 138, **139**, 140, 232
Marnézia, his *La Nature Champetre*, 299
Marot, Daniel, garden designer, 174, 175, 177
Marquette, Château de, 188
Marsy, sculptor, 110
Martial, quoted, 9
Mary II, Queen, 192, 218, 221
Mascall, Leonard, writer on gardening, 210
Masretier, gardener, 311
Matarazzo, quoted, 39
Max Emmanuel, Elector, 254
Maximilian, Elector, 242
Maximilian II, 260
Mayeline, fountain by, **133**
Mazes, at Fontainebleau, 146; at Seville, 280; and *see* Labyrinths
Medici, Cosimo di, 29, 30, **34**
Medici, Eleonora, 30
Medici, Lorenzo di, 38, 39
Medici, Pier Francesco di, 33
Medici, Villa, Rome, **40, 41**
Melbourne Hall, leaden groups at, 222, 229
Ménager de Paris, The, 21
Menageries, 14, 39, 81, 104, 192, 261
Mercure de France, The, 135

Mercure Galant, The, 136, 141
Merestein, moated house at, 188
Mereville, landscape garden at, **304, 305**
Merian, Matthew, his engravings, 81, 183, 240, **242**, 253
Merovingian villas, 13
Meudon, Château de, 121, 134, **135, 136,** 155
Metz, Guillebert de, his description of Paris, 21
Michelozzi, Michelozzo, architect of Careggio, 29
Middachten, gardens at, 199
Middle Ages, gardens of the, 13–27
Mignard, artist, 86
Mignaux, gardens at, 297
Milan, villas round, 61
Migue, arthitect, 300, 301
Mirabell, Schloss, **248, 251, 252**
Mirador, The, Granada, 274
Mizauld, André, his works on gardening, 78
Moats, 23, 46, 152, 164 187, 188, 239, 241
Mollet, the elder, gardener, 74, 77
Mollet, André, gardener, son of Claude, 77, 248
Mollet, Claude, **1**; garden designer; 77, **78**, 81, 83
Mollett, Claude, **2**; gardener, son of Claude, **1**, 77
Monasteries, gardening in, 12–15, 25, 26, 203
Monceaux, Château of, 77, 300, 306, 307
Mondragone, Villa, **55**, 58, 134
Montacute, gardens at, **206**, 209
Montagu, Wortley, quoted, 184, 185
Montaigne, quoted, 53
Montargis, Château de, 70, **72**, 73, 74
Monte Cassino, Monastery of, 15
Montespan, Madame de, and the Grand Trianon, 126; and Clagny, 135
Montmorency, Anne de, Constable, and Chantilly, 66, 89
Monuments, garden, 304, 311
Moor Park, Herts, garden of, 218
Moorish gardens in Spain, **264**, *et seq.*
Moreau le jeune, pictures by, **139, 148, 151**
Morel, J. B., his *Théorie des Jardins*, 301
Morfontaine, aviary at, **303**
Mottoes on Gazebos, 178, 181
Moulin Joli, Le, Paris, **302**, 303
Mount St Willibald Monastery, 233
Mounts, 41, 169, 172, 192, **204**, 205, 245
Moxon, translates de Caus' work, 234
Munich, gardens at, 242, 245, 253, 308; and *see* Nymphenburg
Muti, Villa, Frascati, 58
Myrtle, Hedges, **283**

Naples, gardens of, 58
Nasr, King, 285
Neckham, Alexander, Abbot of Cirencester, 26
Nesle, gardens at, 75

INDEX

Netherlands, garden design in the, 159 *et seq.*
Nolhac, Pierre de, quoted, 109
Nonsuch Palace, 206, 217
Nost, van, lead modeller, 229
Nun Moncton, garden house at, 226
Nurseries, 160
Nymphaeum, The, 8
Nymphenburg Palace, Munich, 253, **254**, **255**, 257, 261, 308

Olivieri, Orazio, engineer, 53, 54
Olympia, Temple to Dionysius at, 2
Ommeyades, The, 267
Orangeries, at Versailles, 110, **112**, 113, 117; at Meudon, 134-136; at Fontainebleau, **144**; at Liancourt, 152; Dutch, **173**, 174, **176** 178, 187, 188, 191, 199; English, 227, 228; German, 238, **247**; at Cordova, **265**
Oranienbaum, Park of, 309
Orbay, D', garden designer at Fontainebleau, 145
Orcellari, Orti, Florence, 39
Orchards, 14, **15**, 23, 199, 245
Organs, Water, 53, 54, and *see* Waterworks
Orléans, Duchesse d', and La Chapelle, 306; and *see* Henriette
Oxenhoath, Gazebo at, **225**
Oxford, New College, **204**; St. John's College, **207**; Botanic Garden, **212**

Padilla, Maria di, her bathing pool at the Alcazar, Seville, 279; her parterre, 281
Padua, botanic garden at, 201, 212
Pagodas, 225
Palais Royal, Paris, **124**, 152
Palisades, 1, 4, 89, 135, 136
Palissy, Bernard, 66, 78, 81, 183; portrait, **75**; his *Recepte Véritable*, 75-77
Pallavicini, Villa, Frascati, 58
Palmieri, Villa, Florence, 28
Pamphili Doria, Villa, **44**, 45
Paradeisoi, The Persian royal gardens, 3
Paris, town gardens, 21, 78; Champs Elysées, 146, 202
Parkinson, John, 210-212, 217; portrait, **211**
Parma, Margaret Duchess of, and the Villa Madama, 40
Parterres, different varieties defined, 125, *à broderie*, 77, **78**, 79, 82, **84**, 85, 90, 94, 123, 135, 141, **142**, 145, 152; *à l'anglaise*, 123; English, 190, 209, **219**, **220**; Dutch, 161, 162, **166**, **169**, **181**, **183**; German, **233**, 245, 249, 251, 258
Parterres d'eau, *see* Water gardens
Passe, Crispin de, his *Hortus Floridus*, 165, 166
Patios, **265**, **268**, **269**, **277**, **286**, **287**
Pattes d'oie, 90
Paulowsky, Palace, 309

Pavia, Certosa, **14**
Pavilions, *see* Summer-houses
Pedro el Cruel, 279
Peeters, artist, 163
Penshurst, Place, fishponds at, 214
Percier, architect, 46
Perelle, engraver, 93, 99, 123, 145
Pergolas, 7, 12, 24, 28, 62
Peristyle, The, 11
Perrault, Claude, his *Allée d'eau* at Versailles 104; at Sceaux, 141
Peruzzi, artist, 39
Peterhof, garden at, 309
Petersfield, leaden figure at, 229
Petraja, Villa, Florence, 33-**35**, 37
Pfalz, Counts of, 247
Philip II of Spain, 283, 285
Philip V of Spain, 284, 285
Physic gardens, 14, 42, 43, 73, 159-161
Pigeon towers, *see* Dovecotes
Pindar, quoted, 4
Pinturicchio, painter, 28
Pitti Palace, Florence, 30, 79, 82
Pleaching, 1, **29**, 190, 191, 214, 215
Pliny, his villas, 4-7; his writings, 12; 26, 28, 41
Plutarch, on Lucullus' gardens, 4
Poggio a Cajano, Lorenzo di Medici's Villa at, 38
Poland, garden design in, 262
Pompadour, Madame de, and the Grand Trianon, 130
Pompeii, House of Sallust, **9**, **10**; houses of Marcus Lucretius, 10; Nymphaeum, **11**; Roof gardens, 11; atrium, 286
Pope, Alexander, on formal gardening, 218, 288; his Villa at Twickenham, 289
Portland, Duke of, his house at Sorgvliet, 192, 195
Post, Pierre, architect, 196
Potemkin, Prince, his gardening extravagances, 309, 310
Pots for plants, 18, 76, *see also* Vases
Potsdam, gardens at, 259
Poussin, Nicolas, sculptor, 89
Powis Castle, The Terrace, **208**
Praeneste, its roses, 7
Pratolino, Villa, 79
Primaticcio, painter, 65
Pulhawa, landscape garden at, 310
Pulvinus, The, 8
Pyrtaneum, The, 8

Quickset hedges, 159, 207
Quincunxes, 8, 146, 187
Quirini, garden designer, 248

Rademaker, his *Maison de Plaisance*, 187

INDEX

Rainaldi, architect, 42
Rambouillet, Château de, **150, 151**
Raphael, his designs for gardens, 39, 40
Ratisbon, botanic gardens at, 232
Redelyk, Madame, her country-house of Tulpenburg, 189 190
Regnaudin, sculptor, 100
Regnard, his design for the Tuileries, 145, 146
Remier, Jacob de, engraver, 192
Repton, Humphrey, landscape gardener, 291, 292; portrait, **292**
Reux, Château de, 75, **84**
Riairio, Cardinal, his gardens at Trastevere, 40
Riat, Monsieur G., on Kent's theories, 298
Richard (father of Claude), English gardener at Trianon, 300, 306
Richard, Claude, gardener at Trianon, 301, 306
Richmond, royal gardens at, 233, 306
Riviera, The Italian, 62
Rivières d'eau, see Cascades
Robert, Hubert, painting by, 118
Rock shelters, 76
Rockingham, mount at, 205
Romaineville, landscape garden at, 306
Roman, Jacques, garden designer, 174, 175
Roman gardens, 4–12, 39–46
Romaunt de la Rose, fifteenth century MS., **17, 19, 21, 22**
Rome, model of, 10, 53
Ronda, Patio at, **287**
Roof gardens, 11
Rosarium, The, 8
Rose, John, 221
Rosemary hedges, 8, 184
Rosendaal, gardens at, 199
Rosso, Il, architect, 65
Roubillard, Claud, fontanier, 89
Roubo, his *L'Art Du Treillageur*, 125
Rousham, Oxon, gardens designed by Kent, 289
Rousseau, J. J., his influence on gardening, 297, 298, 301
Rowlandson, drawing by, **289**
Rubens, P. P., designs the Fontaine de Medicis, 81
Rucellai, Bernardo, his Orti Orcellari, 39
Rueil, Château de, 87
Ruffini, Cardinal, his Villa Falconieri, 58
Ruines des plus beaux monuments de la Grèce, Les, 298
Rumford, Count, introduces English gardening at Munich, 308
Rupelmonde on the Vecht, **175**
Russia, gardens in, 309
Ryswyck, gardens at, 176, 192, 196, **197**
Ryxdorp, gardens at, 196

St. Catherine's Court, bowling green, **214**; terrace, **215**
St. Cloud, Palace of, 134, 147; cascade at, **122, 145, 146**; the *Jet d'eau* at, **149**; the *Alleé d'eau* at, f. **150**
St. Cyr, Château of, **153**
St. Denis, Abbey of, 79
St. Gall, Abbey of, 14; plan, **15**
St. Germain-en-Laye, 65, 70, 77, 82, 134, 142; parterres, **78, 85**, 144; plan, **83**; terrace, 142
St. James' Park, 121, 221
St. Maur, Château de, 121, 134
St. Petersburg, gardens at and near, 309
St. Pierre, B. de, his *Etudes de la Nature*, 298
Saint Simon, on Marly, 139; on Maisons, 150
St. Willibald, Monastery of, 233
Salisbury, Lord, *see* Cecil
Salvador, Jaime, botanist, 285
Salzburg, Mirabell Schloss at, 252, 253
Sampierdarena, villas and gardens at, 62
San Gallo, Giulio di, his designs for gardens, 38–40
San Juan d'Espe, botanic gardens at, 285
Sandremius, A., his collections of engravings, 163
Sands, coloured, use of, 85, 166
Sans Souci, palace of, at Potsdam, **258**–260, 308
Sarrazin, Jacques, sculptor, 104
Sauval, his description of gardens in Paris, 21
Savage, English gardener in Poland, 310
Saxony, Elector of, 232
Sceaux, Château of, 121, 134, **141**, 143, 142
Schlaumwerth, topiary work at, 245
Schleissheim, Palace of, 257, 258
Schlosshof, Palace of, **260**
Schönborn, Count of, his gardens, 262
Schönbrunn, Palace of, 155, **259**, 260, **261**
Schott, Van der, Dutch garden designer, 261
Schwartzenburg, Prince, his gardens at Vienna, 261
Schwetzingen, Castle, 264, 247
Schynvoet, Simon, garden designer, 174, 175; portrait, **172**
Sckell, Louis, landscape gardener, 308
Screens, **19, 234**, 243
Scudery, Mlle. de, her *Clélie*, 79
Sculpture, **10**, 18, 34, **41**, 46, **49**, 66, **82**, **99**, **101, 107, 109**, 113, **117**, **149**, 177
Seats, 18, 19, 21, 22, **188**
Sedding, J. D., his *Garden Craft*, 211
Segur, Marquis de, his Château of Romaineville, 306
Seignelay, Marquis de, and Sceaux, 141
Sergardi, Villa, Siena, 58
Serlio, Sebastian, architect, 65
Serres, Olivier de, horticulturist, 77, 183, 216
Severn End, The Judge's Study at, 227
Sevigné, Mme. de, quoted, 136
Seville, gardens of, 265, 278, 279, 287
Shrublands, Barry's designs at, 296
Sicily, gardens in, 58

INDEX

Sidonius Apollinarius, Bishop of Clermont, on Gallo-Roman gardens, 13
Siena, villas at, 57, 58
Silver balls, use in Dutch gardens, 200
Silvestre, Israel, his engravings, 82, 94, **95**, 135
Sittich, Archbishop Marcus, and Hellbrunn, 252
Skittle Swing, a, **254**
Smith, Sir J. E., on the Botanic garden, Leyden, 202
Soetendaal on the Vecht, **189**
Solaria, 11
Somerset House, gardens of, 233
Sorgvliet, Château of, 192, **195**
Spanish gardens, 263 *et seq.*
Stanislaus I of Poland, 155, 262
Stanislaus Augustus of Poland, 262
Staunton Harold, bowling green at, 228
Steckhoven, Adrian, gardener, 261
Storks' nests, 166
Stowe, Lord Cobham's seat at, 224, 288, **289**, 290
Strabo, on the early Britons, 25
Stuttgart, Castle Garden at, **239**
Subiaco or Sublaqueum, villas at, 7
Summer-houses, Arbours, Banqueting-houses, Garden-houses, Gazebos, Pavilions or *Triclina*, formed of masonry, 9, **133**, **169**, **170**, **177**, **178**, 206, **225**, **226**, 242; of wood or trellis, 11, **12**, 21, 24, 74, 81, **295**, **296**; in rocks, 76; Greek and Roman, 9, 11, **12**; medieval, 17, 21, 24; French, 69, 73, 74, 76, 81, 123, 152; Dutch, 161, 162, **168**, **169**, **170**, **177**, **178**, 187, 200; English, **206**, 215, **225**, **226**; **295**; **296**; German, **242**, **245**; Moorish, **279**
Sundials, 176, **230**, **231**
Surflet, Richard, his translation of *La Maison Rustique*, 69, 215, 216
Sutton Place, Old Garden-house, f. **226**
Swanenburg, gardens at, 196
Swanstead, orangery at, 228
Sweden, gardens of, 156, 310, 311
Switzer, Stephen, his *Ichnographia Rustica*, 223, 224, 231, 288
Switzerland, gardens of, 311

Tarquinius Superbus, his garden, 4
Taurida Palace, 309, 310
Temple, Sir William, and the gardens at Moor Park, 218
Temples, 2, 173, 188, 225, **289**, **297**, **298**, **304**, **305**
Tents, 16
Terraces, 11, 44, 46, 83, 169, 209, **215**, 237
Theatres, garden, 31, **32**, **55**, **57**, 58, 146, 155, 188, 189, 227, **248**, 251, 253
Théâtres d'eau, 53, 54, 57, 58, 88, **102**, **103**, 145
Theobalds, its garden described, 207
Theophrastus, his Museum at Athens, 2
Thompson, his *Seasons*, 298

Tiltyards, 245
Tivoli, near Rome, 7
Tivoli, near Paris, 299
Toledo, 265; water kiosk at, 267
Topiary work, 8, 17, **30**, 77, **120**, 133, 162, **173**, 176, **183**, 184, 191, 192, 199, 200, 207, 224, 245; parterre of, **196**
Torlonia, Villa, Frascati, 58, **59**, 149
Tower of London, Royal garden at the, 26
Torus, The, 8
Town gardens, 10, 152, **200**
Tradescant, John, gardener, 216; portrait, **217**
Treillage, or Trellis-work, 1, **12**, **19**, **21**, 24, **29**, **30**, 81, **93**, 117, **123**, **124**–**126**, **129**, 141, **184**, 189, 209, **245**, **251**
Trentham, its gardens designed by Barry, 296
Trianon, the Grand, 123, 126, **127**, 129, **130**, **131**, **133**, **134**; Fountain at, f. **130**, Basson de Trianon, f. **134**
Trianon, Petit, 126, **133**, **299**, 306; Hamlet at, **299**, **300**, 301
Tribolo, Il, designs the Boboli gardens, 30, 34, **35**
Triclinia, 8, 9
Trumel, Antoine, gardener, 89
Tsarkoi-Selo, Palace of, 309
Tuby, sculptor, **99**, 100, 109
Tuileries, The, 70, 77, 80, 81, 86, 145, 306; plan, **97**; parterre, 85, **142**
Tulpenberg, Château of, 190
Tunnels, 168, **169**
Tusser, Thomas, his *A hundreth good points of husbandrie*, 210, 211
Twickel, garden at, 199
Twickenham, Pope's Villa at, 288

Ulm, botanic garden at, 232; Furttenbach's garden at, **239**

Valencia, gardens in, 286
Valkenborch, painting by, **233**
Vanbrugh, Sir John, his plan of Stowe, 289
Vansanzio, Giovanni, architect, 42
Vanweerden, artist, 163
Varese, villas near, 61
Varro, his *De Re Rustica*, 4, 5, 23, 38
Vasari quoted, 29, 30
Vases, **46**, **62**, **115**, 149, **230**, 237
Vatican gardens, 8, 38, **39**, **40**; Villa Pia, **37**, 50
Vauquelin des Yveteaux, gardens of, 74
Vaux-le-Vicomte, Château of, 87, **88**, f. **88**, 89, 94, 121, 134
Vecht, villas on the, 175, 186
Vegetable gardens, *see* Herb gardens
Velasquez, his picture of Aranjuez, 283
Velsen, garden chair at, **188**
Venne, A. de, his garden, **167**

Vergers, see Castle gardens
Vermakhoven or pleasure yards, 159
Verneuil, Château de, **69**, 70
Versailles, 85, 88–90, **94**, **95**, 130, 134, 140, 232; fountains and waterworks, 97, 99, **100**, **102**, 103–105, **107**, 109, 113, 114, 115, **116**, **117**, 145; sculpture, 99, 100, **101**, **104**, **107**, 109, 110, 113, 115, 117; plan, 112–113; orangery, 112, 113; colonnades, 114, 117; Salle du bal, 116, 117; in 1775, 118
Vicobello, Siena, **58**
Vienna, gardens at or near, 240, **241**, 261, 262
Vignola, Giacomo, architect, 46, 49, 65
Villa rustica, the, 6
Villa urbana, the, 7
Vincennes, Château de, 70, 134
Vineyards, 8, 204
Viniers, Château of, 23
Virgil, 4
Visscher, Nicholas, engraver, 192, 199
Vitruvius, on the *xystos*, 8
Vogel, artist, 310
Volières, see Aviaries
Volkamen, J. C., his *Nurnbergische Hesperides*, 246
Voltaire, on Lunéville, 155; at Enghien, 172; at Sans Souci, 260; at Delices, 311
Voorst, the Count of Albemarle's garden at, 175
Vouët, Simon, painter, 86, 87
Vredeman de Vries, Jan, portrait, **158**; garden designs by, **160**, **161**, 162
Vrendenburg, garden at, 196
Vyvers, 167, 172, and see Fish-ponds

Wakefield Lodge, 290
Wallace, Sir Richard, and Bagatelle, 307
Walls, 1, 4, 238, 241; painted, 159, 192
Walpole, Horace, quoted, 224, 298
Watalet, C. H., his *Essai sur les Jardins*, 302
Water devices, jokes and surprises, 53, **76**, 77, 81, 83, 122, 205, 206, 213, 234, 237, 253, 267
Water gardens, 1, 18, **22**, **33**, **34**, **47**, 53, 54, 58, 99, 101, 107, 117, 188, **222**, 223, 241, 253, 278, 280, 281

Waterland, water garden at, 188
Watervliet, avenue at, 188
Watteau, picture by, **125**
Weimar, mount at the Castle of, 245
Weissenstein, garden at, 262
Well-head, 58
Westbury Court, water garden at, **222**, 223
Westerhof, aviary at, **181**
Westerwyk, garden theatre at, 188, 189
Westminster, royal gardens at, 26
Whitehall Palace, gardens of, 26; trick sundial at, 213
Wilhelmshöhe, English gardens at, 308
William III, his gardens in Holland, 170, 175, 191, 192, 221; at Hampton Court, 218; statues of, 299
William, Landgrave of Hesse, 232
Wilton, "Lady Pembroke's Boys" at, **299**
Wimbledon, garden at, 217
Windsor, royal gardens at, 26; orangery at, 227
Wise, Henry, (with London), his *The Retired Gardener*, 222, 223
Wolff, Jeremias, engraver, 259
Wolsey, Cardinal, and Hampton Court, 205
Woodstock, Palace of, 26
Wooton, garden designed by Evelyn at, 222
Wren, Sir Christopher, architect, 218
Wrest, leaden statue at, 299; sundial at, 231
Wurzburg, Bishop of, his gardens at Dresden, 259

Xenophon, his Temple to Dionysus, 2
Xystos, the, 5. 8

Yocteaux, Nicholas, d', his garden near Paris, 79

Zaandam, Lilliputian gardens at, 200
Zandyck, leaden figures at, 200
Zeiller, Castle, 241
Zeyst, pleached alley at, **190**
Zouche, Lord, his garden at Hackney, 217
Zuylesteyn, gardens at, 199

www.ingramcontent.com/pod-product-compliance
Lightning Source LLC
Chambersburg PA
CBHW080541230426
43663CB00015B/2667